MEMOIRS OF A CAVALIER

DANIEL DEFOE

PREFACE TO THE FIRST EDITION.

As an evidence that 'tis very probable these Memorials were written many years ago, the persons now concerned in the publication assure the reader that they have had them in their possession finished, as they now appear, above twenty years; that they were so long ago found by great accident, among other valuable papers, in the closet of an eminent public minister, of no less figure than one of King William's secretaries of state.

As it is not proper to trace them any farther, so neither is there any need to trace them at all, to give reputation to the story related, seeing the actions here mentioned have a sufficient sanction from all the histories of the times to which they relate, with this addition, that the admirable manner of relating them and the wonderful variety of incidents with which they are beautified in the course of a private gentleman's story, add such delight in the reading, and give such a lustre, as well to the accounts themselves as to the person who was the actor, that no story, we believe, extant in the world ever came abroad with such advantage.

It must naturally give some concern in the reading that the name of a person of so much gallantry and honour, and so many ways valuable to the world, should be lost to the readers. We assure them no small labour has been thrown away upon the inquiry, and all we have been able to arrive to of discovery in this affair is, that a memorandum was found with this manuscript, in these words, but not signed by any name, only the two letters of a name, which gives us no light into the matter, which memoir was as follows:--

Memorandum. "I found this manuscript among my father's writings, and I understand that he got them as plunder, at, or after, the fight at Worcester, where he served as major of ---- 's regiment of horse on the side of the Parliament. I.K."

As this has been of no use but to terminate the inquiry after the person, so, however, it seems most naturally to give an authority to the original of the work, viz., that it was born of a soldier; and indeed it is through every part related with so soldierly a style, and in the very language of the field, that it seems impossible anything but the very person who was present in every action here related, could be the relater of them.

The accounts of battles, the sieges, and the several actions of which this work is so full, are all recorded in the histories of those times; such as the great battle of Leipsic, the sacking of Magdeburg, the siege of Nuremburg, the passing the river Lech in Bavaria; such also as the battle of Kineton, or Edgehill, the battles of Newbury, Marston Moor, and Naseby, and the like: they are all, we say, recorded in other histories, and written by those who lived in those times, and perhaps had good authority for what they wrote.

But do those relations give any of the beautiful ideas of things formed in this account? Have they one half of the circumstances and incidents of the actions themselves that this man's eyes were witness to, and which his memory has thus preserved? He that has read the best accounts of those battles will be surprised to see the particulars of the story so preserved, so nicely and so agreeably described, and will confess what we allege, that the story is inimitably told; and even the great actions of the glorious King GUSTAVUS ADOLPHUS receive a lustre from this man's relations which the world was never made sensible of before, and which the present age has much wanted of late, in order to give their affections a turn in favour of his late glorious successor.

2

In the story of our own country's unnatural wars, he carries on the same spirit. How effectually does he record the virtues and glorious actions of King Charles the First, at the same time that he frequently enters upon the mistakes of his Majesty's conduct, and of his friends, which gave his enemies all those fatal advantages against him, which ended in the overthrow of his armies, the loss of his crown and life, and the ruin of the constitution!

In all his accounts he does justice to his enemies, and honours the merit of those whose cause he fought against; and many accounts recorded in his story, are not to be found even in the best histories of those times.

What applause does he give to gallantry of Sir Thomas Fairfax, to his modesty, to his conduct, under which he himself was subdued, and to the justice he did the king's troops when they laid down their arms!

His description of the Scots troops in the beginning of the war, and the behaviour of the party under the Earl of Holland, who went over against them, are admirable; and his censure of their conduct, who pushed the king upon the quarrel, and then would not let him fight, is no more than what many of the king's friends (though less knowing as soldiers) have often complained of.

In a word, this work is a confutation of many errors in all the writers upon the subject of our wars in England, and even in that extraordinary history written by the Earl of Clarendon; but the editors were so just that when, near twenty years ago, a person who had written a whole volume in folio, by way of answer to and confutation of Clarendon's "History of the Rebellion," would have borrowed the clauses in this account, which clash with that history, and confront it,--we say the editors were so just as to refuse them.

There can be nothing objected against the general credit of this work, seeing its truth is established upon universal history; and almost all the facts, especially those of moment, are confirmed for their general part by all the writers of those times. If they are here embellished with particulars, which are nowhere else to be found, that is the beauty we boast of; and that it is that much recommend this work to all the men of sense and judgment that read it.

The only objection we find possible to make against this work is, that it is not carried on farther, or, as we may say finished, with the finishing the war of the time; and this we complain of also. But then we complain of it as a misfortune to the world, not as a fault in the author; for how do we know but that this author might carry it on, and have another part finished which might not fall into the same hands, or may still remain with some of his family, and which they cannot indeed publish, to make it seem anything perfect, for want of the other parts which we have, and which we have now made public? Nor is it very improbable but that if any such farther part is in being, the publishing these two parts may occasion the proprietors of the third to let the world see it, and that by such a discovery the name of the person may also come to be known, which would, no doubt, be a great satisfaction to the reader as well as us.

This, however, must be said, that if the same author should have written another part of this work, and carried it on to the end of those times, yet as the residue of those melancholy days, to the Restoration, were filled with the intrigues of government, the political management of illegal power, and the dissensions and factions of a people who were then even in themselves but a faction, and that there was very little action in the field, it is more than probable that our author, who was a man of arms, had little share in those things, and might not care to trouble himself with looking at them.

But besides all this, it might happen that he might go abroad again at that time, as most of the gentlemen of quality, and who had an abhorrence for the power that then governed here, did. Nor are we certain that he might live to the end of that time, so we can give no account whether he had any share in the subsequent actions of that time.

'Tis enough that we have the authorities above to recommend this part to us that is now published. The relation, we are persuaded, will recommend itself, and nothing more can be needful, because nothing more can invite than the story itself, which, when the reader enters into, he will find it very hard to get out of till he has gone through it.

MEMOIRS OF A CAVALIER. PART I.

It may suffice the reader, without being very inquisitive after my name, that I was born in the county of Salop, in the year 1608, under the government of what star I was never astrologer enough to examine; but the consequences of my life may allow me to suppose some extraordinary influence affected my birth.

My father was a gentleman of a very plentiful fortune, having an estate of above £5000 per annum, of a family nearly allied to several of the principal nobility, and lived about six miles from the town; and my mother being at

---- on some particular occasion, was surprised there at a friend's house, and brought me very safe into the world.

I was my father's second son, and therefore was not altogether so much slighted as younger sons of good families generally are. But my father saw something in my genius also which particularly pleased him, and so made him take extraordinary care of my education.

I was taught, therefore, by the best masters that could be had, everything that was needful to accomplish a young gentleman for the world; and at seventeen years old my tutor told my father an academic education was very proper for a person of quality, and he thought me very fit for it: so my father entered me of ---- College in Oxford, where I continued three years.

A collegiate life did not suit me at all, though I loved books well enough. It was never designed that I should be either a lawyer, physician, or divine; and I wrote to my father that I thought I had stayed there long enough for a gentleman, and with his leave I desired to give him a visit.

During my stay at Oxford, though I passed through the proper exercises of the house, yet my chief reading was upon history and geography, as that which pleased my mind best, and supplied me with ideas most suitable to my genius; by one I understood what great actions had been done in the world, and by the other I understood where they had been done. My father readily complied with my desire of coming home; for besides that he thought, as I did, that three years' time at the university was enough, he also most passionately loved me, and began to think of my settling near him.

At my arrival I found myself extraordinarily caressed by my father, and he seemed to take a particular delight in my conversation. My mother, who lived in perfect union with him both in desires and affection, received me very passionately. Apartments were provided for me by myself, and horses and servants allowed me in particular.

My father never went a-hunting, an exercise he was exceeding fond of, but he would have me with him; and it pleased him when he found me like the sport. I lived thus, in all the pleasures 'twas possible for me to enjoy, for about a year more, when going out one morning with my father to hunt a stag, and having had a very hard chase, and gotten a great way off from home, we had leisure enough to ride gently back; and as we returned my father took occasion to enter into a serious discourse with me concerning the manner of my settling in the world.

He told me, with a great deal of passion, that he loved me above all the rest of his children, and that therefore he intended to do very well for me; and that my eldest brother being already married and settled, he had designed the same for me, and proposed a very advantageous match for me, with a young lady of very extraordinary fortune and merit, and offered to make a settlement of £2000 per annum on me, which he said he would purchase for me without diminishing his paternal estate.

There was too much tenderness in this discourse not to affect me exceedingly. I told him I would perfectly resign myself unto his disposal. But as my father had, together with his love for me, a very nice judgment in his discourse, he fixed his eyes very attentively on me, and though my answer was without the least reserve, yet he thought he saw some uneasiness in me at the proposal, and from thence concluded that my compliance was rather an act of discretion than inclination; and that, however I seemed so absolutely given up to what he had proposed, yet my answer was really an effect of my obedience rather than my choice.

So he returned very quick upon me: "Look you, son, though I give you my own thoughts in the matter, yet I would have you be very plain with me; for if your own choice does not agree with mine, I will be your adviser, but will never impose upon you, and therefore let me know your mind freely." "I don't reckon myself capable, sir," said I, with a great deal of respect, "to make so good a choice for myself as you can for me; and though my opinion differed from yours, its being your opinion would reform mine, and my judgment would as readily comply as my duty." "I gather at least from thence," said my father, "that your designs lay another way before, however they may comply with mine; and therefore I would know what it was you would have asked of me if I had not offered this to you; and you must not deny me your obedience in this, if you expect I should believe your readiness in the other."

"Sir," said I, "'twas impossible I should lay out for myself just what you have proposed; but if my inclinations were never so contrary, though at your command you shall know them, yet I declare them to be wholly subjected to your order. I confess my thoughts did not tend towards marriage or a settlement; for, though I had no reason to question your care of me, yet I thought a gentleman ought always to see something of the world before he confined himself to any part of it. And if I had been to ask your consent to anything, it should have been to give me leave to travel for a short time, in order to qualify myself to appear at home like a son to so good a father."

"In what capacity would you travel?" replied my father. "You must go abroad either as a private gentleman, as a scholar, or as a soldier." "If it were in the latter capacity, sir," said I, returning pretty quick, "I hope I should not misbehave myself; but I am not so determined as not to be ruled by your judgment." "Truly," replied my father, "I see no war abroad at this time worth while for a man to appear in, whether we talk of the cause or the encouragement; and indeed, son, I am afraid you need not go far for adventures of that nature, for times seem to look as if this part of Europe would find us work enough." My father spake then relating to the quarrel likely to happen between the King of England and the Spaniard,' [1] for I believe he had no notions of a civil war in his head.

In short, my father, perceiving my inclinations very forward to go abroad, gave me leave to travel, upon condition I would promise to return in two years at farthest, or sooner, if he sent for me.

While I was at Oxford I happened into the society of a young gentleman, of a good family, but of a low fortune, being a younger brother, and who had indeed instilled into me the first desires of going abroad, and who, I knew, passionately longed to travel, but had not sufficient allowance to defray his expenses as a gentleman. We had contracted a very close friendship, and our humours being very agreeable to one another, we daily enjoyed the conversation of letters. He was of a generous free temper, without the least affectation or deceit, a handsome proper person, a strong body, very good mien, and brave to the last degree. His name was Fielding and we called him Captain, though it be a very unusual title in a college; but fate had some hand in the title, for he had certainly the lines of a soldier drawn in his countenance. I imparted to him the resolutions I had taken, and how I had my father's consent to go abroad, and would know his mind whether he would go with me. He sent me word he would go with all his heart.

My father, when he saw him, for I sent for him immediately to come to me, mightily approved my choice; so we got our equipage ready, and came away for London.

'Twas on the 22nd of April 1630, when we embarked at Dover, landed in a few hours at Calais, and immediately took post for Paris. I shall not trouble the reader with a journal of my travels, nor with the description of places, which every geographer can do better than I; but these Memoirs being only a relation of what happened either to ourselves, or in our own knowledge, I shall confine myself to that part of it.

We had indeed some diverting passages in our journey to Paris, as first, the horse my comrade was upon fell so very lame with a slip that he could not go, and hardly stand, and the fellow that rid with us express, pretended to ride away to a town five miles off to get a fresh horse, and so left us on the road with one horse between two of us. We followed as well as we could, but being strangers, missed the way, and wandered a great way out the road. Whether the man performed in reasonable time or not we could not be sure, but if it had not been for an old priest, we had never found him. We met this man, by a very good accident, near a little village whereof he was curate. We spoke Latin enough just to make him understand us, and he did not speak it much better himself; but he carried us into the village to his house, gave us wine and bread, and entertained us with wonderful courtesy. After this he sent into the village, hired a peasant, and a horse for my captain, and sent him to guide us into the road. At parting he made a great many compliments to us in French, which we could just understand; but the sum was, to excuse him for a question he had a mind to ask us. After leave to ask what he pleased, it was if we wanted any money for our journey, and pulled out two pistoles, which he offered either to give or lend us.

I mention this exceeding courtesy of the curate because, though civility is very much in use in France, and especially to strangers, yet 'tis a very unusual thing to have them part with their money.

We let the priest know, first, that we did not want money, and next that we were very sensible of the obligation he had put upon us; and I told him in particular, if I lived to see him again, I would acknowledge it.

This accident of our horse was, as we afterwards found, of some use to us. We had left our two servants behind us at Calais to bring our baggage after us, by reason of some dispute between the captain of the packet and the custom-house officer, which could not be adjusted, and we were willing to be at Paris. The fellows followed as fast as they could, and, as near as we could learn, in the time we lost our way, were robbed, and our portmanteaus opened. They took what they pleased; but as there was no money there, but linen and necessaries, the loss was not great.

Our guide carried us to Amiens, where we found the express and our two servants, who the express meeting on the road with a spare horse, had brought back with him thither. We took this for a good omen of our successful journey, having escaped a danger which might have been greater to us than it was to our servants; for the highwaymen in France do not always give a traveller the civility of bidding him stand and deliver his money, but frequently fire on him first, and then take his money.

We stayed one day at Amiens, to adjust this little disorder, and walked about the town, and into the great church, but saw nothing very remarkable there; but going across a broad street near the great church, we saw a crowd of people gazing at a mountebank doctor, who made a long harangue to them with a thousand antic postures, and gave out bills this way, and boxes of physic that way, and had a great trade, when on a sudden the people raised a cry, "_Larron, Larron_!" (in English, "Thief, thief"), on the other side the street, and all the auditors ran away, from Mr Doctor to see what the matter was. Among the rest we went to see, and the case was plain and short enough. Two English gentlemen and a Scotchman, travellers as we were, were standing gazing at this prating doctor, and one of them catched a fellow picking his pocket. The fellow had got some of his money, for he dropped two or three pieces just by him, and had got hold of his watch, but being surprised let it slip again. But the reason of telling this story is for the management of it. This thief had his seconds so ready, that as soon as the Englishman had seized him they fell in, pretended to be mighty zealous for the stranger, takes the fellow by the throat, and makes a great bustle; the gentleman not doubting but the man was secured let go his own hold of him, and left him to them. The hubbub was great, and 'twas these fellows cried, "_Larron, larron_!" but with a dexterity peculiar to themselves had let the right fellow go, and pretended to be all upon one of their own gang. At last they bring the man to the gentleman to ask him what the fellow had done, who, when he saw the person they seized on, presently told them that was not the man. Then they seemed to be in more consternation than before, and spread themselves all over the street, crying, "_Larron, larron_!" pretending to search for the fellow; and so one one way, one another, they were all gone, the noise went over, the gentlemen stood looking one at another, and the bawling doctor began to have the crowd about him again. This was the first French trick I had the opportunity of seeing, but I was told they have a great many more as dexterous as this. We soon got acquaintance with these gentlemen, who were going to Paris, as well as we; so the next day we made up our company with them, and were a pretty troop of five gentlemen and four servants.

As we had really no design to stay long at Paris, so indeed, excepting the city itself, there was not much to be seen there. Cardinal Richelieu, who was not only a supreme minister in the Church, but Prime Minister in the State, was now made also General of the King's Forces, with a title never known in France before nor since, viz., Lieutenant-General "au place du Roi," in the king's stead, or, as some have since translated it, representing the person of the king.

Under this character he pretended to execute all the royal powers in the army without appeal to the king, or without waiting for orders; and having parted from Paris the winter before had now actually begun the war against the Duke of Savoy, in the process of which he restored the Duke of Mantua, and having taken Pignerol from the duke, put it into such a state of defence as the duke could never force it out of his hands, and reduced the duke, rather by manage and conduct than by force, to make peace without it; so as annexing it to the crown of France it has ever since been a thorn in his foot that has always made the peace of Savoy lame and precarious, and France has since made Pignerol one of the strongest fortresses in the world.

As the cardinal, with all the military part of the court, was in the field, so the king, to be near him, was gone with the queen and all the court, just before I reached Paris, to reside at Lyons. All these considered, there was nothing to do at Paris; the court looked like a citizen's house when the family was all gone into the country, and I thought the whole city looked very melancholy, compared to all the fine things I had heard of it.

The queen-mother and her party were chagrined at the cardinal, who, though he owed his grandeur to her immediate favour, was now grown too great any longer to be at the command of her Majesty, or indeed in her interest; and therefore the queen was under dissatisfaction and her party looked very much down. The Protestants were everywhere disconsolate, for the losses they had received at Rochelle, Nimes, and Montpelier had reduced them to an absolute dependence on the king's will, without all possible hopes of ever recovering themselves, or being so much as in a condition to take arms for their religion, and therefore the wisest of them plainly foresaw their own entire reduction, as it since came to pass. And I remember very well that a Protestant gentleman told me once, as we were passing from Orleans to Lyons, that the English had ruined them; and therefore, says he, "I think the next occasion the king takes to use us ill, as I know 'twill not be long before he does, we must all fly over to England, where you are bound to maintain us for having helped to turn us out of our own country." I asked him what he meant by saying the English had done it? He returned short upon me: "I do not mean," says he, "by not relieving Rochelle, but by helping to ruin Rochelle, when you and the Dutch lent ships to beat our fleet, which all the ships in France could not have done without you."

I was too young in the world to be very sensible of this before, and therefore was something startled at the charge; but when I came to discourse with this gentleman, I soon saw the truth of what he said was undeniable, and have since reflected on it with regret, that the naval power of the Protestants, which was then superior to the royal, would certainly have been the recovery of all their fortunes, had it not been unhappily broke by their brethren of England and Holland, the former lending seven men-of-war, and the latter twenty, for the destruction of the Rochellers' fleet; and by these very ships the Rochellers' fleet were actually beaten and destroyed, and they never afterwards recovered their force at sea, and by consequence sunk under the siege, which the English afterwards in vain attempted to prevent.

These things made the Protestants look very dull, and expected the ruin of all their party, which had certainly happened had the cardinal lived a few years longer.

We stayed in Paris, about three weeks, as well to see the court and what rarities the place afforded, as by an occasion which had like to have put a short period to our ramble. Walking one morning before the gate of the Louvre, with a design to see the Swiss drawn up, which they always did, and exercised just before they relieved the guards, a page came up to me, and speaking English to me, "Sir," says he, "the captain must needs have your immediate assistance." I, that had not the knowledge of any person in Paris but my own companion, whom I called captain, had no room to question, but it was he that sent for me; and crying out hastily to him, "Where?" followed the fellow as fast as 'twas possible. He led me through several passages which I knew not, and at last through a tennis-court and into a large room, where three men, like gentlemen, were engaged very briskly two against one. The room was very dark, so that I could not easily know them asunder, but being fully possessed with an opinion before of my captain's danger, I ran into the room with my sword in my hand. I had not particularly engaged any of them, nor so much as made a pass at any, when I received a very dangerous thrust in my thigh, rather occasioned by my too hasty running in, than a real design of the person; but enraged at the hurt, without examining who it was hurt me, I threw myself upon him, and run my sword quite through his body.

The novelty of the adventure, and the unexpected fall of the man by a stranger come in nobody knew how, had becalmed the other two, that they really stood gazing at me. By this time I had discovered that my captain was not there, and that 'twas some strange accident brought me thither. I could speak but little French, and supposed they could speak no English, so I stepped to the door to see for the page that brought me thither, but seeing nobody there and the passage clear, I made off as fast as I could, without speaking a word; nor did the other two gentlemen offer to stop me.

But I was in a strange confusion when, coming into those entries and passages which the page led me through, I could by no means find my way out. At last seeing a door open that looked through a house into the street, I went in, and out at the other door; but then I was at as great a loss to know where I was, and which was the way to my lodgings. The wound in my thigh bled apace, and I could feel the blood in my breeches. In this interval came by a chair; I called, and went into it, and bid them, as well as I could, go to the Louvre; for though I knew not the name of the street where I lodged, I knew I could find the way to it when I was at the Bastille. The chairmen went on their own way, and being stopped by a company of the guards as they went, set me down till the soldiers were marched by; when looking out I found I was just at my own lodging, and the captain was standing at the door looking for me. I beckoned him to me, and, whispering, told him I was very much hurt, but bid him pay the chairmen, and ask no questions but come to me.

I made the best of my way upstairs, but had lost so much blood, that I had hardly spirits enough to keep me from swooning till he came in. He was equally concerned with me to see me in such a bloody condition, and presently called up our landlord, and he as quickly called in his neighbours, that I had a room full of people about me in a quarter of an hour. But this had like to have been of worse consequence to me than the other, for by this time there was great inquiring after the person who killed a man at the tennis-court. My landlord was then sensible of his mistake, and came to me and told me the danger I was in, and very honestly offered to convey me to a friend's of his, where I should be very secure; I thanked him, and suffered myself to be carried at midnight whither he pleased. He visited me very often, till I was well enough to walk about, which was not in less than ten days, and then we thought fit to be gone, so we took post for Orleans. But when I came upon the road I found myself in a new error, for my wound opened again with riding, and I was in a worse condition than before, being forced to take up at a little village on the road, called ----, about ---- miles from Orleans, where there was no surgeon to be had, but a sorry country barber, who nevertheless dressed me as well as he could, and in about a week more I was able to walk to Orleans at three times. Here I stayed till I was quite well, and took coach for Lyons and so through Savoy into Italy.

I spent nearly two years' time after this bad beginning in travelling through Italy, and to the several courts of Rome, Naples, Venice, and Vienna.

When I came to Lyons the king was gone from thence to Grenoble to meet the cardinal, but the queens were both at Lyons. The French affairs seemed at this time to have but an indifferent aspect. There was no life in anything but where the cardinal was: he pushed on everything with extraordinary conduct, and generally with success; he had taken Susa and Pignerol from the Duke of Savoy, and was preparing to push the duke even out of all his dominions.

But in the meantime everywhere else things looked ill; the troops were ill-paid, the magazines empty, the people mutinous, and a general disorder seized the minds of the court; and the cardinal, who was the soul of everything, desired this interview at Grenoble, in order to put things into some better method.

This politic minister always ordered matters so, that if there was success in anything the glory was his, but if things miscarried it was all laid upon the king. This conduct was so much the more nice, as it is the direct contrary to the custom in like cases, where kings assume the glory of all the success in an action, and when a thing miscarries make themselves easy by sacrificing their ministers and favourites to the complaints and resentments of the people; but this accurate refined statesman got over this point.

While we were at Lyons, and as I remember, the third day after our coming thither, we had like to have been involved in a state broil, without knowing where we were. It was of a Sunday in the evening, the people of Lyons, who had been sorely oppressed in taxes, and the war in Italy pinching their trade, began to be very tumultuous. We found the day before the mob got together in great crowds, and talked oddly; the king was everywhere reviled, and spoken disrespectfully of, and the magistrates of the city either winked at, or durst not attempt to meddle, lest they should provoke the people.

But on Sunday night, about midnight, we were waked by a prodigious noise in the street. I jumped out of bed, and running to the window, I saw the street as full of mob as it could hold, some armed with muskets and halberds, matched in very good order; others in disorderly crowds, all shouting and crying out, "Du paix le roi," and the like. One that led a great party of this rabble carried a loaf of bread upon the top of a pike, and other lesser loaves, signifying the smallness of their bread, occasioned by dearness.

By morning this crowd was gathered to a great height; they ran roving over the whole city, shut up all the shops, and forced all the people to join with them from thence. They went up to the castle, and renewing the clamour, a strange consternation seized all the princes.

They broke open the doors of the officers, collectors of the new taxes, and plundered their houses, and had not the persons themselves fled in time they had been very ill-treated.

The queen-mother, as she was very much displeased to see such consequences of the government, in whose management she had no share, so I suppose she had the less concern upon her. However, she came into the court of the castle and showed herself to the people, gave money amongst them, and spoke gently to them; and by a way peculiar to herself, and which obliged all she talked with, she pacified the mob gradually, sent them home with promises of redress and the like; and so appeased this tumult in two days by her prudence, which the guards in the castle had small mind to meddle with, and if they had, would in all probability have made the better side the worse.

11

There had been several seditions of the like nature in sundry other parts of France, and the very army began to murmur, though not to mutiny, for want of provisions.

This sedition at Lyons was not quite over when we left the place, for, finding the city all in a broil, we considered we had no business there, and what the consequence of a popular tumult might be we did not see, so we prepared to be gone. We had not rid above three miles out of the city but we were brought as prisoners of war, by a party of mutineers, who had been abroad upon the scout, and were charged with being messengers sent to the cardinal for forces to reduce the citizens. With these pretences they brought us back in triumph, and the queen-mother, being by this time grown something familiar to them, they carried us before her. When they inquired of us who we were, we called ourselves Scots; for as the English were very much out of favour in France at this time, the peace having been made not many months, and not supposed to be very durable, because particularly displeasing to the people of England, so the Scots were on the other extreme with the French. Nothing was so much caressed as the Scots, and a man had no more to do in France, if he would be well received there, than to say he was a Scotchman.

When we came before the queen-mother she seemed to receive us with some stiffness at first, and caused her guards to take us into custody; but as she was a lady of most exquisite politics, she did this to amuse the mob, and we were immediately after dismissed; and the queen herself made a handsome excuse to us for the rudeness we had suffered, alleging the troubles of the times; and the next morning we had three dragoons of the guards to convoy us out of the jurisdiction of Lyons.

I confess this little adventure gave me an aversion to popular tumults all my life after, and if nothing else had been in the cause, would have biassed me to espouse the king's party in England when our popular heats carried all before it at home.

But I must say, that when I called to mind since, the address, the management, the compliance in show, and in general the whole conduct of the queen-mother with the mutinous people of Lyons, and compared it with the conduct of my unhappy master the King of England, I could not but see that the queen understood much better than King Charles the management of politics and the clamours of the people.

Had this princess been at the helm in England, she would have prevented all the calamities of the Civil War here, and yet not have parted with what that good prince yielded in order to peace neither. She would have yielded gradually, and then gained upon them gradually; she would have managed them to the point she had designed them, as she did all parties in France; and none could effectually subject her but the very man she had raised to be her principal support--I mean the cardinal. We went from hence to Grenoble, and arrived there the same day that the king and the cardinal with the whole court went out to view a body of 6000 Swiss foot, which the cardinal had wheedled the cantons to grant to the king to help to ruin their neighbour the Duke of Savoy.

The troops were exceeding fine, well-accoutred, brave, clean-limbed, stout fellows indeed. Here I saw the cardinal; there was an air of church gravity in his habit, but all the vigour of a general, and the sprightliness of a vast genius in his face. He affected a little stiffness in his behaviour, but managed all his affairs with such clearness, such steadiness, and such application, that it was no wonder he had such success in every undertaking.

Here I saw the king, whose figure was mean, his countenance hollow, and always seemed dejected, and every way discovering that weakness in his countenance that appeared in his actions.

If he was ever sprightly and vigorous it was when the cardinal was with him, for he depended so much on everything he did, he that was at the utmost dilemma when he was absent, always timorous, jealous, and irresolute.

After the review the cardinal was absent some days, having been to wait on the queen-mother at Lyons, where, as it was discoursed, they were at least seemingly reconciled.

I observed while the cardinal was gone there was no court, the king was seldom to be seen, very small attendance given, and no bustle at the castle; but as soon as the cardinal returned, the great councils were assembled, the coaches of the ambassadors went every day to the castle, and a face of business appeared upon the whole court.

Here the measures of the Duke of Savoy's ruin were concerted, and in order to it the king and the cardinal put themselves at the head of the army, with which they immediately reduced all Savoy, took Chamberri and the whole duchy except Montmelian. The army that did this was not above 22,000 men, including the Swiss, and but indifferent troops neither, especially the French foot, who, compared to the infantry I have since seen in the German and Swedish armies, were not fit to be called soldiers. On the other hand, considering the Savoyards and Italian troops, they were good troops; but the cardinal's conduct made amends for all these deficiencies.

From hence I went to Pignerol, which was then little more than a single fortification on the hill near the town called St Bride's, but the situation of that was very strong. I mention this because of the prodigious works since added to it, by which it has since obtained the name of "the right hand of France." They had begun a new line below the hill, and some works were marked out on the side of the town next the fort; but the cardinal afterwards drew the plan of the works with his own hand, by which it was made one of the strongest fortresses in Europe.

While I was at Pignerol, the governor of Milan, for the Spaniards, came with an army and sat down before Casale. The grand quarrel, and for which the war in this part of Italy was begun, was this: The Spaniards and Germans pretended to the duchy of Mantua; the Duke of Nevers, a Frenchman, had not only a title to it, but had got possession of it; but being ill-supported by the French, was beaten out by the Imperialists, and after a long siege the Germans took Mantua itself, and drove the poor duke quite out of the country.

The taking of Mantua elevated the spirits of the Duke of Savoy, and the Germans and Spaniards being now at more leisure, with a complete army came to his assistance, and formed the siege of Montferrat.

For as the Spaniards pushed the Duke of Mantua, so the French by way of diversion lay hard upon the Duke of Savoy. They had seized Montferrat, and held it for the Duke of Mantua, and had a strong French garrison under Thoiras, a brave and experienced commander; and thus affairs stood when we came into the French army. I had no business there as a soldier, but having passed as a Scotch gentleman with the mob at Lyons, and after with her Majesty the queen-mother, when we obtained the guard of her dragoons, we had also her Majesty's pass, with which we came and went where we pleased. And the cardinal, who was then not on very good terms with the queen, but willing to keep smooth water there, when two or three times our passes came to be examined, showed a more than ordinary respect to us on that very account, our passes being from the queen.

Casale being besieged, as I have observed, began to be in danger, for the cardinal, who 'twas thought had formed a design to ruin Savoy, was more intent upon that than upon the succour of the Duke of Mantua; but necessity calling upon him to deliver so great a captain as Thoiras, and not to let such a place as Casale fall into the hands of the enemy, the king, or cardinal rather, ordered the Duke of Montmorency, and the Maréchal D'Effiat, with 10,000 foot and 2000 horse, to march and join the Maréchals De La Force and Schomberg, who lay already with an army on the frontiers of Genoa, but too weak to attempt the raising the siege of Casale.

As all men thought there would be a battle between the French and the Spaniards, I could not prevail with myself to lose the opportunity, and therefore by the help of the passes above mentioned, I came to the French army under the Duke of Montmorency. We marched through the enemy's country with great boldness and no small hazard, for the Duke of Savoy appeared frequently with great bodies of horse on the rear of the army, and frequently skirmished with our troops, in one of which I had the folly--I can call it no better, for I had no business there--to go out and see the sport, as the French gentlemen called it. I was but a raw soldier, and did not like the sport at all, for this party was surrounded by the Duke of Savoy, and almost all killed, for as to quarter they neither asked nor gave. I ran away very fairly, one of the first, and my companion with me, and by the goodness of our horses got out of the fray, and being not much known in the army, we came into the camp an hour or two after, as if we had been only riding abroad for the air. This little rout made the general very cautious, for the Savoyards were stronger in horse by three or four thousand, and the army always marched in a body, and kept their parties in or very near hand.

I escaped another rub in this French army about five days after, which had like to have made me pay dear for my curiosity.

The Duke de Montmorency and the Maréchal Schomberg joined their army about four or five days after, and immediately, according to the cardinal's instructions, put themselves on the march for the relief of Casale.

The army had marched over a great plain, with some marshy grounds on the right and the Po on the left, and as the country was so well discovered that 'twas thought impossible any mischief should happen, the generals observed the less caution. At the end of this plain was a long wood and a lane or narrow defile through the middle of it.

Through this pass the army was to march, and the van began to file through it about four o'clock. By three hours' time all the army was got through, or into the pass, and the artillery was just entered when the Duke of Savoy with 4000 horse and 1500 dragoons with every horseman a footman behind him, whether he had swam the Po or passed it above at a bridge, and made a long march after, was not examined, but he came boldly up the plain and charged our rear with a great deal of fury.

Our artillery was in the lane, and as it was impossible to turn them about and make way for the army, so the rear was obliged to support themselves and maintain the fight for above an hour and a half.

In this time we lost abundance of men, and if it had not been for two accidents all that line had been cut off. One was, that the wood was so near that those regiments which were disordered presently sheltered themselves in the wood; the other was, that by this time the Maréchal Schomberg, with the horse of the van, began to get back through the lane, and to make good the ground from whence the other had been beaten, till at last by this means it came to almost a pitched battle. There were two regiments of French dragoons who did excellent service in this action, and maintained their ground till they were almost all killed.

Had the Duke of Savoy contented himself with the defeat of five regiments on the right, which he quite broke and drove into the wood, and with the slaughter and havoc which he had made among the rest, he had come off with honour, and might have called it a victory; but endeavouring to break the whole party and carry off some cannon, the obstinate resistance of these few dragoons lost him his advantages, and held him in play till so many fresh troops got through the pass again as made us too strong for him, and had not night parted them he had been entirely defeated.

At last, finding our troops increase and spread themselves on his flank, he retired and gave over. We had no great stomach to pursue him neither, though some horse were ordered to follow a little way.

The duke lost about a thousand men, and we almost twice as many, and but for those dragoons had lost the whole rear-guard and half our cannon. I was in a very sorry case in this action too. I was with the rear in the regiment of horse of Perigoort, with a captain of which regiment I had contracted some acquaintance. I would have rid off at first, as the captain desired me, but there was no doing it, for the cannon was in the lane, and the horse and dragoons of the van eagerly pressing back through the lane must have run me down or carried me with them. As for the wood, it was a good shelter to save one's life, but was so thick there was no passing it on horseback.

Our regiment was one of the first that was broke, and being all in confusion, with the Duke of Savoy's men at our heels, away we ran into the wood. Never was there so much disorder among a parcel of runaways as when we came to this wood; it was so exceeding bushy and thick at the bottom there was no entering it, and a volley of small shot from a regiment of Savoy's dragoons poured in upon us at our breaking into the wood made terrible work among our horses.

For my part I was got into the wood, but was forced to quit my horse, and by that means, with a great deal of difficulty, got a little farther in, where there was a little open place, and being quite spent with labouring among the bushes I sat down resolving to take my fate there, let it be what it would, for I was not able to go any farther. I had twenty or thirty more in the same condition come to me in less than half-an-hour, and here we waited very securely the success of the battle, which was as before.

It was no small relief to those with me to hear the Savoyards were beaten, for otherwise they had all been lost; as for me, I confess, I was glad as it was because of the danger, but otherwise I cared not much which had the better, for I designed no service among them.

One kindness it did me, that I began to consider what I had to do here, and as I could give but a very slender account of myself for what it was I run all these risks, so I resolved they should fight it among themselves, for I would come among them no more.

15

The captain with whom, as I noted above, I had contracted some acquaintance in this regiment, was killed in this action, and the French had really a great blow here, though they took care to conceal it all they could; and I cannot, without smiling, read some of the histories and memoirs of this action, which they are not ashamed to call a victory.

We marched on to Saluzzo, and the next day the Duke of Savoy presented himself in battalia on the other side of a small river, giving us a fair challenge to pass and engage him. We always said in our camp that the orders were to fight the Duke of Savoy wherever we met him; but though he braved us in our view we did not care to engage him, but we brought Saluzzo to surrender upon articles, which the duke could not relieve without attacking our camp, which he did not care to do.

The next morning we had news of the surrender of Mantua to the Imperial army. We heard of it first from the Duke of Savoy's cannon, which he fired by way of rejoicing, and which seemed to make him amends for the loss of Saluzzo. As this was a mortification to the French, so it quite damped the success of the campaign, for the Duke de Montmorency imagining that the Imperial general would send immediate assistance to the Marquis Spinola, who besieged Casale, they called frequent councils of war what course to take, and at last resolved to halt in Piedmont. A few days after their resolutions were changed again by the news of the death of the Duke of Savoy, Charles Emanuel, who died, as some say, agitated with the extremes of joy and grief.

This put our generals upon considering again whether they should march to the relief of Casale, but the chimera of the Germans put them by, and so they took up quarters in Piedmont. They took several small places from the Duke of Savoy, making advantage of the consternation the duke's subjects were in on the death of their prince, and spread themselves from the seaside to the banks of the Po. But here an enemy did that for them which the Savoyards could not, for the plague got into their quarters and destroyed abundance of people, both of the army and of the country.

I thought then it was time for me to be gone, for I had no manner of courage for that risk; and I think verily I was more afraid of being taken sick in a strange country than ever I was of being killed in battle. Upon this resolution I procured a pass to go for Genoa, and accordingly began my journey, but was arrested at Villa Franca by a slow lingering fever, which held me about five days, and then turned to a burning malignancy, and at last to the plague. My friend, the captain, never left me night nor day; and though for four days more I knew nobody, nor was capable of so much as thinking of myself, yet it pleased God that the distemper gathered in my neck, swelled and broke. During the swelling I was raging mad with the violence of pain, which being so near my head swelled that also in proportion, that my eyes were swelled up, and for the twenty-four hours my tongue and mouth; then, as my servant told me, all the physicians gave me over, as past all remedy, but by the good providence of God the swelling broke.

The prodigious collection of matter which this swelling discharged gave me immediate relief, and I became sensible in less than an hour's time; and in two hours or thereabouts fell into a little slumber which recovered my spirits and sensibly revived me. Here I lay by it till the middle of September. My captain fell sick after me, but recovered quickly. His man had the plague, and died in two days; my man held it out well.

16

About the middle of September we heard of a truce concluded between all parties, and being unwilling to winter at Villa Franca, I got passes, and though we were both but weak, we began to travel in litters for Milan.

And here I experienced the truth of an old English proverb, that standers-by see more than the gamesters.

The French, Savoyards, and Spaniards made this peace or truce all for separate and several grounds, and every one were mistaken.

The French yielded to it because they had given over the relief of Casale, and were very much afraid it would fall into the hands of the Marquis Spinola. The Savoyards yielded to it because they were afraid the French would winter in Piedmont; the Spaniards yielded to it because the Duke of Savoy being dead, and the Count de Colalto, the Imperial general, giving no assistance, and his army weakened by sickness and the fatigues of the siege, he foresaw he should never take the town, and wanted but to come off with honour.

The French were mistaken, because really Spinola was so weak that had they marched on into Montferrat the Spaniards must have raised the siege; the Duke of Savoy was mistaken, because the plague had so weakened the French that they durst not have stayed to winter in Piedmont; and Spinola was mistaken, for though he was very slow, if he had stayed before the town one fortnight longer, Thoiras the governor must have surrendered, being brought to the last extremity.

Of all these mistakes the French had the advantage, for Casale, was relieved, the army had time to be recruited, and the French had the best of it by an early campaign. I passed through Montferrat in my way to Milan just as the truce was declared, and saw the miserable remains of the Spanish army, who by sickness, fatigue, hard duty, the sallies of the garrison and such like consequences, were reduced to less than 2000 men, and of them above 1000 lay wounded and sick in the camp.

Here were several regiments which I saw drawn out to their arms that could not make up above seventy or eighty men, officers and all, and those half starved with hunger, almost naked, and in a lamentable condition. From thence I went into the town, and there things were still in a worse condition, the houses beaten down, the walls and works ruined, the garrison, by continual duty, reduced from 4500 men to less than 800, without clothes, money, or provisions, the brave governor weak with continual fatigue, and the whole face of things in a miserable case.

The French generals had just sent them 30,000 crowns for present supply, which heartened them a little, but had not the truce been made as it was, they must have surrendered upon what terms the Spaniards had pleased to make them.

Never were two armies in such fear of one another with so little cause; the Spaniards afraid of the French whom the plague had devoured, and the French afraid of the Spaniards whom the siege had almost ruined.

The grief of this mistake, together with the sense of his master, the Spaniards, leaving him without supplies to complete the siege of Casale, so affected the Marquis Spinola, that he died for grief, and in him fell the last of that rare breed of Low Country soldiers, who gave the world so great and just a character of the Spanish infantry, as the best soldiers of the world; a character which we see them so very much degenerated from since, that they hardly deserve the name of soldiers.

I tarried at Milan the rest of the winter, both for the recovery of my health, and also for supplies from England. Here it was I first heard the name of Gustavus Adolphus, the king of Sweden, who now began his war with the emperor; and while the king of France was at Lyons, the league with Sweden was made, in which the French contributed 1,200,000 crowns in money, and 600,000 per annum to the attempt of Gustavus Adolphus. About this time he landed in Pomerania, took the towns of Stettin and Stralsund, and from thence proceeded in that prodigious manner of which I shall have occasion to be very particular in the prosecution of these Memoirs.

I had indeed no thoughts of seeing that king or his armies. I had been so roughly handled already, that I had given over the thoughts of appearing among the fighting people, and resolved in the spring to pursue my journey to Venice, and so for the rest of Italy. Yet I cannot deny that as every Gazette gave us some accounts of the conquests and victories of this glorious prince, it prepossessed my thoughts with secret wishes of seeing him, but these were so young and unsettled, that I drew no resolutions from them for a long while after.

About the middle of January I left Milan and came to Genoa, from thence by sea to Leghorn, then to Naples, Rome, and Venice, but saw nothing in Italy that gave me any diversion.

As for what is modern, I saw nothing but lewdness, private murders, stabbing men at the corner of a street, or in the dark, hiring of bravos, and the like. These were to me the modern excellencies of Italy; and I had no gust to antiquities.

'Twas pleasant indeed when I was at Rome to say here stood the Capitol, there the Colossus of Nero, here was the Amphitheatre of Titus, there the Aqueduct of----, here the Forum, there the Catacombs, here the Temple of Venus, there of Jupiter, here the Pantheon, and the like; but I never designed to write a book. As much as was useful I kept in my head, and for the rest, I left it to others.

I observed the people degenerated from the ancient glorious inhabitants, who were generous, brave, and the most valiant of all nations, to a vicious baseness of soul, barbarous, treacherous, jealous and revengeful, lewd and cowardly, intolerably proud and haughty, bigoted to blind, incoherent devotion, and the grossest of idolatry.

Indeed, I think the unsuitableness of the people made the place unpleasant to me, for there is so little in a country to recommend it when the people disgrace it, that no beauties of the creation can make up for the want of those excellencies which suitable society procure the defect of. This made Italy a very unpleasant country to me; the people were the foil to the place, all manner of hateful vices reigning in their general way of living.

I confess I was not very religious myself, and being come abroad into the world young enough, might easily have been drawn into evils that had recommended themselves with any tolerable agreeableness to nature and common manners; but when wickedness presented itself full-grown in its grossest freedoms and liberties, it quite took away all the gust to vice that the devil had furnished me with.

The prodigious stupid bigotry of the people also was irksome to me; I thought there was something in it very sordid. The entire empire the priests have over both the souls and bodies of the people, gave me a specimen of that meanness of spirit, which is nowhere else to be seen but in Italy, especially in the city of Rome.

At Venice I perceived it quite different, the civil authority having a visible superiority over the ecclesiastic, and the Church being more subject there to the State than in any other part of Italy.

For these reasons I took no pleasure in filling my memoirs of Italy with remarks of places or things. All the antiquities and valuable remains of the Roman nation are done better than I can pretend to by such people who made it more their business; as for me, I went to see, and not to write, and as little thought then of these Memoirs as I ill furnished myself to write them. I left Italy in April, and taking the tour of Bavaria, though very much out of the way, I passed through Munich, Passau, Lintz, and at last to Vienna.

I came to Vienna the 10th of April 1631, intending to have gone from thence down the Danube into Hungary, and by means of a pass, which I had obtained from the English ambassador at Constantinople, I designed to have seen all the great towns on the Danube, which were then in the hands of the Turks, and which I had read much of in the history of the war between the Turks and the Germans; but I was diverted from my design by the following occasion.

There had been a long bloody war in the empire of Germany for twelve years, between the emperor, the Duke of Bavaria, the King of Spain, and the Popish princes and electors on the one side, and the Protestant princes on the other; and both sides having been exhausted by the war, and even the Catholics themselves beginning to dislike the growing power of the house of Austria, 'twas thought all parties were willing to make peace. Nay, things were brought to that pass that some of the Popish princes and electors began to talk of making alliances with the King of Sweden.

Here it is necessary to observe, that the two Dukes of Mecklenburg having been dispossessed of most of their dominions by the tyranny of the Emperor Ferdinand, and being in danger of losing the rest, earnestly solicited the King of Sweden to come to their assistance; and that prince, as he was related to the house of Mecklenburg, and especially as he was willing to lay hold of any opportunity to break with the emperor, against whom he had laid up an implacable prejudice, was very ready and forward to come to their assistance.

The reasons of his quarrel with the emperor were grounded upon the Imperialists concerning themselves in the war of Poland, where the emperor had sent 8000 foot and 2000 horse to join the Polish army against the king, and had thereby given some check to his arms in that war.

In pursuance, therefore, of his resolution to quarrel with the emperor, but more particularly at the instances of the princes above-named, his Swedish Majesty had landed the year before at Stralsund with about 12,000 men, and having joined with some forces which he had left in Polish Prussia, all which did not make 30,000 men, he began a war with the emperor, the greatest in event, filled with the most famous battles, sieges, and extraordinary actions, including its wonderful success and happy conclusion, of any war ever maintained in the world.

19

The King of Sweden had already taken Stettin, Stralsund, Rostock, Wismar, and all the strong places on the Baltic, and began to spread himself in Germany. He had made a league with the French, as I observed in my story of Saxony; he had now made a treaty with the Duke of Brandenburg, and, in short, began to be terrible to the empire.

In this conjuncture the emperor called the General Diet of the empire to be held at Ratisbon, where, as was pretended, all sides were to treat of peace and to join forces to beat the Swedes out of the empire. Here the emperor, by a most exquisite management, brought the affairs of the Diet to a conclusion, exceedingly to his own advantage, and to the farther oppression of the Protestants; and, in particular, in that the war against the King of Sweden was to be carried on in such manner as that the whole burden and charge would lie on the Protestants themselves, and they be made the instruments to oppose their best friends. Other matters also ended equally to their disadvantage, as the methods resolved on to recover the Church lands, and to prevent the education of the Protestant clergy; and what remained was referred to another General Diet to be held at

Frankfort-au-Main in August 1631.

I won't pretend to say the other Protestant princes of Germany had never made any overtures to the King of Sweden to come to their assistance, but 'tis plain they had entered into no league with him; that appears from the difficulties which retarded the fixing of the treaties afterward, both with the Dukes of Brandenburg and Saxony, which unhappily occasioned the ruin of Magdeburg.

But 'tis plain the Swede was resolved on a war with the emperor. His Swedish majesty might, and indeed could not but foresee that if he once showed himself with a sufficient force on the frontiers of the empire, all the Protestant princes would be obliged by their interest or by his arms to fall in with him, and this the consequence made appear to be a just conclusion, for the Electors of Brandenburg and Saxony were both forced to join with him.

First, they were willing to join with him--at least they could not find in their hearts to join with the emperor, of whose power they had such just apprehensions. They wished the Swedes success, and would have been very glad to have had the work done at another man's charge, but, like true Germans, they were more willing to be saved than to save themselves, and therefore hung back and stood upon terms.

Secondly, they were at last forced to it. The first was forced to join by the King of Sweden himself, who being come so far was not to be dallied with, and had not the Duke of Brandenburg complied as he did, he had been ruined by the Swede. The Saxon was driven into the arms of the Swede by force, for Count Tilly, ravaging his country, made him comply with any terms to be saved from destruction.

Thus matters stood at the end of the Diet at Ratisbon. The King of Sweden began to see himself leagued against at the Diet both by Protestant and Papist; and, as I have often heard his Majesty say since, he had resolved to try to force them off from the emperor, and to treat them as enemies equally with the rest if they did not.

But the Protestants convinced him soon after, that though they were tricked into the outward appearance of a league against him at Ratisbon, they had no such intentions; and by their ambassadors to him let him know that they only wanted his powerful assistance to defend their councils, when they would soon convince him that they had a due sense of the emperor's designs, and would do their utmost for their liberty. And these I take to be the first invitations the King of Sweden had to undertake the Protestant cause as such, and which entitled him to say he fought for the liberty and religion of the German nation. I have had some particular opportunities to hear these things form the mouths of some of the very princes themselves, and therefore am the forwarder to relate them; and I place them here because, previous to the part I acted on this bloody scene, 'tis necessary to let the reader into some part of that story, and to show him in what manner and on what occasions this terrible war began.

The Protestants, alarmed at the usage they had met with at the former Diet, had secretly proposed among themselves to form a general union or confederacy, for preventing that ruin which they saw, unless some speedy remedies were applied, would be inevitable. The Elector of Saxony, the head of the Protestants, a vigorous and politic prince, was the first that moved it; and the Landgrave of Hesse, a zealous and gallant prince, being consulted with, it rested a great while between those two, no method being found practicable to bring it to pass, the emperor being so powerful in all parts, that they foresaw the petty princes would not dare to negotiate an affair of such a nature, being surrounded with the Imperial forces, who by their two generals, Wallenstein and Tilly, kept them in continual subjection and terror.

This dilemma had like to have stifled the thoughts of the union as a thing impracticable, when one Seigensius, a Lutheran minister, a person of great abilities, and one whom the Elector of Saxony made great use of in matters of policy as well as religion, contrived for them this excellent expedient.

I had the honour to be acquainted with this gentleman while I was at Leipsic. It pleased him exceedingly to have been the contriver of so fine a structure as the Conclusions of Leipsic, and he was glad to be entertained on that subject. I had the relation from his own mouth, when, but very modestly, he told me he thought 'twas an inspiration darted on a sudden into his thoughts, when the Duke of Saxony calling him into his closet one morning, with a face full of concern, shaking his head, and looking very earnestly, "What will become of us, doctor?" said the duke; "we shall all be undone at Frankfort-au-Main." "Why so, please your highness?" says the doctor. "Why, they will fight with the King of Sweden with our armies and our money," says the duke, "and devour our friends and ourselves by the help of our friends and ourselves." "But what is become of the confederacy, then," said the doctor, "which your highness had so happily framed in your thoughts, and which the Landgrave of Hesse was so pleased with?" "Become of it?" says the duke, "'tis a good thought enough, but 'tis impossible to bring it to pass among so many members of the Protestant princes as are to be consulted with, for we neither have time to treat, nor will half of them dare to negotiate the matter, the Imperialists being quartered in their very bowels." "But may not some expedient be found out," says the doctor, "to bring them all together to treat of it in a general meeting?" "'Tis well proposed," says the duke, "but in what town or city shall they assemble where the very deputies shall not be besieged by Tilly or Wallenstein in fourteen days' time, and sacrificed to the cruelty and fury of the Emperor Ferdinand?" "Will your highness be the easier in it," replies the doctor, "if a way may be found out to call such an assembly upon other causes, at which the emperor may have no umbrage, and perhaps give his assent? You know the Diet at Frankfort is at hand; 'tis necessary the Protestants should have an assembly of their own to prepare matters for the General Diet, and it may be no difficult matter to obtain it." The duke, surprised with joy at the motion, embraced the doctor with an extraordinary transport. "Thou hast done it, doctor," said he, and immediately caused him to draw a form of a letter to the emperor, which he did with the utmost dexterity of style, in which he was a great master, representing to his Imperial Majesty that, in order to put an end to the troubles of Germany, his Majesty would be pleased to permit the Protestant princes of the empire to hold a Diet to themselves, to consider of such matters as they were to treat of at the General Diet, in order to conform themselves to the will and pleasure of his Imperial Majesty, to drive out foreigners, and settle a lasting peace in the empire. He also insinuated something of their resolutions unanimously to give their suffrages in favour of the King of Hungary at the election of a king of the Romans, a thing which he knew the emperor had in his thought, and would push at with all his might at the Diet. This letter was sent, and the bait so neatly concealed, that the Electors of Bavaria and Mentz, the King of Hungary, and several of the Popish princes, not foreseeing that the ruin of them all lay in the bottom of it, foolishly advised the emperor to consent to it. In consenting to this the emperor signed his own destruction, for here began the conjunction of the German Protestants with the Swede, which was the fatalest blow to Ferdinand, and which he could never recover.

Accordingly the Diet was held at Leipsic, February 8, 1630, where the Protestants agreed on several heads for their mutual defence, which were the grounds of the following war. These were the famous Conclusions of Leipsic, which so alarmed the emperor and the whole empire, that to crush it in the beginning, the emperor commanded Count Tilly immediately to fall upon the Landgrave of Hesse and the Duke of Saxony as the principal heads of the union; but it was too late.

The Conclusions were digested into ten heads:--

1. That since their sins had brought God's judgments upon the whole Protestant Church, they should command public prayers to be made to Almighty God for the diverting the calamities that attended them.

2. That a treaty of peace might be set on foot, in order to come to a right understanding with the Catholic princes.

3. That a time for such a treaty being obtained, they should appoint an assembly of delegates to meet preparatory to the treaty.

4. That all their complaints should be humbly represented to his Imperial Majesty and the Catholic Electors, in order to a peaceable accommodation.

5. That they claim the protection of the emperor, according to the laws of the empire, and the present emperor's solemn oath and promise.

6. That they would appoint deputies who should meet at certain times to consult of their common interest, and who should be always empowered to conclude of what should be thought needful for their safety.

7. That they will raise a competent force to maintain and defend their liberties, rights, and religion. 8. That it is agreeable to the Constitution of the empire, concluded in the Diet at Augsburg, to do so.

9. That the arming for their necessary defence shall by no means hinder their obedience to his Imperial Majesty, but that they will still continue their loyalty to him.

10. They agree to proportion their forces, which in all amounted to 70,000 men.

The emperor, exceedingly startled at the Conclusions, issued out a severe proclamation or ban against them, which imported much the same thing as a declaration of war, and commanded Tilly to begin, and immediately to fall on the Duke of Saxony with all the fury imaginable, as I have already observed.

Here began the flame to break out; for upon the emperor's ban, the Protestants send away to the King of Sweden for succour.

His Swedish Majesty had already conquered Mecklenburg, and part of Pomerania, and was advancing with his victorious troops, increased by the addition of some regiments raised in those parts, in order to carry on the war against the emperor, having designed to follow up the Oder into Silesia, and so to push the war home to the emperor's hereditary countries of Austria and Bohemia, when the first messengers came to him in this case; but this changed his measures, and brought him to the frontiers of Brandenburg resolved to answer the desires of the Protestants. But here the Duke of Brandenburg began to halt, making some difficulties and demanding terms, which drove the king to use some extremities with him, and stopped the Swedes for a while, who had otherwise been on the banks of the Elbe as soon as Tilly, the Imperial general, had entered Saxony, which if they had done, the miserable destruction of Magdeburg had been prevented, as I observed before. The king had been invited into the union, and when he first came back from the banks of the Oder he had accepted it, and was preparing to back it with all his power. The Duke of Saxony had already a good army which he had with infinite diligence recruited, and mustered them under the cannon of Leipsic. The King of Sweden having, by his ambassador at Leipsic, entered into the union of the Protestants, was advancing victoriously to their aid, just as Count Tilly had entered the Duke of Saxony's dominions. The fame of the Swedish conquests, and of the hero who commanded them, shook my resolution of travelling into Turkey, being resolved to see the conjunction of the Protestant armies, and before the fire was broke out too far to take the advantage of seeing both sides.

While I remained at Vienna, uncertain which way I should proceed, I remember I observed they talked of the King of Sweden as a prince of no consideration, one that they might let go on and tire himself in Mecklenburg and thereabout, till they could find leisure to deal with him, and then might be crushed as they pleased; but 'tis never safe to despise an enemy, so this was not an enemy to be despised, as they afterwards found.

As to the Conclusions of Leipsic, indeed, at first they gave the Imperial court some uneasiness, but when they found the Imperial armies, began to fright the members out of the union, and that the several branches had no considerable forces on foot, it was the general discourse at Vienna, that the union at Leipsic only gave the emperor an opportunity to crush absolutely the Dukes of Saxony, Brandenburg, and the Landgrave of Hesse, and they looked upon it as a thing certain.

I never saw any real concern in their faces at Vienna till news came to court that the King of Sweden had entered into the union; but as this made them very uneasy, they began to move the powerfulest methods possible to divert this storm; and upon this news Tilly was hastened to fall into Saxony before this union could proceed to a conjunction of forces. This was certainly a very good resolution, and no measure could have been more exactly concerted, had not the diligence of the Saxons prevented it.

The gathering of this storm, which from a cloud began to spread over the empire, and from the little duchy of Mecklenburg began to threaten all Germany, absolutely determined me, as I noted before, as to travelling, and laying aside the thoughts of Hungary, I resolved, if possible, to see the King of Sweden's army.

I parted from Vienna the middle of May, and took post for Great Glogau in Silesia, as if I had purposed to pass into Poland, but designing indeed to go down the Oder to Custrim in the marquisate of Brandenburg, and so to Berlin. But when I came to the frontiers of Silesia, though I had passes, I could go no farther, the guards on all the frontiers were so strict, so I was obliged to come back into Bohemia, and went to Prague. From hence I found I could easily pass through the Imperial provinces to the lower Saxony, and accordingly took passes for Hamburg, designing, however, to use them no farther than I found occasion.

By virtue of these passes I got into the Imperial army, under Count Tilly, then at the siege of Magdeburg, May the 2nd.

I confess I did not foresee the fate of this city, neither, I believe, did Count Tilly himself expect to glut his fury with so entire a desolation, much less did the people expect it. I did believe they must capitulate, and I perceived by discourse in the army that Tilly would give them but very indifferent conditions; but it fell out otherwise. The treaty of surrender was, as it were, begun, nay, some say concluded, when some of the out-guards of the Imperialists finding the citizens had abandoned the guards of the works, and looked to themselves with less diligence than usual, they broke in, carried an half-moon, sword in hand, with little resistance; and though it was a surprise on both sides, the citizens neither fearing, nor the army expecting the occasion, the garrison, with as much resolution as could be expected under such a fright, flew to the walls, twice beat the Imperialists off, but fresh men coming up, and the administrator of Magdeburg himself being wounded and taken, the enemy broke in, took the city by storm, and entered with such terrible fury, that, without respect to age or condition, they put all the garrison and inhabitants, man, woman, and child, to the sword, plundered the city, and when they had done this set it on fire.

This calamity sure was the dreadfulest sight that ever I saw; the rage of the Imperial soldiers was most intolerable, and not to be expressed. Of 25,000, some said 30,000 people, there was not a soul to be seen alive, till the flames drove those that were hid in vaults and secret places to seek death in the streets rather than perish in the fire. Of these miserable creatures some were killed too by the furious soldiers, but at last they saved the lives of such as came out of their cellars and holes, and so about two thousand poor desperate creatures were left. The exact number of those that perished in this city could never be known, because those the soldiers had first butchered the flames afterwards devoured.

I was on the outer side of the Elbe when this dreadful piece of butchery was done. The city of Magdeburg had a sconce or fort over against it called the toll-house, which joined to the city by a very fine bridge of boats. This fort was taken by the Imperialists a few days before, and having a mind to see it, and the rather because from thence I could have a very good view of the city, I was going over Tilley's bridge of boats to view this fort. About ten o'clock in the morning I perceived they were storming by the firing, and immediately all ran to the works; I little thought of the taking the city, but imagined it might be some outwork attacked, for we all expected the city would surrender that day, or next, and they might have capitulated upon very good terms.

Being upon the works of the fort, on a sudden I heard the dreadfulest cry raised in the city that can be imagined; 'tis not possible to express the manner of it, and I could see the women and children running about the streets in a most lamentable condition.

24

The city wall did not run along the side where the river was with so great a height, but we could plainly see the market-place and the several streets which run down to the river. In about an hour's time after this first cry all was in confusion; there was little shooting, the execution was all cutting of throats and mere house murders. The resolute garrison, with the brave Baron Falkenberg, fought it out to the last, and were cut in pieces, and by this time the Imperial soldiers having broke open the gates and entered on all sides, the slaughter was very dreadful. We could see the poor people in crowds driven down the streets, flying from the fury of the soldiers, who followed butchering them as fast as they could, and refused mercy to anybody, till driving them to the river's edge, the desperate wretches would throw themselves into the river, where thousands of them perished, especially women and children. Several men that could swim got over to our side, where the soldiers not heated with fight gave them quarter, and took them up, and I cannot but do this justice to the German officers in the fort: they had five small flat boats, and they gave leave to the soldiers to go off in them, and get what booty they could, but charged them not to kill anybody, but take them all prisoners.

Nor was their humanity ill rewarded, for the soldiers, wisely avoiding those places where their fellows were employed in butchering the miserable people, rowed to other places, where crowds of people stood crying out for help, and expecting to be every minute either drowned or murdered; of these at sundry times they fetched over near six hundred, but took care to take in none but such as offered them good pay.

Never was money or jewels of greater service than now, for those that had anything of that sort to offer were soonest helped.

There was a burgher of the town who, seeing a boat coming near him, but out of his call, by the help of a speaking trumpet, told the soldiers in it he would give them 20,000 dollars to fetch him off. They rowed close to the shore, and got him with his wife and six children into the boat, but such throngs of people got about the boat that had like to have sunk her, so that the soldiers were fain to drive a great many out again by main force, and while they were doing this some of the enemies coming down the street desperately drove them all into the water.

The boat, however, brought the burgher and his wife and children safe, and though they had not all that wealth about them, yet in jewels and money he gave them so much as made all the fellows very rich.

I cannot pretend to describe the cruelty of this day: the town by five in the afternoon was all in a flame; the wealth consumed was inestimable, and a loss to the very conqueror. I think there was little or nothing left but the great church and about a hundred houses. This was a sad welcome into the army for me, and gave me a horror and aversion to the emperor's people, as well as to his cause. I quitted the camp the third day after this execution, while the fire was hardly out in the city; and from thence getting safe-conduct to pass into the Palatinate, I turned out of the road at a small village on the Elbe, called Emerfield, and by ways and towns I can give but small account of, having a boor for our guide, whom we could hardly understand, I arrived at Leipsic on the 17th of May.

We found the elector intense upon the strengthening of his army, but the people in the greatest terror imaginable, every day expecting Tilly with the German army, who by his cruelty at Magdeburg was become so dreadful to the Protestants that they expected no mercy wherever he came.

The emperor's power was made so formidable to all the Protestants, particularly since the Diet at Ratisbon left them in a worse case than it found them, that they had not only formed the Conclusions of Leipsic, which all men looked on as the effect of desperation rather than any probable means of their deliverance, but had privately implored the protection and assistance of foreign powers, and particularly the King of Sweden, from whom they had promises of a speedy and powerful assistance. And truly if the Swede had not with a very strong hand rescued them, all their Conclusions at Leipsic had served but to hasten their ruin. I remember very well when I was in the Imperial army they discoursed with such contempt of the forces of the Protestant, that not only the Imperialists but the Protestants themselves gave them up as lost. The emperor had not less than 200,000 men in several armies on foot, who most of them were on the back of the Protestants in every corner. If Tilly did but write a threatening letter to any city or prince of the union, they presently submitted, renounced the Conclusions of Leipsic, and received Imperial garrisons, as the cities of Ulm and Memmingen, the duchy of Wirtemberg, and several others, and almost all Suaben.

Only the Duke of Saxony and the Landgrave of Hesse upheld the drooping courage of the Protestants, and refused all terms of peace, slighted all the threatenings of the Imperial generals, and the Duke of Brandenburg was brought in afterward almost by force. The Duke of Saxony mustered his forces under the walls of Leipsic, and I having returned to Leipsic, two days before, saw them pass the review. The duke, gallantly mounted, rode through the ranks, attended by his

field-marshal Arnheim, and seemed mighty well pleased with them, and indeed the troops made a very fine appearance; but I that had seen Tilly's army and his old weather-beaten soldiers, whose discipline and exercises were so exact, and their courage so often tried, could not look on the Saxon army without some concern for them when I considered who they had to deal with. Tilly's men were rugged surly fellows, their faces had an air of hardy courage, mangled with wounds and scars, their armour showed the bruises of musket bullets, and the rust of the winter storms. I observed of them their clothes were always dirty, but their arms were clean and bright; they were used to camp in the open fields, and sleep in the frosts and rain; their horses were strong and hardy like themselves, and well taught their exercises; the soldiers knew their business so exactly that general orders were enough; every private man was fit to command, and their wheelings, marchings, counter-marchings and exercise were done with such order and readiness, that the distinct words of command were hardly of any use among them; they were flushed with victory, and hardly knew what it was to fly.

There had passed some messages between Tilly and the duke, and he gave always such ambiguous answers as he thought might serve to gain time; but Tilly was not to be put off with words, and drawing his army towards Saxony, sends four propositions to him to sign, and demands an immediate reply. The propositions were positive.

1. To cause his troops to enter into the emperor's service, and to march in person with them against the King of Sweden.

2. To give the Imperial army quarters in his country, and supply them with necessary provisions.

3. To relinquish the union of Leipsic, and disown the ten Conclusions.

4. To make restitution of the goods and lands of the Church. The duke being pressed by Tilly's trumpeter for an immediate answer sat all night, and part of the next day, in council with his privy councillors, debating what reply to give him, which at last was concluded, in short, that he would live and die in defence of the Protestant religion, and the Conclusions of Leipsic, and bade Tilly defiance.

The die being thus cast, he immediately decamped with his whole army for Torgau, fearing that Tilly should get there before him, and so prevent his conjunction with the Swede. The duke had not yet concluded any positive treaty with the King of Swedeland, and the Duke of Brandenburg having made some difficulty of joining, they both stood on some niceties till they had like to have ruined themselves all at once.

Brandenburg had given up the town of Spandau to the king by a former treaty to secure a retreat for his army, and the king was advanced as far as Frankfort-upon-the-Oder, when on a sudden some small difficulties arising, Brandenburg seems cold in the matter, and with a sort of indifference demands to have his town of Spandau restored to him again. Gustavus Adolphus, who began presently to imagine the duke had made his peace with the emperor, and so would either be his enemy or pretend a neutrality, generously delivered him his town of Spandau, but immediately turns about, and with his whole army besieges him in his capital city of Berlin.

This brought the duke to know his error, and by the interpositions of the ladies, the Queen of Sweden being the duke's sister, the matter was accommodated, and the duke joined his forces with the king.

But the duke of Saxony had like to have been undone by this delay, for the Imperialists, under Count de Furstenberg, were entered his country, and had possessed themselves of Halle, and Tilly was on his march to join him, as he afterwards did, and ravaging the whole country laid siege to Leipsic itself. The duke driven to this extremity rather flies to the Swede than treats with him, and on the 2nd of September the duke's army joined with the King of Sweden.

I had not come to Leipsic but to see the Duke of Saxony's army, and that being marched, as I have said, for Torgau, I had no business there, but if I had, the approach of Tilly and the Imperial army was enough to hasten me away, for I had no occasion to be besieged there; so on the 27th of August I left the town, as several of the principal inhabitants had done before, and more would have done had not the governor published a proclamation against it, and besides they knew not whither to fly, for all places were alike exposed. The poor people were under dreadful apprehensions of a siege, and of the merciless usage of the Imperial soldiers, the example of Magdeburg being fresh before them, the duke and his army gone from them, and the town, though well furnished, but indifferently fortified.

In this condition I left them, buying up stores of provisions, working hard to scour their moats, set up palisadoes, repair their fortifications, and preparing all things for a siege; and following the Saxon army to Torgau, I continued in the camp till a few days before they joined the King of Sweden.

I had much ado to persuade my companion from entering into the service of the Duke of Saxony, one of whose colonels, with whom we had contracted a particular acquaintance, offering him a commission to be cornet in one of the old regiments of horse; but the difference I had observed between this new army and Tilly's old troops had made such an impression on me, that I confess I had yet no manner of inclination for the service, and therefore persuaded him to wait a while till we had seen a little further into affairs, and particularly till we had seen the Swedish army which we had heard so much of.

The difficulties which the Elector-Duke of Saxony made of joining with the king were made up by a treaty concluded with the king on the 2nd of September at Coswig, a small town on the Elbe, whither the king's army was arrived the night before; for General Tilly being now entered into the duke's country, had plundered and ruined all the lower part of it, and was now actually besieging the capital city of Leipsic. These necessities made almost any conditions easy to him; the greatest difficulty was that the King of Sweden demanded the absolute command of the army, which the duke submitted to with less goodwill than he had reason to do, the king's experience and conduct considered. I had not patience to attend the conclusions of their particular treaties, but as soon as ever the passage was clear I quitted the Saxon camp and went to see the Swedish army. I fell in with the out-guards of the Swedes at a little town called Beltsig, on the river Wersa, just as they were relieving the guards and going to march, and having a pass from the English ambassador was very well received by the officer who changed the guards, and with him I went back into the army. By nine in the morning the army was in full march, the king himself at the head of them on a grey pad, and riding from one brigade to another, ordered the march of every line himself.

When I saw the Swedish troops, their exact discipline, their order, the modesty and familiarity of their officers, and the regular living of the soldiers, their camp seemed a well-ordered city; the meanest country woman with her market ware was as safe from violence as in the streets of Vienna. There were no women in the camp but such as being known to the provosts to be the wives of the soldiers, who were necessary for washing linen, taking care of the soldiers' clothes, and dressing their victuals.

The soldiers were well clad, not gay, furnished with excellent arms, and exceedingly careful of them; and though they did not seem so terrible as I thought Tilly's men did when I first saw them, yet the figure they made, together with what we had heard of them, made them seem to me invincible: the discipline and order of their marchings, camping, and exercise was excellent and singular, and, which was to be seen in no armies but the king's, his own skill, judgment, and vigilance having added much to the general conduct of armies then in use.

As I met the Swedes on their march I had no opportunity to acquaint myself with anybody till after the conjunction of the Saxon army, and then it being but four days to the great battle of Leipsic, our acquaintance was but small, saving what fell out accidentally by conversation.

I met with several gentlemen in the king's army who spoke English very well; besides that there were three regiments of Scots in the army, the colonels whereof I found were extraordinarily esteemed by the king, as the Lord Reay, Colonel Lumsdell, and Sir John Hepburn. The latter of these, after I had by an accident become acquainted with, I found had been for many years acquainted with my father, and on that account I received a great deal of civility from him, which afterwards grew into a kind of intimate friendship. He was a complete soldier indeed, and for that reason so well beloved by that gallant king, that he hardly knew how to go about any great action without him.

It was impossible for me now to restrain my young comrade from entering into the Swedish service, and indeed everything was so inviting that I could not blame him. A captain in Sir John Hepburn's regiment had picked acquaintance with him, and he having as much gallantry

28

in his face as real courage in his heart, the captain had persuaded him to take service, and promised to use his interest to get him a company in the Scotch brigade. I had made him promise me not to part from me in my travels without my consent, which was the only obstacle to his desires of entering into the Swedish pay; and being one evening in the captain's tent with him and discoursing very freely together, the captain asked him very short but friendly, and looking earnestly at me, "Is this the gentleman, Mr Fielding, that has done so much prejudice to the King of Sweden's service?" I was doubly surprised at the expression, and at the colonel, Sir John Hepburn, coming at that very moment into the tent. The colonel hearing something of the question, but knowing nothing of the reason of it, any more than as I seemed a little to concern myself at it, yet after the ceremony due to his character was over, would needs know what I had done to hinder his Majesty's service. "So much truly," says the captain, "that if his Majesty knew it he would think himself very little beholden to him." "I am sorry, sir," said I, "that I should offend in anything, who am but a stranger; but if you would please to inform me, I would endeavour to alter anything in my behaviour that is prejudicial to any one, much less to his Majesty's service." "I shall take you at your word, sir," says the captain; "the King of Sweden, sir, has a particular request to you." "I should be glad to know two things, sir," said I; "first, how that can be possible, since I am not yet known to any man in the army, much less to his Majesty? and secondly, what the request can be?" "Why, sir, his Majesty desires you would not hinder this gentleman from entering into his service, who it seems desires nothing more, if he may have your consent to it." "I have too much honour for his Majesty," returned I, "to deny anything which he pleases to command me; but methinks 'tis some hardship you should make that the king's order, which 'tis very probable he knows nothing of." Sir John Hepburn took the case up something gravely, and drinking a glass of Leipsic beer to the captain, said, "Come, captain, don't press these gentlemen; the king desires no man's service but what is purely volunteer." So we entered into other discourse, and the colonel perceiving by my talk that I had seen Tilly's army, was mighty curious in his questions, and seeming very well satisfied with the account I gave him.

The next day the army having passed the Elbe at Wittenberg, and joined the Saxon army near Torgau, his Majesty caused both armies to draw up in battalia, giving every brigade the same post in the lines as he purposed to fight in. I must do the memory of that glorious general this honour, that I never saw an army drawn up with so much variety, order, and exact regularity since, though I have seen many armies drawn up by some of the greatest captains of the age. The order by which his men were directed to flank and relieve one another, the methods of receiving one body of men if disordered into another, and rallying one squadron without disordering another was so admirable; the horse everywhere flanked lined and defended by the foot, and the foot by the horse, and both by the cannon, was such that if those orders were but as punctually obeyed, 'twere impossible to put an army so modelled into any confusion.

The view being over, and the troops returned to their camps, the captain with whom we drank the day before meeting me told me I must come and sup with him in his tent, where he would ask my pardon for the affront he gave me before. I told him he needed not put himself to the trouble, I was not affronted at all; that I would do myself the honour to wait on him, provided he would give me his word not to speak any more of it as an affront.

We had not been a quarter of an hour in his tent but Sir John Hepburn came in again, and addressing to me, told me he was glad to find me there; that he came to the captain's tent to inquire how to send to me; and that I must do him the honour to go with him to wait on the king, who had a mind to hear the account I could give him of the Imperial army from my own mouth. I must confess I was at some loss in my mind how to make my address to his Majesty, but I had heard so much of the conversable temper of the king, and his particular sweetness of humour with the meanest soldier, that I made no more difficulty, but having paid my respects to Colonel Hepburn, thanked him for the honour he had done me, and offered to rise and wait upon him. "Nay," says the Colonel, "we will eat first, for I find Gourdon," which was the captain's name, "has got something for supper, and the king's order is at seven o'clock." So we went to supper, and Sir John, becoming very friendly, must know my name; which, when I had told him, and of what place and family, he rose from his seat, and embracing me, told me he knew my father very well, and had been intimately acquainted with him, and told me several passages wherein my father had particularly obliged him. After this we went to supper, and the king's health being drank round, the colonel moved the sooner because he had a mind to talk with me.

When we were going to the king he inquired of me where I had been, and what occasion brought me to the army. I told him the short history of my travels, and that I came hither from Vienna on purpose to see the King of Sweden and his army. He asked me if there was any service he could do me, by which he meant, whether I desired an employment. I pretended not to take him so, but told him the protection his acquaintance would afford me was more than I could have asked, since I might thereby have opportunity to satisfy my curiosity, which was the chief end of my coming abroad. He perceiving by this that I had no mind to be a soldier, told me very kindly I should command him in anything; that his tent and equipage, horses and servants should always have orders to be at my service; but that as a piece of friendship, he would advise me to retire to some place distant from the army, for that the army would march to-morrow, and the king was resolved to fight General Tilly, and he would not have me hazard myself; that if I thought fit to take his advice, he would have me take that interval to see the court at Berlin, whither he would send one of his servants to wait on me. His discourse was too kind not to extort the tenderest acknowledgment from me that I was capable of. I told him his care of me was so obliging, that I knew not what return to make him, but if he pleased to leave me to my choice I desired no greater favour than to trail a pike under his command in the ensuing battle. "I can never answer it to your father," says he, "to suffer you to expose yourself so far." I told him my father would certainly acknowledge his friendship in the proposal made me; but I believed he knew him better than to think he would be well pleased with me if I should accept of it; that I was sure my father would have rode post five hundred miles to have been at such a battle under such a general, and it should never be told him that his son had rode fifty miles to be out of it. He seemed to be something concerned at the resolution I had taken, and replied very quickly upon me, that he approved very well of my courage; "but," says he, "no man gets any credit by running upon needless adventures, nor loses any by shunning hazards which he has no order for. 'Tis enough," says he, "for a gentleman to behave well when he is commanded upon any service; I have had fighting enough," says he, "upon these points of honour, and I never got anything but reproof for it from the king himself."

"Well, sir," said I, "however if a man expects to rise by his valour, he must show it somewhere; and if I were to have any command in an army, I would first try whether I could deserve it. I have never yet seen any service, and must have my induction some time or other. I shall never have a better schoolmaster than yourself, nor a better school than such an army." "Well," says Sir John, "but you may have the same school and the same teaching after this battle is over; for I must tell you beforehand, this will be a bloody touch. Tilly has a great army of old lads that are used to boxing, fellows with iron faces, and 'tis a little too much to engage so hotly the first entrance into the wars. You may see our discipline this winter, and make your campaign with us next summer, when you need not fear but we shall have fighting enough, and you will be better acquainted with things. We do never put our common soldiers upon pitched battles the first campaign, but place our new men in garrisons and try them in parties first." "Sir," said I, with a little more freedom, "I believe I shall not make a trade of the war, and therefore need not serve an apprenticeship to it; 'tis a hard battle where none escapes. If I come off, I hope I shall not disgrace you, and if not, 'twill be some satisfaction to my father to hear his son died fighting under the command of Sir John Hepburn, in the army of the King of Sweden, and I desire no better epitaph upon my tomb."

"Well," says Sir John, and by this time we were just come to the king's quarters, and the guards calling to us interrupted his reply; so we went into the courtyard where the king was lodged, which was in an indifferent house of one of the burghers of Dieben, and Sir John stepping up, met the king coming down some steps into a large room which looked over the town wall into a field where part of the artillery was drawn up. Sir John Hepburn sent his man presently to me to come up, which I did; and Sir John without any ceremony carries me directly up to the king, who was leaning on his elbow in the window. The king turning about, "This is the English gentleman," says Sir John, "who I told your Majesty had been in the Imperial army." "How then did he get hither," says the king, "without being taken by the scouts?" At which question, Sir John saying nothing, "By a pass, and please your Majesty, from the English ambassador's secretary at Vienna," said I, making a profound reverence. "Have you then been at Vienna?" says the king. "Yes, and please your Majesty," said I; upon which the king, folding up a letter he had in his hand, seemed much more earnest to talk about Vienna than about Tilly. "And, pray, what news had you at Vienna?" "Nothing, sir," said I, "but daily accounts one in the neck of another of their own misfortunes, and your Majesty's conquests, which makes a very melancholy court there." "But, pray," said the king, "what is the common opinion there about these affairs?" "The common people are terrified to the last degree," said I, "and when your Majesty took

Frankfort-upon-Oder, if your army had marched but twenty miles into Silesia, half the people would have run out of Vienna, and I left them fortifying the city." "They need not," replied the king, smiling; "I have no design to trouble them, it is the Protestant countries I must be for."

Upon this the Duke of Saxony entered the room, and finding the king engaged, offered to retire; but the king, beckoning with his hand, called to him in French; "Cousin," says the king, "this gentleman has been travelling and comes from Vienna," and so made me repeat what I had said before; at which the king went on with me, and Sir John Hepburn informing his Majesty that I spoke High Dutch, he changed his language, and asked me in Dutch where it was that I saw General Tilly's army. I told his Majesty at the siege of Magdeburg. "At Magdeburg!" said the king, shaking his head; "Tilly must answer to me some day for that city, and if not to me, to a greater King than I. Can you guess what army he had with him?" said the king. "He had two armies with him," said I, "but one I suppose will do your Majesty no harm." "Two armies!" said the king. "Yes, sir, he has one army of about 26,000 men," said I, "and another of about 15,000 women and their attendants," at which the king laughed heartily. "Ay, ay," says the king, "those 15,000 do us as much harm as the 26,000, for they eat up the country, and devour the poor Protestants more than the men. Well," says the king, "do they talk of fighting us?" "They talk big enough, sir," said I, "but your Majesty has not been so often fought with as beaten in their discourse." "I know not for the men," says the king, "but the old man is as likely to do it as talk of it, and I hope to try them in a day or two."

The king inquired after that several matters of me about the Low Countries, the Prince of Orange, and of the court and affairs in England; and Sir John Hepburn informing his Majesty that I was the son of an English gentleman of his acquaintance, the king had the goodness to ask him what care he had taken of me against the day of battle. Upon which Sir John repeated to him the discourse we had together by the way; the king seeming particularly pleased with it, began to take me to task himself. "You English gentlemen," says he, "are too forward in the wars, which makes you leave them too soon again." "Your Majesty," replied I, "makes war in so pleasant a manner as makes all the world fond of fighting under your conduct." "Not so pleasant neither," says the king, "here's a man can tell you that sometimes it is not very pleasant." "I know not much of the warrior, sir," said I, "nor of the world, but if always to conquer be the pleasure of the war, your Majesty's soldiers have all that can be desired." "Well," says the king, "but however, considering all things, I think you would do well to take the advice Sir John Hepburn has given you." "Your Majesty may command me to anything, but where your Majesty and so many gallant gentlemen hazard their lives, mine is not worth mentioning; and I should not dare to tell my father at my return into England that I was in your Majesty's army, and made so mean a figure that your Majesty would not permit me to fight under that royal standard." "Nay," replied the king, "I lay no commands upon you, but you are young." "I can never die, sir," said I, "with more honour than in your Majesty's service." I spake this with so much freedom, and his Majesty was so pleased with it, that he asked me how I would choose to serve, on horseback or on foot. I told his Majesty I should be glad to receive any of his Majesty's commands, but if I had not that honour I had purposed to trail a pike under Sir John Hepburn, who had done me so much honour as to introduce me into his Majesty's presence. "Do so, then," replied the king, and turning to Sir John Hepburn, said, "and pray, do you take care of him." At which, overcome with the goodness of his discourse, I could not answer a word, but made him a profound reverence and retired.

The next day but one, being the 7th of September, before day the army marched from Dieben to a large field about a mile from Leipsic, where we found Tilly's army in full battalia in admirable order, which made a show both glorious and terrible. Tilly, like a fair gamester, had taken up but one side of the plain, and left the other free, and all the avenues open for the king's army; nor did he stir to the charge till the king's army was completely drawn up and advanced toward him. He had in his army 44,000 old soldiers, every way answerable to what I have said of them before; and I shall only add, a better army, I believe, never was so soundly beaten.

The king was not much inferior in force, being joined with the Saxons, who were reckoned 22,000 men, and who drew up on the left, making a main battle and two wings, as the king did on the right.

The king placed himself at the right wing of his own horse, Gustavus Horn had the main battle of the Swedes, the Duke of Saxony had the main battle of his own troops, and General Arnheim the right wing of his horse. The second line of the Swedes consisted of the two Scotch brigades, and three Swedish, with the Finland horse in the wings.

In the beginning of the fight, Tilly's right wing charged with such irresistible fury upon the left of the king's army where the Saxons were posted, that nothing could withstand them. The Saxons fled amain, and some of them carried the news over the country that all was lost, and the king's army overthrown; and indeed it passed for an oversight with some that the king did not place some of his old troops among the Saxons, who were new-raised men. The Saxons lost here near 2000 men, and hardly ever showed their faces again all the battle, except some few of their horse.

I was posted with my comrade, the captain, at the head of three Scottish regiments of foot, commanded by Sir John Hepburn, with express directions from the colonel to keep by him. Our post was in the second line, as a reserve to the King of Sweden's main battle, and, which was strange, the main battle, which consisted of four great brigades of foot, were never charged during the whole fight; and yet we, who had the reserve, were obliged to endure the whole weight of the Imperial army. The occasion was, the right wing of the Imperialists having defeated the Saxons, and being eager in the chase, Tilly, who was an old soldier, and ready to prevent all mistakes, forbids any pursuit. "Let them go," says he, "but let us beat the Swedes, or we do nothing." Upon this the victorious troops fell in upon the flank of the king's army, which, the Saxons being fled, lay open to them. Gustavus Horn commanded the left wing of the Swedes, and having first defeated some regiments which charged him, falls in upon the rear of the Imperial right wing, and separates them from the van, who were advanced a great way forward in pursuit of the Saxons, and having routed the said rear or reserve, falls on upon Tilly's main battle, and defeated part of them; the other part was gone in chase of the Saxons, and now also returned, fell in upon the rear of the left wing of the Swedes, charging them in the flank, for they drew up upon the very ground which the Saxons had quitted. This changed the whole front, and made the Swedes face about to the left, and made a great front on their flank to make this good. Our brigades, who were placed as a reserve for the main battle, were, by special order from the king, wheeled about to the left, and placed for the right of this new front to charge the Imperialists; they were about 12,000 of their best foot, besides horse, and flushed with the execution of the Saxons, fell on like furies. The king by this time had almost defeated the Imperialists' left wing; their horse, with more haste than good speed, had charged faster than their foot could follow, and having broke into the king's first line, he let them go, where, while the second line bears the shock, and bravely resisted them, the king follows them on the crupper with thirteen troops of horse, and some musketeers, by which being hemmed in, they were all cut down in a moment as it were, and the army never disordered with them.

This fatal blow to the left wing gave the king more leisure to defeat the foot which followed, and to send some assistance to Gustavus Horn in his left wing, who had his hands full with the main battle of the Imperialists.

But those troops who, as I said, had routed the Saxons, being called off from the pursuit, had charged our flank, and were now grown very strong, renewed the battle in a terrible manner. Here it was I saw our men go to wreck. Colonel Hall, a brave soldier, commanded the rear of the Swede's left wing; he fought like a lion, but was slain, and most of his regiment cut off, though not unrevenged, for they entirely ruined Furstenberg's regiment of foot. Colonel Cullembach, with his regiment of horse, was extremely overlaid also, and the colonel and many brave officers killed, and in short all that wing was shattered, and in an ill condition.

In this juncture came the king, and having seen what havoc the enemy made of Cullembach's troops, he comes riding along the front of our three brigades, and himself led us on to the charge; the colonel of his guards, the Baron Dyvel, was shot dead just as the king had given him some orders.

When the Scots advanced, seconded by some regiments of horse which the king also sent to the charge, the bloodiest fight began that ever men beheld, for the Scottish brigades,

33

giving fire three ranks at a time over one another's heads, poured in their shot so thick, that the enemy were cut down like grass before a scythe; and following into the thickest of their foot with the clubs of their muskets made a most dreadful slaughter, and yet was there no flying. Tilly's men might be killed and knocked down, but no man turned his back, nor would give an inch of ground, but as they were wheeled, or marched, or retreated by their officers.

There was a regiment of cuirassiers which stood whole to the last, and fought like lions; they went ranging over the field when all their army was broken, and nobody cared for charging them; they were commanded by Baron Kronenburg, and at last went off from the battle whole. These were armed in black armour from head to foot, and they carried off their general. About six o'clock the field was cleared of the enemy, except at one place on the king's side, where some of them rallied, and though they knew all was lost would take no quarter, but fought it out to the last man, being found dead the next day in rank and file as they were drawn up.

I had the good fortune to receive no hurt in this battle, excepting a small scratch on the side of my neck by the push of a pike; but my friend received a very dangerous wound when the battle was as good as over. He had engaged with a German colonel, whose name we could never learn, and having killed his man, and pressed very close upon him, so that he had shot his horse, the horse in the fall kept the colonel down, lying on one of his legs; upon which he demanded quarter, which Captain Fielding granting, helped him to quit his horse, and having disarmed him, was bringing him into the line, when the regiment of cuirassiers, which I mentioned, commanded by Baron Kronenburg, came roving over the field, and with a flying charge saluted our front with a salvo of carabine shot, which wounded us a great many men, and among the rest the captain received a shot in his thigh, which laid him on the ground, and being separated from the line, his prisoner got away with them.

This was the first service I was in, and indeed I never saw any fight since maintained with such gallantry, such desperate valour, together with such dexterity of management, both sides being composed of soldiers fully tried, bred to the wars, expert in everything, exact in their order, and incapable of fear, which made the battle be much more bloody than usual. Sir John Hepburn, at my request, took particular care of my comrade, and sent his own surgeon to look after him; and afterwards, when the city of Leipsic was retaken, provided him lodgings there, and came very often to see him; and indeed I was in great care for him too, the surgeons being very doubtful of him a great while; for having lain in the field all night among the dead, his wound, for want of dressing, and with the extremity of cold, was in a very ill condition, and the pain of it had thrown him into a fever. 'Twas quite dusk before the fight ended, especially where the last rallied troops fought so long, and therefore we durst not break our order to seek out our friends, so that 'twas near seven o'clock the next morning before we found the captain, who, though very weak by the loss of blood, had raised himself up, and placed his back against the buttock of a dead horse. I was the first that knew him, and running to him, embraced him with a great deal of joy; he was not able to speak, but made signs to let me see he knew me, so we brought him into the camp, and Sir John Hepburn, as I noted before, sent his own surgeons to look after him.

The darkness of the night prevented any pursuit, and was the only refuge the enemy had left: for had there been three hours more daylight ten thousand more lives had been lost, for the Swedes (and Saxons especially) enraged by the obstinacy of the enemy, were so thoroughly heated that they would have given quarter but to few. The retreat was not sounded till seven o'clock, when the king drew up the whole army upon the field of battle, and gave strict command that none should stir from their order; so the army lay under their arms all night, which was another reason why the wounded soldiers suffered very much by the cold; for the king, who had a bold enemy to deal with, was not ignorant what a small body of desperate men rallied together might have done in the darkness of the night, and therefore he lay in his coach all night at the head of the line, though it froze very hard.

As soon as the day began to peep the trumpets sounded to horse, and all the dragoons and light-horse in the army were commanded to the pursuit. The cuirassiers and some commanded musketeers advanced some miles, if need were, to make good their retreat, and all the foot stood to their arms for a reverse; but in half-an-hour word was brought to the king that the enemy were quite dispersed, upon which detachments were made out of every regiment to search among the dead for any of our friends that were wounded; and the king himself gave a strict order, that if any were found wounded and alive among the enemy none should kill them, but take care to bring them into the camp--a piece of humanity which saved the lives of near a thousand of the enemies.

This piece of service being over, the enemy's camp was seized upon, and the soldiers were permitted to plunder it; all the cannon, arms, and ammunition was secured for the king's use, the rest was given up to the soldiers, who found so much plunder that they had no reason to quarrel for shares. For my share, I was so busy with my wounded captain that I got nothing but a sword, which I found just by him when I first saw him; but my man brought me a very good horse with a furniture on him, and one pistol of extraordinary workmanship.

I bade him get upon his back and make the best of the day for himself, which he did, and I saw him no more till three days after, when he found me out at Leipsic, so richly dressed that I hardly knew him; and after making his excuse for his long absence, gave me a very pleasant account where he had been. He told me that, according to my order, being mounted on the horse he had brought me, he first rid into the field among the dead to get some clothes suitable to the equipage of his horse, and having seized on a laced coat, a helmet, a sword, and an extraordinary good cane, was resolved to see what was become of the enemy; and following the track of the dragoons, which he could easily do by the bodies on the road, he fell in with a small party of twenty-five dragoons, under no command but a corporal, making to a village where some of the enemies' horse had been quartered. The dragoons, taking him for an officer by his horse, desired him to command them, told him the enemy was very rich, and they doubted not a good booty. He was a bold, brisk fellow, and told them, with all his heart, but said he had but one pistol, the other being broken with firing; so they lent him a pair of pistols, and a small piece they had taken, and he led them on. There had been a regiment of horse and some troops of Crabats in the village, but they were fled on the first notice of the pursuit, excepting three troops, and these, on sight of this small party, supposing them to be only the first of a greater number, fled in the greatest confusion imaginable.

They took the village, and about fifty horses, with all the plunder of the enemy, and with the heat of the service he had spoiled my horse, he said, for which he had brought me two more; for he, passing for the commander of the party, had all the advantage the custom of war gives an officer in like cases.

I was very well pleased with the relation the fellow gave me, and, laughing at him, "Well, captain," said I, "and what plunder have ye got?" "Enough to make me a captain, sir," says he, "if you please, and a troop ready raised too; for the party of dragoons are posted in the village by my command, till they have farther orders." In short, he pulled out sixty or seventy pieces of gold, five or six watches, thirteen or fourteen rings, whereof two were diamond rings, one of which was worth fifty dollars, silver as much as his pockets would hold; besides that he had brought three horses, two of which were laden with baggage, and a boor he had hired to stay with them at Leipsic till he had found me out. "But I am afraid, captain," says I, "you have plundered the village instead of plundering the enemy." "No indeed, not we," says he, "but the Crabats had done it for us and we light of them just as they were carrying it off." "Well," said I, "but what will you do with your men, for when you come to give them orders they will know you well enough?" "No, no," says he, "I took care of that, for just now I gave a soldier five dollars to carry them news that the army was marched to Merseburg, and that they should follow thither to the regiment."

Having secured his money in my lodgings, he asked me if I pleased to see his horses, and to have one for myself? I told him I would go and see them in the afternoon; but the fellow being impatient goes and fetches them.

There were three horses, one whereof was a very good one, and by the furniture was an officer's horse of the Crabats, and that my man would have me accept, for the other he had spoiled, as he said. I was but indifferently horsed before, so I accepted of the horse, and went down with him to see the rest of his plunder there. He had got three or four pair of pistols, two or three bundles of officers' linen, and lace, a field-bed, and a tent, and several other things of value; but at last, coming to a small fardel, "And this," says he, "I took whole from a Crabat running away with it under his arm," so he brought it up into my chamber. He had not looked into it, he said, but he understood 'twas some plunder the soldiers had made, and finding it heavy took it by consent. We opened it and found it was a bundle of some linen, thirteen or fourteen pieces of plate, and in a small cup, three rings, a fine necklace of pearl and the value of 100 rix-dollars in money.

The fellow was amazed at his own good fortune, and hardly knew what to do with himself; I bid him go take care of his other things, and of his horses, and come again. So he went and discharged the boor that waited and packed up all his plunder, and came up to me in his old clothes again. "How now, captain," says I, "what, have you altered your equipage already?" "I am no more ashamed, sir, of your livery," answered he, "than of your service, and nevertheless your servant for what I have got by it." "Well," says I to him, "but what will you do now with all your money?" "I wish my poor father had some of it," says he, "and for the rest I got it for you, sir, and desire you would take it." He spoke it with so much honesty and freedom that I could not but take it very kindly; but, however, I told him I would not take a farthing from him as his master, but I would have him play the good husband with it, now he had such good fortune to get it. He told me he would take my directions in everything. "Why, then," said I, "I'll tell you what I would advise you to do, turn it all into ready money, and convey it by return home into England, and follow yourself the first opportunity, and with good management you may put yourself in a good posture of living with it." The fellow, with a sort of dejection in his looks, asked me if he had disobliged me in anything? "Why?" says I. "That I was willing to turn him out of his service." "No, George" (that was his name), says I, "but you may live on this money without being a servant." "I'd throw it all into the Elbe," says he, "over Torgau bridge, rather than leave your service; and besides," says he, "can't I save my money without going from you? I got it in your service, and I'll never spend it out of your service, unless you put me away. I hope my money won't make me the worse servant; if I thought it would, I'd soon have little enough." "Nay, George," says I, "I shall not oblige you to it, for I am not willing to lose you neither: come, then," says I, "let us put it all together, and see what it will come to." So he laid it all together on the table, and by our computation he had gotten as much plunder as was worth about 1400 rix-dollars, besides three horses with their furniture, a tent, a bed, and some wearing linen. Then he takes the necklace of pearl, a very good watch, a diamond ring, and 100 pieces of gold, and lays them by themselves, and having, according to our best calculation, valued the things, he put up all the rest, and as I was going to ask him what they were left out for, he takes them up in his hand, and coming round the table, told me, that if I did not think him unworthy of my service and favour, he begged I would give him leave to make that present to me; that it was my first thought his going out, that he had got it all in my service, and he should think I had no kindness for him if I should refuse it. I was resolved in my mind not to take it from him, and yet I could find no means to resist his importunity. At last I told him, I would accept of part of his present, and that I esteemed his respect in that as much as the whole, and that I would not have him importune me farther; so I took the ring and watch, with the horse and furniture as before, and made him turn all the rest into money at Leipsic, and not suffering him to wear his livery, made him put himself into a tolerable equipage, and taking a young Leipsicer into my service, he attended me as a gentleman from that time forward.

The king's army never entered Leipsic, but proceeded to Merseberg, and from thence to Halle, and so marched on into Franconia, while the Duke of Saxony employed his forces in recovering Leipsic and driving the Imperialists out of his country. I continued at Leipsic twelve days, being not willing to leave my comrade till he was recovered; but Sir John Hepburn so often importuned me to come into the army, and sent me word that the king had very often inquired for me, that at last I consented to go without him; so having made our appointment where to meet, and how to correspond by letters, I went to wait on Sir John Hepburn, who then lay with the king's army at the city of Erfurt in Saxony. As I was riding between Leipsic and Halle, I observed my horse went very awkwardly and uneasy, and sweat very much, though the weather was cold, and we had rid but very softly; I fancied therefore that the saddle might hurt the horse, and calls my new captain up. "George," says I, "I believe this saddle hurts the horse." So we alighted, and looking under the saddle found the back of the horse extremely galled; so I bid him take off the saddle, which he did, and giving the horse to my young Leipsicer to lead, we sat down to see if we could mend it, for there was no town near us. Says George, pointing with his finger, "If you please to cut open the pannel there, I'll get something to stuff into it which will bear it from the horse's back." So while he looked for something to thrust in, I cut a hole in the pannel of the saddle, and, following it with my finger, I felt something hard, which seemed to move up and down. Again, as I thrust it with my finger, "Here's something that should not be here," says I, not yet imagining what afterwards fell out, and calling, "Run back," bade him put up his finger. "Whatever 'tis," says he, "'tis this hurts the horse, for it bears just on his back when the saddle is set on." So we strove to take hold on it, but could not reach it; at last we took the upper part of the saddle quite from the pannel, and there lay a small silk purse wrapped in a piece of leather, and full of gold ducats. "Thou art born to be rich, George," says I to him, "here's more money." We opened the purse and found in it four hundred and thirty-eight small pieces of gold.

There I had a new skirmish with him whose the money should be. I told him 'twas his, he told me no; I had accepted of the horse and furniture, and all that was about him was mine, and solemnly vowed he would not have a penny of it. I saw no remedy, but put up the money for the present, mended our saddle, and went on. We lay that night at Halle, and having had such a booty in the saddle, I made him search the saddles of the other two horses, in one of which we found three French crowns, but nothing in the other.

We arrived at Erfurt the 28th of September, but the army was removed, and entered into Franconia, and at the siege of Koningshoven we came up with them. The first thing I did was to pay my civilities to Sir John Hepburn, who received me very kindly, but told me withal that I had not done well to be so long from him, and the king had particularly inquired for me, had commanded him to bring me to him at my return. I told him the reason of my stay at Leipsic, and how I had left that place and my comrade, before he was cured of his wounds, to wait on him according to his letters. He told me the king had spoken some things very obliging about me, and he believed would offer me some command in the army, if I thought well to accept of it. I told him I had promised my father not to take service in an army without his leave, and yet if his Majesty should offer it, I neither knew how to resist it, nor had I an inclination to anything more than the service, and such a leader, though I had much rather have served as a volunteer at my own charge (which, as he knew, was the custom of our English gentlemen) than in any command. He replied, "Do as you think fit; but some gentlemen would give 20,000 crowns to stand so fair for advancement as you do."

The town of Koningshoven capitulated that day, and Sir John was ordered to treat with the citizens, so I had no further discourse with him then; and the town being taken, the army immediately advanced down the river Maine, for the king had his eye upon Frankfort and Mentz, two great cities, both which he soon became master of, chiefly by the prodigious expedition of his march; for within a month after the battle, he was in the lower parts of the empire, and had passed from the Elbe to the Rhine, an incredible conquest, had taken all the strong cities, the bishoprics of Bamberg, of Wurtzburg, and almost all the circle of Franconia, with part of Schawberland--a conquest large enough to be seven years a-making by the common course of arms.

Business going on thus, the king had not leisure to think of small matters, and I being not thoroughly resolved in my mind, did not press Sir John to introduce me. I had wrote to my father with an account of my reception in the army, the civilities of Sir John Hepburn, the particulars of the battle, and had indeed pressed him to give me leave to serve the King of Sweden, to which particular I waited for an answer, but the following occasion determined me before an answer could possibly reach me.

The king was before the strong castle of Marienburg, which commands the city of Wurtzburg. He had taken the city, but the garrison and richer part of the burghers were retired into the castle, and trusting to the strength of the place, which was thought impregnable, they bade the Swedes do their worst; 'twas well provided with all things, and a strong garrison in it, so that the army indeed expected 'twould be a long piece of work. The castle stood on a high rock, and on the steep of the rock was a bastion which defended the only passage up the hill into the castle; the Scots were chose out to make this attack, and the king was an eye-witness of their gallantry. In the action Sir John was not commanded out, but Sir James Ramsey led them on; but I observed that most of the Scotch officers in the other regiments prepared to serve as volunteers for the honour of their countrymen, and Sir John Hepburn led them on. I was resolved to see this piece of service, and therefore joined myself to the volunteers. We were armed with partisans, and each man two pistols at our belt. It was a piece of service that seemed perfectly desperate, the advantage of the hill, the precipice we were to mount, the height of the bastion, the resolute courage and number of the garrison, who from a complete covert made a terrible fire upon us, all joined to make the action hopeless. But the fury of the Scots musketeers was not to be abated by any difficulties; they mounted the hill, scaled the works like madmen, running upon the enemies' pikes, and after two hours' desperate fight in the midst of fire and smoke, took it by storm, and put all the garrison to the sword. The volunteers did their part, and had their share of the loss too, for thirteen or fourteen were killed out of thirty-seven, besides the wounded, among whom I received a hurt more troublesome than dangerous by a thrust of a halberd into my arm, which proved a very painful wound, and I was a great while before it was thoroughly recovered.

The king received us as we drew off at the foot of the hill, calling the soldiers his brave Scots, and commending the officers by name. The next morning the castle was also taken by storm, and the greatest booty that ever was found in any one conquest in the whole war; the soldiers got here so much money that they knew not what to do with it, and the plunder they got here and at the battle of Leipsic made them so unruly, that had not the king been the best master of discipline in the world, they had never been kept in any reasonable bounds.

The king had taken notice of our small party of volunteers, and though I thought he had not seen me, yet he sent the next morning for Sir John Hepburn, and asked him if I were not come to the army? "Yes," says Sir John, "he has been here two or three days." And as he was forming an excuse for not having brought me to wait on his Majesty, says the king, interrupting him, "I wonder you would let him thrust himself into a hot piece of service as storming the Port Graft. Pray let him know I saw him, and have a very good account of his behaviour." Sir John returned with this account to me, and pressed me to pay my duty to his Majesty the next morning; and accordingly, though I had but an ill night with the pain of my wound, I was with him at the levee in the castle.

I cannot but give some short account of the glory of the morning; the castle had been cleared of the dead bodies of the enemies, and what was not pillaged by the soldiers was placed under a guard. There was first a magazine of very good arms for about 18,000 or 20,000 foot, and 4000 horse, a very good train of artillery of about eighteen pieces of battery, thirty-two brass field-pieces, and four mortars. The bishop's treasure, and other public monies not plundered by the soldiers, was telling out by the officers, and amounted to 400,000 florins in money; and the burghers of the town in solemn procession, bareheaded, brought the king three tons of gold as a composition to exempt the city from plunder. Here was also a stable of gallant horses which the king had the curiosity to go and see.

When the ceremony of the burghers was over, the king came down into the castle court, walked on the parade (where the great train of artillery was placed on their carriages) and round the walls, and gave order for repairing the bastion that was stormed by the Scots; and as at the entrance of the parade Sir John Hepburn and I made our reverence to the king, "Ho, cavalier!" said the king to me, "I am glad to see you," and so passed forward. I made my bow very low, but his Majesty said no more at that time.

When the view was over the king went up into the lodgings, and Sir John and I walked in an antechamber for about a quarter of an hour, when one of the gentlemen of the bedchamber came out to Sir John, and told him the king asked for him; he stayed but a little with the king, and come out to me and told me the king had ordered him to bring me to him.

His Majesty, with a countenance full of honour and goodness, interrupted my compliment, and asked me how I did; at which answering only with a bow, says the king, "I am sorry to see you are hurt; I would have laid my commands on you not to have shown yourself in so sharp a piece of service, if I had known you had been in the camp." "Your Majesty does me too much honour," said I, "in your care of a life that has yet done nothing to deserve your favour." His Majesty was pleased to say something very kind to me relating to my behaviour in the battle of Leipsic, which I have not vanity enough to write; at the conclusion whereof, when I replied very humbly that I was not sensible that any service I had done, or could do, could possibly merit so much goodness, he told me he had ordered me a small testimony of his esteem, and withal gave me his hand to kiss. I was now conquered, and with a sort of surprise told his Majesty I found myself so much engaged by his goodness, as well as my own inclination, that if his Majesty would please to accept of my devoir, I was resolved to serve in his army, or wherever he pleased to command me. "Serve me," says the king, "why, so you do, but I must not have you be a musketeer; a poor soldier at a dollar a week will do that." "Pray, Sir John," says the king, "give him what commission he desires." "No commission, sir," says I, "would please me better than leave to fight near your Majesty's person, and to serve you at my own charge till I am qualified by more experience to receive your commands." "Why, then, it shall be so," said the king, "and I charge you, Hepburn," says he, "when anything offers that is either fit for him, or he desires, that you tell me of it;" and giving me his hand again to kiss, I withdrew.

I was followed before I had passed the castle gate by one of the king's pages, who brought me a warrant, directed to Sir John Hepburn, to go to the master of the horse for an immediate delivery of things ordered by the king himself for my account, where being come, the equerry produced me a very good coach with four horses, harness, and equipage, and two very fine saddle-horses, out of the stable of the bishop's horses afore-mentioned; with these there was a list for three servants, and a warrant to the steward of the king's baggage to defray me, my horses, and servants at the king's charge till farther order. I was very much at a loss how to manage myself in this so strange freedom of so great a prince, and consulting with Sir John Hepburn, I was proposing to him whether it was not proper to go immediately back to pay my duty to his Majesty, and acknowledge his bounty in the best terms I could; but while we were resolving to do so, the guards stood to their arms, and we saw the king go out at the gate in his coach to pass into the city, so we were diverted from it for that time. I acknowledge the bounty of the king was very surprising, but I must say it was not so very strange to me when I afterwards saw the course of his management. Bounty in him was his natural talent, but he never distributed his favours but where he thought himself both loved and faithfully served, and when he was so, even the single actions of his private soldiers he would take particular notice of himself, and publicly own, acknowledge, and reward them, of which I am obliged to give some instances.

A private musketeer at the storming the castle of Wurtzburg, when all the detachment was beaten off, stood in the face of the enemy and fired his piece, and though he had a thousand shot made at him, stood unconcerned, and charged his piece again, and let fly at the enemy, continuing to do so three times, at the same time beckoning with his hand to his fellows to come on again, which they did, animated by his example, and carried the place for the king.

When the town was taken the king ordered the regiment to be drawn out, and calling for that soldier, thanked him before them all for taking the town for him, gave him a thousand dollars in money, and a commission with his own hand for a foot company, or leave to go home, which he would. The soldier took the commission on his knees, kissed it, and put it into his bosom, and told the king, he would never leave his service as long as he lived.

This bounty of the king's, timed and suited by his judgment, was the reason that he was very well served, entirely beloved, and most punctually obeyed by his soldiers, who were sure to be cherished and encouraged if they did well, having the king generally an eye-witness of their behaviour.

My indiscretion rather than valour had engaged me so far at the battle of Leipsic, that being in the van of Sir John Hepburn's brigade, almost three whole companies of us were separated from our line, and surrounded by the enemies' pikes. I cannot but say also that we were disengaged rather by a desperate charge Sir John made with the whole regiment to fetch us off, than by our own valour, though we were not wanting to ourselves neither, but this part of the action being talked of very much to the advantage of the young English volunteer, and possibly more than I deserved, was the occasion of all the distinction the king used me with ever after.

I had by this time letters from my father, in which, though with some reluctance, he left me at liberty to enter into arms if I thought fit, always obliging me to be directed, and, as he said, commanded by Sir John Hepburn. At the same time he wrote to Sir John Hepburn, commending his son's fortunes, as he called it, to his care, which letters Sir John showed the king unknown to me. I took care always to acquaint my father of every circumstance, and forgot not to mention his Majesty's extraordinary favour, which so affected my father, that he obtained a very honourable mention of it in a letter from King Charles to the King of Sweden, written by his own hand.

I had waited on his Majesty, with Sir John Hepburn, to give him thanks for his magnificent present, and was received with his usual goodness, and after that I was every day among the gentlemen of his ordinary attendance. And if his Majesty went out on a party, as he would often do, or to view the country, I always attended him among the volunteers, of whom a great many always followed him; and he would often call me out, talk with me, send me upon messages to towns, to princes, free cities, and the like, upon extraordinary occasions.

The first piece of service he put me upon had like to have embroiled me with one of his favourite colonels. The king was marching through the Bergstraet, a low country on the edge of the Rhine, and, as all men thought, was going to besiege Heidelberg, but on a sudden orders a party of his guards, with five companies of Scots, to be drawn out; while they were drawing out this detachment the king calls me to him, "Ho, cavalier," says he, that was his usual word, "you shall command this party;" and thereupon gives me orders to march back all night, and in the morning, by break of day, to take post under the walls of the fort of Oppenheim, and immediately to entrench myself as well as I could. Grave Neels, the colonel of his guards, thought himself injured by this command, but the king took the matter upon himself, and Grave Neels told me very familiarly afterwards, "We have such a master," says he, "that no man can be affronted by. I thought myself wronged," says he, "when you commanded my men over my head; and for my life," says he, "I knew not which way to be angry."

I executed my commission so punctually that by break of day I was set down within musket-shot of the fort, under covert of a little mount, on which stood a windmill, and had indifferently fortified myself, and at the same time had posted some of my men on two other passes, but at farther distance from the fort, so that the fort was effectually blocked up on the land side. In the afternoon the enemy sallied on my first entrenchment, but being covered from their cannon, and defended by a ditch which I had drawn across the road, they were so well received by my musketeers that they retired with the loss of six or seven men.

The next day Sir John Hepburn was sent with two brigades of foot to carry on the work, and so my commission ended. The king expressed himself very well pleased with what I had done, and when he was so was never sparing of telling of it, for he used to say that public commendations were a great encouragement to valour.

While Sir John Hepburn lay before the fort and was preparing to storm it, the king's design was to get over the Rhine, but the Spaniards which were in Oppenheim had sunk all the boats they could find. At last the king, being informed where some lay that were sunk, caused them to be weighed with all the expedition possible, and in the night of the 7th of December, in three boats, passed over his regiment of guards, about three miles above the town, and, as the king thought, secure from danger; but they were no sooner landed, and not drawn into order, but they were charged by a body of Spanish horse, and had not the darkness given them opportunity to draw up in the enclosures in several little parties, they had been in great danger of being disordered; but by this means they lined the hedges and lanes so with musketeers, that the remainder had time to draw up in battalia, and saluted the horse with their muskets, so that they drew farther off.

The king was very impatient, hearing his men engaged, having no boats nor possible means to get over to help them. At last, about eleven o'clock at night, the boats came back, and the king thrust another regiment into them, and though his officers dissuaded him, would go over himself with them on foot, and did so. This was three months that very day when the battle of Leipsic was fought, and winter time too, that the progress of his arms had spread from the Elbe, where it parts Saxony and Brandenburg, to the Lower Palatine and the Rhine.

I went over in the boat with the king. I never saw him in so much concern in my life, for he was in pain for his men; but before we got on shore the Spaniards retired. However, the king landed, ordered his men, and prepared to entrench, but he had not time, for by that time the boats were put off again, the Spaniards, not knowing more troops were landed, and being reinforced from Oppenheim, came on again, and charged with great fury; but all things were now in order, and they were readily received and beaten back again. They came on again the third time, and with repeated charges attacked us; but at last finding us too strong for them they gave it over. By this time another regiment of foot was come over, and as soon as day appeared the king with the three regiments marched to the town, which surrendered at the first summons, and the next day the fort yielded to Sir John Hepburn.

The castle at Oppenheim held out still with a garrison of 800 Spaniards, and the king, leaving 200 Scots of Sir James Ramsey's men in the town, drew out to attack the castle. Sir James Ramsey being left wounded at Wurtzburg, the king gave me the command of those 200 men, which were a regiment, that is to say, all that were left of a gallant regiment of 2000 Scots, which the king brought out of Sweden with him, under that brave colonel. There was about thirty officers, who, having no soldiers, were yet in pay, and served as reformadoes with the regiment, and were over and above the 200 men.

The king designed to storm the castle on the lower side by the way that leads to Mentz, and Sir John Hepburn landed from the other side and marched up to storm on the Rhine port.

My reformado Scots, having observed that the town port of the castle was not so well guarded as the rest, all the eyes of the garrison being bent towards the king and Sir John Hepburn, came running to me, and told me they believed they could enter the castle, sword in hand, if I would give them leave. I told them I durst not give them orders, my commission being only to keep and defend the town; but they being very importunate, I told them they were volunteers, and might do what they pleased, that I would lend them fifty men, and draw up the rest to second

42

them, or bring them off, as I saw occasion, so as I might not hazard the town. This was as much as they desired; they sallied immediately, and in a trice the volunteers scaled the port, cut in pieces the guard, and burst open the gate, at which the fifty entered. Finding the gate won, I advanced immediately with 100 musketeers more, having locked up all the gates of the town but the castle port, and leaving fifty still for a reserve just at that gate; the townsmen, too, seeing the castle, as it were, taken, ran to arms, and followed me with above 200 men. The Spaniards were knocked down by the Scots before they knew what the matter was, and the king and Sir John Hepburn, advancing to storm, were surprised when, instead of resistance, they saw the Spaniards throwing themselves over the walls to avoid the fury of the Scots. Few of the garrison got away, but were either killed or taken, and having cleared the castle, I set open the port on the king's side, and sent his Majesty word the castle was his own. The king came on, and entered on foot. I received him at the head of the Scots reformadoes; who all saluted him with their pikes. The king gave them his hat, and turning about, "Brave Scots, brave Scots," says he smiling, "you were too quick for me;" then beckoning to me, made me tell him how and in what manner we had managed the storm, which he was exceeding well pleased with, but especially at the caution I had used to bring them off if they had miscarried, and secured the town.

From hence the army marched to Mentz, which in four days' time capitulated, with the fort and citadel, and the city paid his Majesty 300,000 dollars to be exempted from the fury of the soldiers. Here the king himself drew the plan of those invincible fortifications which to this day makes it one of the strongest cities in Germany.

Friburg, Koningstien, Neustadt, Kaiserslautern, and almost all the Lower Palatinate, surrendered at the very terror of the King of Sweden's approach, and never suffered the danger of a siege.

The king held a most magnificent court at Mentz, attended by the Landgrave of Hesse, with an incredible number of princes and lords of the empire, with ambassadors and residents of foreign princes; and here his Majesty stayed till March, when the queen, with a great retinue of Swedish nobility, came from Erfurt to see him. The king, attended by a gallant train of German nobility, went to Frankfort, and from thence on to Hoest, to meet the queen, where her Majesty arrived February 8. During the king's stay in these parts, his armies were not idle, his troops, on one side under the Rhinegrave, a brave and ever-fortunate commander, and under the Landgrave of Hesse, on the other, ranged the country from Lorraine to Luxemburg, and past the Moselle on the west, and the Weser on the north. Nothing could stand before them: the Spanish army which came to the relief of the Catholic Electors was everywhere defeated and beaten quite out of the country, and the Lorraine army quite ruined. 'Twas a most pleasant court sure as ever was seen, where every day expresses arrived of armies defeated, towns surrendered, contributions agreed upon, parties routed, prisoners taken, and princes sending ambassadors to sue for truces and neutralities, to make submissions and compositions, and to pay arrears and contributions.

Here arrived, February 10, the King of Bohemia from England, and with him my Lord Craven, with a body of Dutch horse, and a very fine train of English volunteers, who immediately, without any stay, marched on to Hoest to wait upon his Majesty of Sweden, who received him with a great deal of civility, and was treated at a noble collation by the king and queen at Frankfort. Never had the unfortunate king so fair a prospect of being restored to his inheritance of the Palatinate as at that time, and had King James, his father-in-law, had a soul answerable to the occasion, it had been effected before, but it was a strange thing to see him equipped from the English court with one lord and about forty or fifty English gentlemen in his attendance, whereas had the King of England now, as 'tis well known he might have done, furnished him with 10,000 or 12,000 English foot, nothing could have hindered him taking a full possession of his country; and yet even without that help did the King of Sweden clear almost his whole country of Imperialists, and after his death reinstal his son in the Electorate; but no thanks to us.

The Lord Craven did me the honour to inquire for me by name, and his Majesty of Sweden did me yet more by presenting me to the King of Bohemia, and my Lord Craven gave me a letter from my father. And speaking something of my father having served under the Prince of Orange in the famous battle of Nieuport, the king, smiling, returned, "And pray tell him from me his son has served as well in the warm battle of Leipsic." My father being very much pleased with the honour I had received from so great a king, had ordered me to acquaint his Majesty that, if he pleased to accept of their service, he would raise him a regiment of English horse at his own charge to be under my command, and to be sent over into Holland; and my Lord Craven had orders from the King of England to signify his consent to the said levy. I acquainted my old friend Sir John Hepburn with the contents of the letter in order to have his advice, who being pleased with the proposal, would have me go to the king immediately with the letter, but present service put it off for some days.

The taking of Creutznach was the next service of any moment. The king drew out in person to the siege of this town. The town soon came to parley, but the castle seemed a work of difficulty, for its situation was so strong and so surrounded with works behind and above one and another, that most people thought the king would receive a check from it; but it was not easy to resist the resolution of the King of Sweden.

He never battered it but with two small pieces, but having viewed the works himself, ordered a mine under the first ravelin, which being sprung with success, he commands a storm. I think there was not more commanded men than volunteers, both English, Scots, French, and Germans. My old comrade was by this time recovered of his wound at Leipsic, and made one. The first body of volunteers, of about forty, were led on by my Lord Craven, and I led the second, among whom were most of the reformado Scots officers who took the castle of Oppenheim. The first party was not able to make anything of it; the garrison fought with so much fury that many of the volunteer gentlemen being wounded, and some killed, the rest were beaten off with loss. The king was in some passion at his men, and rated them for running away, as he called it, though they really retreated in good order, and commanded the assault to be renewed. 'Twas our turn to fall on next. Our Scots officers, not being used to be beaten, advanced immediately, and my Lord Craven with his volunteers pierced in with us, fighting gallantly in the breach with a pike in his hand; and, to give him the honour due to his bravery, he was with the first on the top of the rampart, and gave his hand to my comrade, and lifted him up after him. We helped one another up, till at last almost all the volunteers had gained the height of the ravelin, and maintained it with a great deal of resolution, expecting when the commanded men had gained the same height to advance upon the enemy; when one of the enemy's captains called to my Lord Craven, and told him if they might have honourable terms they would capitulate, which my lord telling him he would engage for, the garrison fired no more, and the captain, leaping down from the next rampart, came with my Lord Craven into the camp, where the conditions were agreed on, and the castle surrendered.

After the taking of this town, the king, hearing of Tilly's approach, and how he had beaten Gustavus Horn, the king's field-marshal, out of Bamberg, began to draw his forces together, and leaving the care of his conquests in these parts to his chancellor Oxenstiern, prepares to advance towards Bavaria.

I had taken an opportunity to wait upon his Majesty with Sir John Hepburn and being about to introduce the discourse of my father's letter, the king told me he had received a compliment on my account in a letter from King Charles. I told him his Majesty had by his exceeding generosity bound me and all my friends to pay their acknowledgments to him, and that I supposed my father had obtained such a mention of it from the King of England, as gratitude moved him to that his Majesty's favour had been shown in me to a family both willing and ready to serve him, that I had received some commands from my father, which, if his Majesty pleased to do me the honour to accept of, might put me in a condition to acknowledge his Majesty's goodness in a manner more proportioned to the sense I had of his favour; and with that I produced my father's letter, and read that clause in it which related to the regiment of horse, which was as follows:--

"I read with a great deal of satisfaction the account you give of the great and extraordinary conquests of the King of Sweden, and with more his Majesty's singular favour to you; I hope you will be careful to value and deserve so much honour. I am glad you rather chose to serve as a volunteer at your own charge, than to take any command, which, for want of experience, you might misbehave in. "I have obtained of the king that he will particularly thank his Majesty of Sweden for the honour he has done you, and if his Majesty gives you so much freedom, I could be glad you should in the humblest manner thank his Majesty in the name of an old broken soldier.

"If you think yourself officer enough to command them, and his Majesty pleased to accept them, I would have you offer to raise his Majesty a regiment of horse, which, I think, I may near complete in our neighbourhood with some of your old acquaintance, who are very willing to see the world. If his Majesty gives you the word, they shall receive his commands in the Maes, the king having promised me to give them arms, and transport them for that service into Holland; and I hope they may do his Majesty such service as may be for your honour and the advantage of his Majesty's interest and glory."

"YOUR LOVING FATHER."

"'Tis an offer like a gentleman and like a soldier," says the king," and I'll accept of it on two conditions: first," says the king, "that I will pay your father the advance money for the raising the regiment; and next, that they shall be landed in the Weser or the Elbe; for which, if the King of England will not, I will pay the passage; for if they land in Holland, it may prove very difficult to get them to us when the army shall be marched out of this part of the country."

I returned this answer to my father, and sent my man George into England to order that regiment, and made him quartermaster. I sent blank commissions for the officers, signed by the king, to be filled up as my father should think fit; and when I had the king's order for the commissions, the secretary told me I must go back to the king with them. Accordingly I went back to the king, who, opening the packet, laid all the commissions but one upon a table before him, and bade me take them, and keeping that one still in his hand, "Now," says he, "you are one of my soldiers," and therewith gave me his commission, as colonel of horse in present pay. I took the commission kneeling, and humbly thanked his Majesty. "But," says the king, "there is one article-of-war I expect of you more than of others." "Your Majesty can expect nothing of me which I shall not willingly comply with," said I, "as soon as I have the honour to understand what it is." "Why, it is," says the king, "that you shall never fight but when you have orders, for I shall not be willing to lose my colonel before I have the regiment." "I shall be ready at all times, sir," returned I, "to obey your Majesty's orders."

I sent my man express with the king's answer and the commission to my father, who had the regiment completed in less than two months' time, and six of the officers, with a list of the rest, came away to me, whom I presented to his Majesty when he lay before Nuremberg, where they kissed his hand.

One of the captains offered to bring the whole regiment travelling as private men into the army in six weeks' time, and either to transport their equipage, or buy it in Germany, but 'twas thought impracticable. However, I had so many come in that manner that I had a complete troop always about me, and obtained the king's order to muster them as a troop.

On the 8th of March the king decamped, and, marching up the river Maine, bent his course directly for Bavaria, taking several small places by the way, and expecting to engage with Tilly, who he thought would dispute his entrance into Bavaria, kept his army together; but Tilly, finding himself too weak to encounter him, turned away, and leaving Bavaria open to the king, marched into the Upper Palatinate. The king finding the country clear of the Imperialists comes to Nuremberg, made his entrance into that city the 21st of March, and being nobly treated by the citizens, he continued his march into Bavaria, and on the 26th sat down before Donauwerth. The town was taken the next day by storm, so swift were the conquests of this invincible captain. Sir John Hepburn, with the Scots and the English volunteers at the head of them, entered the town first, and cut all the garrison to pieces, except such as escaped over the bridge.

I had no share in the business of Donauwerth, being now among the horse, but I was posted on the roads with five troops of horse, where we picked up a great many stragglers of the garrison, whom we made prisoners of war. 'Tis observable that this town of Donauwerth is a very strong place and well fortified, and yet such expedition did the king make, and such resolution did he use in his first attacks, that he carried the town without putting himself to the trouble of formal approaches. 'Twas generally his way when he came before any town with a design to besiege it; he never would encamp at a distance and begin his trenches a great way off, but bring his men immediately within half musket-shot of the place; there getting under the best cover he could, he would immediately begin his batteries and trenches before their faces; and if there was any place possibly to be attacked, he would fall to storming immediately. By this resolute way of coming on he carried many a town in the first heat of his men, which would have held out many days against a more regular siege.

This march of the king broke all Tilly's measures, for now he was obliged to face about, and leaving the Upper Palatinate, to come to the assistance of the Duke of Bavaria; for the king being 20,000 strong, besides 10,000 foot and 4000 horse and dragoons which joined him from the Duringer Wald, was resolved to ruin the duke, who lay now open to him, and was the most powerful and inveterate enemy of the Protestants in the empire.

Tilly was now joined with the Duke of Bavaria, and might together make about 22,000 men, and in order to keep the Swedes out of the country of Bavaria, had planted themselves along the banks of the river Lech, which runs on the edge of the duke's territories; and having fortified the other side of the river, and planted his cannon for several miles at all the convenient places on the river, resolved to dispute the king's passage.

I shall be the longer in relating this account of the Lech, being esteemed in those days as great an action as any battle or siege of that age, and particularly famous for the disaster of the gallant old General Tilly; and for that I can be more particular in it than other accounts, having been an eye-witness to every part of it.

The king being truly informed of the disposition of the Bavarian army, was once of the mind to have left the banks of the Lech, have repassed the Danube, and so setting down before Ingolstadt, the duke's capital city, by the taking that strong town to have made his entrance into Bavaria, and the conquest of such a fortress, one entire action; but the strength of the place and the difficulty of maintaining his leaguer in an enemy's country while Tilly was so strong in the field, diverted him from that design; he therefore concluded that Tilly was first to be beaten out of the country, and then the siege of Ingolstadt would be the easier.

Whereupon the king resolved to go and view the situation of the enemy. His Majesty went out the 2nd of April with a strong party of horse, which I had the honour to command. We marched as near as we could to the banks of the river, not to be too much exposed to the enemy's cannon, and having gained a little height, where the whole course of the river might be seen, the king halted, and commanded to draw up. The king alighted, and calling me to him, examined every reach and turning of the river by his glass, but finding the river run a long and almost a straight course he could find no place which he liked; but at last turning himself north, and looking down the stream, he found the river, stretching a long reach, doubles short upon itself, making a round and very narrow point. "There's a point will do our business," says the king, "and if the ground be good I'll pass there, let Tilly do his worst."

He immediately ordered a small party of horse to view the ground, and to bring him word particularly how high the bank was on each side and at the point. "And he shall have fifty dollars," says the king, "that will bring me word how deep the water is." I asked his Majesty leave to let me go, which he would by no means allow of; but as the party was drawing out, a sergeant of dragoons told the king, if he pleased to let him go disguised as a boor, he would bring him an account of everything he desired. The king liked the notion well enough, and the fellow being very well acquainted with the country, puts on a ploughman's habit, and went away immediately with a long pole upon his shoulder. The horse lay all this while in the woods, and the king stood undiscerned by the enemy on the little hill aforesaid. The dragoon with his long pole comes down boldly to the bank of the river, and calling to the sentinels which Tilly had placed on the other bank, talked with them, asked them if they could not help him over the river, and pretended he wanted to come to them. At last being come to the point where, as I said, the river makes a short turn, he stands parleying with them a great while, and sometimes, pretending to wade over, he puts his long pole into the water, then finding it pretty shallow he pulls off his hose and goes in, still thrusting his pole in before him, till being gotten up to his middle, he could reach beyond him, where it was too deep, and so shaking his head, comes back again. The soldiers on the other side, laughing at him, asked him if he could swim? He said, "No," "Why, you fool you," says one of the sentinels, "the channel of the river is twenty feet deep." "How do you know that?" says the dragoon. "Why, our engineer," says he, "measured it yesterday." This was what he wanted, but not yet fully satisfied, "Ay, but," says he, "maybe it may not be very broad, and if one of you would wade in to meet me till I could reach you with my pole, I'd give him half a ducat to pull me over." The innocent way of his discourse so deluded the soldiers, that one of them immediately strips and goes in up to the shoulders, and our dragoon goes in on this side to meet him; but the stream took t' other soldier away, and he being a good swimmer, came swimming over to this side. The dragoon was then in a great deal of pain for fear of being discovered, and

47

was once going to kill the fellow, and make off; but at last resolved to carry on the humour, and having entertained the fellow with a tale of a tub, about the Swedes stealing his oats, the fellow being a-cold wanted to be gone, and he as willing to be rid of him, pretended to be very sorry he could not get over the river, and so makes off.

By this, however, he learned both the depth and breadth of the channel, the bottom and nature of both shores, and everything the king wanted to know. We could see him from the hill by our glasses very plain, and could see the soldier naked with him. Says the king, "He will certainly be discovered and knocked on the head from the other side: he is a fool," says the king, "he does not kill the fellow and run off." But when the dragoon told his tale, the king was extremely well satisfied with him, gave him a hundred dollars, and made him a quartermaster to a troop of cuirassiers.

The king having farther examined the dragoon, he gave him a very distinct account of the shore and the ground on this side, which he found to be higher than the enemy's by ten or twelve foot, and a hard gravel. Hereupon the king resolves to pass there, and in order to it gives, himself, particular directions for such a bridge as I believe never army passed a river on before nor since.

His bridge was only loose planks laid upon large tressels in the same homely manner as I have seen bricklayers raise a low scaffold to build a brick wall; the tressels were made higher than one another to answer to the river as it became deeper or shallower, and was all framed and fitted before any appearance was made of attempting to pass.

When all was ready the king brings his army down to the bank of the river, and plants his cannon as the enemy had done, some here and some there, to amuse them.

At night, April 4th, the king commanded about 2000 men to march to the point, and to throw up a trench on either side, and quite round it with a battery of six pieces of cannon at each end, besides three small mounts, one at the point and one of each side, which had each of them two pieces upon them. This work was begun so briskly and so well carried on, the king firing all the night from the other parts of the river, that by daylight all the batteries at the new work were mounted, the trench lined with 2000 musketeers, and all the utensils of the bridge lay ready to be put together.

Now the Imperialists discovered the design, but it was too late to hinder it; the musketeers in the great trench, and the five new batteries, made such continual fire that the other bank, which, as before, lay twelve feet below them, was too hot for the Imperialists; whereupon Tilly, to be provided for the king at his coming over, falls to work in a wood right against the point, and raises a great battery for twenty pieces of cannon, with a breastwork or line, as near the river as he could, to cover his men, thinking that when the king had built his bridge he might easily beat it down with his cannon.

But the king had doubly prevented him, first by laying his bridge so low that none of Tilly's shot could hurt it; for the bridge lay not above half a foot above the water's edge, by which means the king, who in that showed himself an excellent engineer, had secured it from any batteries to be made within the land, and the angle of the bank secured it from the remoter batteries on the other side, and the continual fire of the cannon and small shot beat the Imperialists from their station just against it, they having no works to cover them.

And in the second place, to secure his passage he sent over about 200 men, and after that 200 more, who had orders to cast up a large ravelin on the other bank, just where he designed to land his bridge. This was done with such expedition too, that it was finished before night, and in condition to receive all the shot of Tilly's great battery, and effectually covered his bridge. While this was doing the king on his side lays over his bridge. Both sides wrought hard all day and night, as if the spade, not the sword, had been to decide the controversy, and that he had got the victory whose trenches and batteries were first ready. In the meanwhile the cannon and musket bullets flew like hail, and made the service so hot that both sides had enough to do to make their men stand to their work. The king, in the hottest of it, animated his men by his presence, and Tilly, to give him his due, did the same; for the execution was so great, and so many officers killed, General Altringer wounded, and two sergeant-majors killed, that at last Tilly himself was obliged to expose himself, and to come up to the very face of our line to encourage his men, and give his necessary orders.

And here about one o'clock, much about the time that the king's brigade and works were finished, and just as they said he had ordered to fall on upon our ravelin with 3000 foot, was the brave old Tilly slain with a musket ball in the thigh. He was carried off to Ingolstadt, and lived some days after, but died of that wound the same day as the king had his horse shot under him at the siege of that town.

We made no question of passing the river here, having brought everything so forward, and with such extraordinary success; but we should have found it a very hot piece of work if Tilly had lived one day more, and, if I may give my opinion of it, having seen Tilly's battery and breastwork, in the face of which we must have passed the river, I must say that, whenever we had marched, if Tilly had fallen in with his horse and foot, placed in that trench, the whole army would have passed as much danger as in the face of a strong town in the storming a counterscarp. The king himself, when he saw with what judgment Tilly had prepared his works, and what danger he must have run, would often say that day's success was every way equal to the victory of Leipsic.

Tilly being hurt and carried off, as if the soul of the army had been lost, they began to draw off. The Duke of Bavaria took horse and rid away as if he had fled out of battle for his life.

The other generals, with a little more caution, as well as courage, drew off by degrees, sending their cannon and baggage away first, and leaving some to continue firing on the bank of the river, to conceal their retreat. The river preventing any intelligence, we knew nothing of the disaster befallen them; and the king, who looked for blows, having finished his bridge and ravelin, ordered to run a line with palisadoes to take in more ground on the bank of the river, to cover the first troops he should send over. This being finished the same night, the king sends over a party of his guards to relieve the men who were in the ravelin, and commanded 600 musketeers to man the new line out of the Scots brigade.

Early in the morning a small party of Scots, commanded by one Captain Forbes, of my Lord Reay's regiment, were sent out to learn something of the enemy, the king observing they had not fired all night; and while this party were abroad, the army stood in battalia; and my old friend Sir John Hepburn, whom of all men the king most depended upon for any desperate service, was ordered to pass the bridge with his brigade, and to draw up without the line, with command to advance as he found the horse, who were to second him, come over.

Sir John being passed without the trench, meets Captain Forbes with some prisoners, and the good news of the enemy's retreat. He sends him directly to the king, who was by this time at the head of his army, in full battalia, ready to follow his vanguard, expecting a hot day's work of it. Sir John sends messenger after messenger to the king, entreating him to give him orders to advance; but the king would not suffer him, for he was ever upon his guard, and would not venture a surprise; so the army continued on this side the Lech all day and the next night. In the morning the king sent for me, and ordered me to draw out 300 horse, and a colonel with 600 horse, and a colonel with 800 dragoons, and ordered us to enter the wood by three ways, but so as to be able to relieve one another; and then ordered Sir John Hepburn with his brigade to advance to the edge of the wood to secure our retreat, and at the same time commanded another brigade of foot to pass the bridge, if need were, to second Sir John Hepburn, so warily did this prudent general proceed.

We advanced with our horse into the Bavarian camp, which we found forsaken. The plunder of it was inconsiderable, for the exceeding caution the king had used gave them time to carry off all their baggage. We followed them three or four miles, and returned to our camp.

I confess I was most diverted that day with viewing the works which Tilly had cast up, and must own again that had he not been taken off we had met with as desperate a piece of work as ever was attempted. The next day the rest of the cavalry came up to us, commanded by Gustavus Horn, and the king and the whole army followed. We advanced through the heart of Bavaria, took Rain at the first summons, and several other small towns, and sat down before Augsburg.

Augsburg, though a Protestant city, had a Popish Bavarian garrison in it of above 5000 men, commanded by a Fugger, a great family in Bavaria. The governor had posted several little parties as out-scouts at the distance of two miles and a half or three miles from the town. The king, at his coming up to this town, sends me with my little troop and three companies of dragoons to beat in these out-scouts. The first party I lighted on was not above sixteen men, who had made a small barricado across the road, and stood resolutely upon their guard. I commanded the dragoons to alight and open the barricado, which, while they resolutely performed, the sixteen men gave them two volleys of their muskets, and through the enclosures made their retreat to a turnpike about a quarter of a mile farther. We passed their first traverse, and coming up to the turnpike, I found it defended by 200 musketeers. I prepared to attack them, sending word to the king how strong the enemy was, and desired some foot to be sent me. My dragoons fell on, and though the enemy made a very hot fire, had beat them from this post before 200 foot, which the king had sent me, had come up. Being joined with the foot, I followed the enemy, who retreated fighting, till they came under the cannon of a strong redoubt, where they drew up, and I could see another body of foot of about 300 join them out of the works; upon which I halted, and considering I was in view of the town, and a great way from the army, I faced about and began to march off. As we marched I found the enemy followed, but kept at a distance, as if only designed to observe me. I had not marched far, but I heard a volley of small shot, answered by two or three more, which I presently apprehended to be at the turnpike, where I had left a small guard of twenty-six men with a lieutenant. Immediately I detached 100 dragoons to relieve my men and secure my retreat, following myself as fast as the foot could march. The lieutenant sent me back word the post was taken by the enemy, and my men cut off. Upon this I doubled my pace, and when I came up I found it as the lieutenant said; for the post was taken and manned with 300 musketeers and three troops of horse. By this time, also, I found the party in my rear made up towards me, so that I was like to be charged in a narrow place both in front and rear.

I saw there was no remedy but with all my force to fall upon that party before me, and so to break through before those from the town could come up with me; wherefore, commanding my dragoons to alight, I ordered them to fall on upon the foot. Their horse were drawn up in an enclosed field on one side of the road, a great ditch securing the other side, so that they thought if I charged the foot in front they would fall upon my flank, while those behind would charge my rear; and, indeed, had the other come in time, they had cut me off. My dragoons made three fair charges on their foot, but were received with so much resolution and so brisk a fire, that they were beaten off, and sixteen men killed. Seeing them so rudely handled, and the horse ready to fall in, I relieved them with 100 musketeers, and they renewed the attack; at the same time, with my troop of horse, flanked on both wings with fifty musketeers, I faced their horse, but did not offer to charge them. The case grew now desperate, and the enemy behind were just at my heels with near 600 men. The captain who commanded the musketeers who flanked my horse came up to me; says he, "If we do not force this pass all will be lost; if you will draw out your troop and twenty of my foot, and fall in, I'll engage to keep off the horse with the rest." "With all my heart," says I.

Immediately I wheeled off my troop, and a small party of the musketeers followed me, and fell in with the dragoons and foot, who, seeing the danger too as well as I, fought like madmen. The foot at the turnpike were not able to hinder our breaking through, so we made our way out, killing about 150 of them, and put the rest into confusion.

But now was I in as great a difficulty as before how to fetch off my brave captain of foot, for they charged home upon him. He defended himself with extraordinary gallantry, having the benefit of a piece of a hedge to cover him, but he lost half his men, and was just upon the point of being defeated when the king, informed by a soldier that escaped from the turnpike, one of twenty-six, had sent a party of 600 dragoons to bring me off; these came upon the spur, and joined with me just as I had broke through the turnpike. The enemy's foot rallied behind their horse, and by this time their other party was come in; but seeing our relief they drew off together.

I lost above 100 men in these skirmishes, and killed them about 180. We secured the turnpike, and placed a company of foot there with 100 dragoons, and came back well beaten to the army. The king, to prevent such uncertain skirmishes, advanced the next day in view of the town, and, according to his custom, sits down with his whole army within cannon-shot of their walls.

The King won this great city by force of words, for by two or three messages and letters to and from the citizens, the town was gained, the garrison not daring to defend them against their wills. His Majesty made his public entrance into the city on the 14th of April, and receiving the compliments of the citizens, advanced immediately to Ingolstadt, which is accounted, and really is, the strongest town in all these parts.

The town had a very strong garrison in it, and the Duke of Bavaria lay entrenched with his army under the walls of it, on the other side of the river. The king, who never loved long sieges, having viewed the town, and brought his army within musket-shot of it, called a council of war, where it was the king's opinion, in short, that the town would lose him more than 'twas worth, and therefore he resolved to raise his siege.

51

Here the king going to view the town had his horse shot with a cannon-bullet from the works, which tumbled the king and his horse over one another, that everybody thought he had been killed; but he received no hurt at all. That very minute, as near as could be learnt, General Tilly died in the town of the shot he received on the bank of the Lech, as aforesaid.

I was not in the camp when the king was hurt, for the king had sent almost all the horse and dragoons, under Gustavus Horn, to face the Duke of Bavaria's camp, and after that to plunder the country; which truly was a work the soldiers were very glad of, for it was very seldom they had that liberty given them, and they made very good use of it when it was, for the country of Bavaria was rich and plentiful, having seen no enemy before during the whole war.

The army having left the siege of Ingolstadt, proceeds to take in the rest of Bavaria. Sir John Hepburn, with three brigades of foot, and Gustavus Horn, with 3000 horse and dragoons, went to the Landshut, and took it the same day. The garrison was all horse, and gave us several camisadoes at our approach, in one of which I lost two of my troops, but when we had beat them into close quarters they presently capitulated. The general got a great sum of money of the town, besides a great many presents to the officers.

And from thence the king went on to Munich, the Duke of Bavaria's court. Some of the general officers would fain have had the plundering of the duke's palace, but the king was too generous. The city paid him 400,000 dollars; and the duke's magazine was there seized, in which was 140 pieces of cannon, and small arms for above 20,000 men. The great chamber of the duke's rarities was preserved, by the king's special order, with a great deal of care. I expected to have stayed here some time, and to have taken a very exact account of this curious laboratory; but being commanded away, I had no time, and the fate of the war never gave me opportunity to see it again. The Imperialists, under the command of Commissary Osta, had besieged Biberach, an Imperial city not very well fortified; and the inhabitants being under the Swedes' protection, defended themselves as well as they could, but were in great danger, and sent several expresses to the king for help.

The king immediately detaches a strong body of horse and foot to relieve Biberach, and would be the commander himself. I marched among the horse, but the Imperialists saved us the labour; for the news of the king's coming frighted away Osta, that he left Biberach, and hardly looked behind him till he got up to the Bodensee, on the confines of Switzerland.

At our return from this expedition the king had the first news of Wallenstein's approach, who, on the death of Count Tilly, being declared generalissimo of the emperor's forces, had played the tyrant in Bohemia, and was now advancing with 60,000 men, as they reported, to relieve the Duke of Bavaria.

The king, therefore, in order to be in a posture to receive this great general, resolves to quit Bavaria, and to expect him on the frontiers of Franconia.

And because he knew the Nurembergers for their kindness to him would be the first sacrifice, he resolved to defend that city against him whatever it cost.

Nevertheless he did not leave Bavaria without a defence; but, on the one hand, he left Sir John Baner with 10,000 men about Augsburg, and the Duke of Saxe-Weimar with another like army about Ulm and Meningen, with orders so to direct their march as that they might join him upon any occasion in a few days.

We encamped about Nuremberg the middle of June. The army, after so many detachments, was not above 19,000 men. The Imperial army, joined with the Bavarian, were not so numerous as was reported, but were really 60,000 men. The king, not strong enough to fight, yet, as he used to say, was strong enough not to be forced to fight, formed his camp so under the cannon of Nuremberg that there was no besieging the town but they must besiege him too; and he fortified his camp in so formidable a manner that Wallenstein never durst attack him. On the 30th of June Wallenstein's troops appeared, and on the 5th of July encamped close by the king, and posted themselves not on the Bavarian side, but between the king and his own friends of Schwaben and Frankenland, in order to intercept his provisions, and, as they thought, to starve him out of his camp.

Here they lay to see, as it were, who could subsist longest. The king was strong in horse, for we had full 8000 horse and dragoons in the army, and this gave us great advantage in the several skirmishes we had with the enemy. The enemy had possession of the whole country, and had taken effectual care to furnish their army with provisions; they placed their guards in such excellent order, to secure their convoys, that their waggons went from stage to stage as quiet as in a time of peace, and were relieved every five miles by parties constantly posted on the road. And thus the Imperial general sat down by us, not doubting but he should force the king either to fight his way through on very disadvantageous terms, or to rise for want of provisions, and leave the city of Nuremberg a prey to his army; for he had vowed the destruction of the city, and to make it a second Magdeburg.

But the king, who was not to be easily deceived, had countermined all Wallenstein's designs. He had passed his honour to the Nurembergers that he would not leave them, and they had undertaken to victual his army, and secure him from want, which they did so effectually, that he had no occasion to expose his troops to any hazard or fatigues for convoys or forage on any account whatever.

The city of Nuremberg is a very rich and populous city, and the king being very sensible of their danger, had given his word for their defence. And when they, being terrified at the threats of the Imperialists, sent their deputies to beseech the king to take care of them, he sent them word he would, and be besieged with them. They, on the other hand, laid in such stores of all sorts of provision, both for men and horse, that had Wallenstein lain before it six months longer, there would have been no scarcity. Every private house was a magazine, the camp was plentifully supplied with all manner of provisions, and the market always full, and as cheap as in times of peace. The magistrates were so careful, and preserved so excellent an order in the disposal of all sorts of provision, that no engrossing of corn could be practised, for the prices were every day directed at the town-house; and if any man offered to demand more money for corn than the stated price, he could not sell, because at the town store-house you might buy cheaper. Here are two instances of good and bad conduct: the city of Magdeburg had been entreated by the king to settle funds, and raise money for their provision and security, and to have a sufficient garrison to defend them, but they made difficulties, either to raise men for themselves, or to admit the king's troops to assist them, for fear of the charge of maintaining them; and this was the cause of the city's ruin.

The city of Nuremberg opened their arms to receive the assistance proffered by the Swedes, and their purses to defend their town and common cause; and this was the saving them absolutely from destruction. The rich burghers and magistrates kept open houses, where the officers of the army were always welcome; and the council of the city took such care of the poor that there was no complaining nor disorders in the whole city. There is no doubt but it cost the city a great deal of money; but I never saw a public charge borne with so much cheerfulness, nor managed with so much prudence and conduct in my life. The city fed above 50,000 mouths every day, including their own poor, besides themselves; and yet when the king had lain thus three months, and finding his armies longer in coming up than he expected, asked the burgrave how their magazines held out, he answered, they desired his Majesty not to hasten things for them, for they could maintain themselves and him twelve months longer if there was occasion. This plenty kept both the army and city in good health, as well as in good heart; whereas nothing was to be had of us but blows, for we fetched nothing from without our works, nor had no business without the line but to interrupt the enemy.

The manner of the king's encampment deserves a particular chapter. He was a complete surveyor and a master in fortification, not to be outdone by anybody. He had posted his army in the suburbs of the town, and drawn lines round the whole circumference, so that he begirt the whole city with his army. His works were large, the ditch deep, flanked with innumerable bastions, ravelins, horn-works, forts, redoubts, batteries, and palisadoes, the incessant work of 8000 men for about fourteen days; besides that, the king was adding something or other to it every day, and the very posture of his camp was enough to tell a bigger army than Wallenstein's that he was not to be assaulted in his trenches.

The king's design appeared chiefly to be the preservation of the city; but that was not all. He had three armies acting abroad in three several places. Gustavus Horn was on the Moselle, the chancellor Oxenstiern about Mentz, Cologne, and the Rhine, Duke William and Duke Bernhard, together with General Baner, in Bavaria. And though he designed they should all join him, and had wrote to them all to that purpose, yet he did not hasten them, knowing that while he kept the main army at bay about Nuremberg, they would, without opposition, reduce those several countries they were acting in to his power. This occasioned his lying longer in the camp at Nuremberg than he would have done, and this occasioned his giving the Imperialists so many alarms by his strong parties of horse, of which he was well provided, that they might not be able to make any considerable detachments for the relief of their friends. And here he showed his mastership in the war, for by this means his conquests went on as effectually as if he had been abroad himself.

In the meantime it was not to be expected two such armies should lie long so near without some action. The Imperial army, being masters of the field, laid the country for twenty miles round Nuremberg in a manner desolate.

What the inhabitants could carry away had been before secured in such strong towns as had garrisons to protect them, and what was left the hungry Crabats devoured or set on fire; but sometimes they were met with by our men, who often paid them home for it. There had passed several small rencounters between our parties and theirs; and as it falls out in such cases, sometimes one side, sometimes the other, got the better. But I have observed there never was any party sent out by the king's special appointment but always came home with victory.

The first considerable attempt, as I remember, was made on a convoy of ammunition. The party sent out was commanded by a Saxon colonel, and consisted of 1000 horse and 500 dragoons, who burnt above 600 waggons loaded with ammunition and stores for the army, besides taking about 2000 muskets, which they brought back to the army.

The latter end of July the king received advice that the Imperialists had formed a magazine for provision at a town called Freynstat, twenty miles from Nuremberg. Hither all the booty and contributions raised in the Upper Palatinate, and parts adjacent, was brought and laid up as in a place of security, a garrison of 600 men being placed to defend it; and when a quantity of provisions was got together, convoys were appointed to fetch it off.

The king was resolved, if possible, to take or destroy this magazine; and sending for Colonel Dubalt, a Swede, and a man of extraordinary conduct, he tells him his design, and withal that he must be the man to put it in execution, and ordered him to take what forces he thought convenient. The colonel, who knew the town very well, and the country about it, told his Majesty he would attempt it with all his heart; but he was afraid 'twould require some foot to make the attack. "But we can't stay for that," says the king; "you must then take some dragoons with you;" and immediately the king called for me. I was just coming up the stairs as the king's page was come out to inquire for me, so I went immediately in to the king. "Here is a piece of hot work for you," says the king, "Dubalt will tell it you; go together and contrive it."

We immediately withdrew, and the colonel told me the design, and what the king and he had discoursed; that, in his opinion, foot would be wanted: but the king had declared there was no time for the foot to march, and had proposed dragoons. I told him, I thought dragoons might do as well; so we agreed to take 1600 horse and 400 dragoons. The king, impatient in his design, came into the room to us to know what we had resolved on, approved our measures, gave us orders immediately; and, turning to me, "You shall command the dragoons," says the king, "but Dubalt must be general in this case, for he knows the country." "Your Majesty," said I, "shall be always served by me in any figure you please." The king wished us good speed, and hurried us away the same afternoon, in order to come to the place in time. We marched slowly on because of the carriages we had with us, and came to Freynstat about one o'clock in the night perfectly undiscovered. The guards were so negligent, that we came to the very port before they had notice of us, and a sergeant with twelve dragoons thrust in upon the out-sentinels, and killed them without noise.

Immediately ladders were placed to the half-moon which defended the gate, which the dragoons mounted and carried in a trice, about twenty-eight men being cut in pieces within. As soon as the ravelin was taken, they burst open the gate, at which I entered at the head of 200 dragoons, and seized the drawbridge. By this time the town was in alarm, and the drums beat to arms, but it was too late, for by the help of a petard we broke open the gate, and entered the town. The garrison made an obstinate fight for about half-an-hour, but our men being all in, and three troops of horse dismounted coming to our assistance with their carabines, the town was entirely mastered by three of the clock, and guards set to prevent anybody running to give notice to the enemy. There were about 200 of the garrison killed, and the rest taken prisoners. The town being thus secured, the gates were opened, and Colonel Dubalt came in with the horse.

The guards being set, we entered the magazine, where we found an incredible quantity of all sorts of provision. There was 150 tons of bread, 8000 sacks of meal, 4000 sacks of oats, and of other provisions in proportion. We caused as much of it as could be loaded to be brought away in such waggons and carriages as we found, and set the rest on fire, town and all. We stayed by it till we saw it past a possibility of being saved, and then drew off with 800 waggons, which we found in the place, most of which we loaded with bread, meal, and oats. While we were doing this we sent a party of dragoons into the fields, who met us again as we came out, with above 1000 head of black cattle, besides sheep.

Our next care was to bring this booty home without meeting with the enemy, to secure which, the colonel immediately despatched an express to the king, to let him know of our success, and to desire a detachment might be made to secure our retreat, being charged with so much plunder. And it was no more than need; for though we had used all the diligence possible to prevent any notice, yet somebody, more forward than ordinary, had escaped away, and carried news of it to the Imperial army. The general, upon this bad news, detaches Major-General Sparr with a body of 6000 men to cut off our retreat. The king, who had notice of this detachment, marches out in person with 3000 men to wait upon General Sparr. All this was the account of one day. The king met General Sparr at the moment when his troops were divided, fell upon them, routed one part of them, and the rest in a few hours after, killed them 1000 men, and took the general prisoner.

In the interval of this action we came safe to the camp with our booty, which was very considerable, and would have supplied our whole army for a month. Thus we feasted at the enemy's cost, and beat them into the bargain.

The king gave all the live cattle to the Nurembergers, who, though they had really no want of provisions, yet fresh meat was not so plentiful as such provisions which were stored up in vessels and laid by.

After this skirmish we had the country more at command than before, and daily fetched in fresh provisions and forage in the fields.

The two armies had now lain a long time in sight of one another, and daily skirmishes had considerably weakened them; and the king, beginning to be impatient, hastened the advancement of his friends to join him, in which also they were not backward; but having drawn together their forces from several parts, and all joined the chancellor Oxenstiern, news came, the 15th of August, that they were in full march to join us; and being come to a small town called Brock, the king went out of the camp with about 1000 horse to view them. I went along with the horse, and the 21st of August saw the review of all the armies together, which were 30,000 men, in extraordinary equipage, old soldiers, and commanded by officers of the greatest conduct and experience in the world. There was the rich chancellor of Sweden, who commanded as general; Gustavus Horn and John Baner, both Swedes and old generals; Duke William and Duke Bernhard of Weimar; the Landgrave of Hesse-Cassel, the Palatine of Birkenfelt, and abundance of princes and lords of the empire.

The armies being joined, the king, who was now a match for Wallenstein, quits his camp and draws up in battalia before the Imperial trenches: but the scene was changed. Wallenstein was no more able to fight now than the king was before; but, keeping within his trenches, stood upon his guard.

The king coming up close to his works, plants batteries, and cannonaded him in his very camp. The Imperialists, finding the king press upon them, retreat into a woody country about three leagues, and, taking possession of an old ruined castle, posted their army behind it.

This old castle they fortified, and placed a very strong guard there. The king, having viewed the place, though it was a very strong post, resolved to attack it with the whole right wing. The attack was made with a great deal of order and resolution, the king leading the first party on with sword in hand, and the fight was maintained on both sides with the utmost gallantry and obstinacy all the day and the next night too, for the cannon and musket never gave over till the

56

morning; but the Imperialists having the advantage of the hill, of their works and batteries, and being continually relieved, and the Swedes naked, without cannon or works, the post was maintained, and the king, finding it would cost him too much blood, drew off in the morning.

This was the famous fight at Altemberg, where the Imperialists boasted to have shown the world the King of Sweden was not invincible. They call it the victory at Altemberg; 'tis true the king failed in his attempt of carrying their works, but there was so little of a victory in it, that the Imperial general thought fit not to venture a second brush, but to draw off their army as soon as they could to a safer quarter.

I had no share in this attack, very few of the horse being in the action, but my comrade, who was always among the Scots volunteers, was wounded and taken prisoner by the enemy. They used him very civilly, and the king and Wallenstein straining courtesies with one another, the king released Major-General Sparr without ransom, and the Imperial general sent home Colonel Tortenson, a Swede, and sixteen volunteer gentlemen, who were taken in the heat of the action, among whom my captain was one.

The king lay fourteen days facing the Imperial army, and using all the stratagems possible to bring them to a battle, but to no purpose, during which time we had parties continually out, and very often skirmishes with the enemy.

I had a command of one of these parties in an adventure, wherein I got no booty, nor much honour. The King had received advice of a convoy of provisions which was to come to the enemy's camp from the Upper Palatinate, and having a great mind to surprise them, he commanded us to waylay them with 1200 horse, and 800 dragoons. I had exact directions given me of the way they were to come, and posting my horse in a village a little out of the road, I lay with my dragoons in a wood, by which they were to pass by break of day. The enemy appeared with their convoy, and being very wary, their out-scouts discovered us in the wood, and fired upon the sentinel I had posted in a tree at the entrance of the wood. Finding myself discovered, I would have retreated to the village where my horse were posted, but in a moment the wood was skirted with the enemy's horse, and 1000 commanded musketeers advanced to beat me out. In this pickle I sent away three messengers one after another for the horse, who were within two miles of me, to advance to my relief; but all my messengers fell into the enemy's hands. Four hundred of my dragoons on foot, whom I had placed at a little distance before me, stood to their work, and beat off two charges of the enemy's foot with some loss on both sides. Meantime 200 of my men faced about, and rushing out of the wood, broke through a party of the enemy's horse, who stood to watch our coming out. I confess I was exceedingly surprised at it, thinking those fellows had done it to make their escape, or else were gone over to the enemy; and my men were so discouraged at it, that they began to look about which way to run to save themselves, and were just upon the point of disbanding to shift for themselves, when one of the captains called to me aloud to beat a parley and treat. I made no answer, but, as if I had not heard him, immediately gave the word for all the captains to come together. The consultation was but short, for the musketeers were advancing to a third charge, with numbers which we were not likely to deal with. In short, we resolved to beat a parley, and demand quarter, for that was all we could expect, when on a sudden the body of horse I had posted in the village, being directed by the noise, had advanced to relieve me, if they saw occasion, and had met the 200 dragoons, who guided them directly to the spot where they had broke through, and altogether fell upon the horse of the enemy, who were posted on that side, and, mastering them before they could be relieved, cut them all to pieces and brought me off. Under the shelter of this party, we made good our retreat to the village, but we lost above 300 men, and were glad to make off from the village too, for the enemy were very much too strong for us.

Returning thence towards the camp, we fell foul with 200 Crabats, who had been upon the plundering account. We made ourselves some amends upon them for our former loss, for we showed them no mercy; but our misfortunes were not ended, for we had but just despatched those Crabats when we fell in with 3000 Imperial horse, who, on the expectation of the aforesaid convoy, were sent out to secure them. All I could do could not persuade my men to stand their ground against this party; so that finding they would run away in confusion, I agreed to make off, and facing to the right, we went over a large common a full trot, till at last fear, which always increases in a flight, brought us to a plain flight, the enemy at our heels. I must confess I was never so mortified in my life; 'twas to no purpose to turn head, no man would stand by us; we run for life, and a great many we left by the way who were either wounded by the enemy's shot, or else could not keep race with us.

At last, having got over the common, which was near two miles, we came to a lane; one of our captains, a Saxon by country, and a gentleman of a good fortune, alighted at the entrance of the lane, and with a bold heart faced about, shot his own horse, and called his men to stand by him and defend the lane. Some of his men halted, and we rallied about 600 men, which we posted as well as we could, to defend the pass; but the enemy charged us with great fury. The Saxon gentleman, after defending himself with exceeding gallantry, and refusing quarter, was killed upon the spot. A German dragoon, as I thought him, gave me a rude blow with the stock of his piece on the side of my head, and was just going to repeat it, when one of my men shot him dead. I was so stunned with the blow, that I knew nothing; but recovering, I found myself in the hands of two of the enemy's officers, who offered me quarter, which I accepted; and indeed, to give them their due, they used me very civilly. Thus this whole party was defeated, and not above 500 men got safe to the army; nor had half the number escaped, had not the Saxon captain made so bold a stand at the head of the lane.

Several other parties of the king's army revenged our quarrel, and paid them home for it; but I had a particular loss in this defeat, that I never saw the king after; for though his Majesty sent a trumpet to reclaim us as prisoners the very next day, yet I was not delivered, some scruple happening about exchanging, till after the battle of Lützen, where that gallant prince lost his life.

The Imperial army rose from their camp about eight or ten days after the king had removed, and I was carried prisoner in the army till they sat down to the siege of Coburg Castle, and then was left with other prisoners of war, in the custody of Colonel Spezuter, in a small castle near the camp called Neustadt. Here we continued indifferent well treated, but could learn nothing of what action the armies were upon, till the Duke of Friedland, having been beaten off from the castle of Coburg, marched into Saxony, and the prisoners were sent for into the camp, as was said, in order to be exchanged.

I came into the Imperial leaguer at the siege of Leipsic, and within three days after my coming, the city was surrendered, and I got liberty to lodge at my old quarters in the town upon my parole.

The King of Sweden was at the heels of the Imperialists, for finding Wallenstein resolved to ruin the Elector of Saxony, the king had re-collected as much of his divided army as he could, and came upon him just as he was going to besiege Torgau. As it is not my design to write a history of any more of these wars than I was actually concerned in, so I shall only note that, upon the king's approach, Wallenstein halted, and likewise called all his troops together, for he apprehended the king would fall on him, and we that were prisoners fancied the Imperial soldiers went unwillingly out, for the very name of the King of Sweden was become terrible to them. In short, they drew all the soldiers of the garrison they could spare out of Leipsic; sent for Pappenheim again, who was gone but three days before with 6000 men on a private expedition. On the 16th of November, the armies met on the plains of Lützen; a long and bloody battle was fought, the Imperialists were entirely routed and beaten, 12,000 slain upon the spot, their cannon, baggage, and 2000 prisoners taken, but the King of Sweden lost his life, being killed at the head of his troops in the beginning of the fight.

It is impossible to describe the consternation the death of this conquering king struck into all the princes of Germany; the grief for him exceeded all manner of human sorrow. All people looked upon themselves as ruined and swallowed up; the inhabitants of two-thirds of all Germany put themselves into mourning for him; when the ministers mentioned him in their sermons or prayers, whole congregations would burst out into tears. The Elector of Saxony was utterly inconsolable, and would for several days walk about his palace like a distracted man, crying the saviour of Germany was lost, the refuge of abused princes was gone, the soul of the war was dead; and from that hour was so hopeless of out-living the war, that he sought to make peace with the emperor.

Three days after this mournful victory, the Saxons recovered the town of Leipsic by stratagem. The Duke of Saxony's forces lay at Torgau, and perceiving the confusion the Imperialists were in at the news of the overthrow of their army, they resolved to attempt the recovery of the town. They sent about twenty scattering troopers, who, pretending themselves to be Imperialists fled from the battle, were let in one by one, and still as they came in, they stayed at the court of guard in the port, entertaining the soldiers with discourse about the fight, and how they escaped, and the like, till the whole number being got in, at a watchword they fell on the guard, and cut them all in pieces; and immediately opening the gate to three troops of Saxon horse, the town was taken in a moment.

It was a welcome surprise to me, for I was at liberty of course; and the war being now on another foot, as I thought, and the king dead, I resolved to quit the service.

I had sent my man, as I have already noted, into England, in order to bring over the troops my father had raised for the King of Sweden. He executed his commission so well, that he landed with five troops at Embden in very good condition; and orders were sent them by the king, to join the Duke of Lunenberg's army, which they did at the siege of Boxtude, in the Lower Saxony. Here by long and very sharp service they were most of them cut off, and though they were several times recruited, yet I understood there were not three full troops left.

The Duke of Saxe-Weimar, a gentleman of great courage, had the command of the army after the king's death, and managed it with so much prudence, that all things were in as much order as could be expected, after so great a loss; for the Imperialists were everywhere beaten, and Wallenstein never made any advantage of the king's death.

I waited on him at Heilbronn, whither he was gone to meet the great chancellor of Sweden, where I paid him my respects, and desired he would bestow the remainder of my regiment on my comrade the captain, which he did with all the civility and readiness imaginable. So I took my leave of him, and prepared to come for England.

I shall only note this, that at this Diet, the Protestant princes of the empire renewed their league with one another, and with the crown of Sweden, and came to several regulations and conclusions for the carrying on the war, which they afterwards prosecuted, under the direction of the said chancellor of Sweden. But it was not the work of a small difficulty nor of a short time. And having been persuaded to continue almost two years afterwards at Frankfort, Heilbronn, and there-about, by the particular friendship of that noble wise man, and extraordinary statesman, Axeli Oxenstiern, chancellor of Sweden, I had opportunity to be concerned in, and present at, several treaties of extraordinary consequence, sufficient for a history, if that were my design.

Particularly I had the happiness to be present at, and have some concern in, the treaty for the restoring the posterity of the truly noble Palsgrave, King of Bohemia. King James of England had indeed too much neglected the whole family; and I may say with authority enough, from my own knowledge of affairs, had nothing been done for them but what was from England, that family had remained desolate and forsaken to this day.

But that glorious king, whom I can never mention without some remark of his extraordinary merit, had left particular instructions with his chancellor to rescue the Palatinate to its rightful lord, as a proof of his design to restore the liberty of Germany, and reinstate the oppressed princes who were subjected to the tyranny of the house of Austria.

Pursuant to this resolution, the chancellor proceeded very much like a man of honour; and though the King of Bohemia was dead a little before, yet he carefully managed the treaty, answered the objections of several princes, who, in the general ruin of the family, had reaped private advantages, settled the capitulations for the quota of contributions very much for their advantage, and fully reinstalled the Prince Charles in the possession of all his dominions in the Lower Palatinate, which afterwards was confirmed to him and his posterity by the peace of Westphalia, where all these bloody wars were finished in a peace, which has since been the foundation of the Protestants' liberty, and the best security of the whole empire.

I spent two years rather in wandering up and down than travelling; for though I had no mind to serve, yet I could not find in my heart to leave Germany; and I had obtained some so very close intimacies with the general officers that I was often in the army, and sometimes they did me the honour to bring me into their councils of war.

Particularly, at that eminent council before the battle of Nördlingen, I was invited to the council of war, both by Duke Bernhard of Weimar and by Gustavus Horn. They were generals of equal worth, and their courage and experience had been so well, and so often tried, that more than ordinary regard was always given to what they said. Duke Bernhard was indeed the younger man, and Gustavus had served longer under our great schoolmaster the king; but it was hard to judge which was the better general, since both had experience enough, and shown undeniable proofs both of their bravery and conduct.

I am obliged, in the course of my relation, so often to mention the great respect I often received from these great men, that it makes me sometimes jealous, lest the reader may think I affect it as a vanity. The truth is, that I am ready to confess, the honours I received, upon all occasions, from persons of such worth, and who had such an eminent share in the greatest action of that age, very much pleased me, and particularly, as they gave me occasions to see everything that was doing on the whole stage of the war.

For being under no command, but at liberty to rove about, I could come to no Swedish garrison or party, but, sending my name to the commanding officer, I could have the word sent me; and if I came into the army, I was often treated as I was now at this famous battle of Nördlingen.

But I cannot but say, that I always looked upon this particular respect to be the effect of more than ordinary regard the great king of Sweden always showed me, rather than any merit of my own; and the veneration they all had for his memory, made them continue to show me all the marks of a suitable esteem.

But to return to the council of war, the great and, indeed, the only question before us was, Shall we give battle to the Imperialists, or not? Gustavus Horn was against it, and gave, as I thought, the most invincible arguments against a battle that reason could imagine.

First, they were weaker than the enemy by above 5000 men.

Secondly, the Cardinal-Infant of Spain, who was in the Imperial army with 8000 men, was but there en passant, being going from Italy to Flanders, to take upon him the government of the Low Countries; and if he saw no prospect of immediate action, would be gone in a few days. Thirdly, they had two reinforcements, one of 5000 men, under the command of Colonel Cratz, and one of 7000 men, under the Rhinegrave, who were just at hand--the last within three days' march of them: and,

Lastly, they had already saved their honour; in that they had put 600 foot into the town of Nördlingen, in the face of the enemy's army, and consequently the town might hold out some days the longer.

Fate, rather than reason, certainly blinded the rest of the generals against such arguments as these. Duke Bernhard and almost all the generals were for fighting, alleging the affront it would be to the Swedish reputation to see their friends in the town lost before their faces.

Gustavus Horn stood stiff to his cautious advice, and was against it, and I thought the Baron D'Offkirk treated him a little indecently; for, being very warm in the matter, he told them, that if Gustavus Adolphus had been governed by such cowardly counsel, he had never been conqueror of half Germany in two years. "No," replied old General Horn, very smartly, "but he had been now alive to have testified for me, that I was never taken by him for a coward: and yet," says he, "the king was never for a victory with a hazard, when he could have it without."

I was asked my opinion, which I would have declined, being in no commission; but they pressed me to speak. I told them I was for staying at least till the Rhinegrave came up, who, at least, might, if expresses were sent to hasten him, be up with us in twenty-four hours. But Offkirk could not hold his passion, and had not he been overruled he would have almost quarrelled with Marshal Horn. Upon which the old general, not to foment him, with a great deal of mildness stood up, and spoke thus--

"Come, Offkirk," says he, "I'll submit my opinion to you, and the majority of our fellow-soldiers. We will fight, but, upon my word, we shall have our hands full."

The resolution thus taken, they attacked the Imperial army. I must confess the counsels of this day seemed as confused as the resolutions of the night. Duke Bernhard was to lead the van of the left wing, and to post himself upon a hill which was on the enemy's right without their entrenchments, so that, having secured that post, they might level their cannon upon the foot, who stood behind the lines, and relieved the town at pleasure. He marched accordingly by break of day, and falling with great fury upon eight regiments of foot, which were posted at the foot of the hill, he presently routed them, and made himself master of the post. Flushed with this success, he never regards his own concerted measures of stopping there and possessing what he had got, but pushes on and falls in with the main body of the enemy's army.

While this was doing, Gustavus Horn attacks another post on the hill, where the Spaniards had posted and lodged themselves behind some works they had cast up on the side of the hill. Here they defended themselves with extreme obstinacy for five hours, and at last obliged the Swedes to give it over with loss. This extraordinary gallantry of the Spaniards was the saving of the Imperial army; for Duke Bernhard having all this while resisted the frequent charges of the Imperialists, and borne the weight of two-thirds of their army, was not able to stand any longer, but sending one messenger on the neck of another to Gustavus Horn for more foot, he, finding he could not carry his point, had given it over, and was in full march to second the duke. But now it was too late, for the King of Hungary seeing the duke's men, as it were, wavering, and having notice of Horn's wheeling about to second him, falls in with all his force upon his flank, and with his Hungarian hussars, made such a furious charge, that the Swedes could stand no longer.

The rout of the left wing was so much the more unhappy, as it happened just upon Gustavus Horn's coming up; for, being pushed on with the enemies at their heels, they were driven upon their own friends, who, having no ground to open and give them way, were trodden down by their own runaway brethren. This brought all into the utmost confusion. The Imperialists cried "Victoria!" and fell into the middle of the infantry with a terrible slaughter. I have always observed, 'tis fatal to upbraid an old experienced officer with want of courage. If Gustavus Horn had not been whetted with the reproaches of the Baron D'Offkirk, and some of the other general officers, I believe it had saved the lives of a thousand men; for when all was thus lost, several officers advised him to make a retreat with such regiments as he had yet unbroken; but nothing could persuade him to stir a foot. But turning his flank into a front, he saluted the enemy, as they passed by him in pursuit of the rest, with such terrible volleys of small shot, as cost them the lives of abundance of their men.

The Imperialists, eager in the pursuit, left him unbroken, till the Spanish brigade came up and charged him. These he bravely repulsed with a great slaughter, and after them a body of dragoons; till being laid at on every side, and most of his men killed, the brave old general, with all the rest who were left, were made prisoners.

The Swedes had a terrible loss here, for almost all their infantry were killed or taken prisoners. Gustavus Horn refused quarter several times; and still those that attacked him were cut down by his men, who fought like furies, and by the example of their general, behaved themselves like lions. But at last, these poor remains of a body of the bravest men in the world were forced to submit. I have heard him say, he had much rather have died than been taken, but that he yielded in compassion to so many brave men as were about him; for none of them would take quarter till he gave his consent.

I had the worst share in this battle that ever I had in any action of my life; and that was to be posted among as brave a body of horse as any in Germany, and yet not be able to succour

our own men; but our foot were cut in pieces (as it were) before our faces, and the situation of the ground was such as we could not fall in. All that we were able to do, was to carry off about 2000 of the foot, who, running away in the rout of the left wing, rallied among our squadrons, and got away with us. Thus we stood till we saw all was lost, and then made the best retreat we could to save ourselves, several regiments having never charged, nor fired a shot; for the foot had so embarrassed themselves among the lines and works of the enemy, and in the vineyards and mountains, that the horse were rendered absolutely unserviceable.

The Rhinegrave had made such expedition to join us, that he reached within three miles of the place of action that night, and he was a great safeguard for us in rallying our dispersed men, who else had fallen into the enemy's hands, and in checking the pursuit of the enemy.

And indeed, had but any considerable body of the foot made an orderly retreat, it had been very probable they had given the enemy a brush that would have turned the scale of victory; for our horse being whole, and in a manner untouched, the enemy found such a check in the pursuit, that 1600 of their forwardest men following too eagerly, fell in with the Rhinegrave's advanced troops the next day, and were cut in pieces without mercy.

This gave us some satisfaction for the loss, but it was but small compared to the ruin of that day. We lost near 8000 men upon the spot, and above 3000 prisoners, all our cannon and baggage, and 120 colours. I thought I never made so indifferent a figure in my life, and so we thought all; to come away, lose our infantry, our general, and our honour, and never fight for it. Duke Bernhard was utterly disconsolate for old Gustavus Horn, for he concluded him killed; he tore the hair from his head like a madman, and telling the Rhinegrave the story of the council of war, would reproach himself with not taking his advice, often repeating it in his passion. "Tis I," said he, "have been the death of the bravest general in Germany;" would call himself fool and boy, and such names, for not listening to the reasons of an old experienced soldier. But when he heard he was alive in the enemy's hands he was the easier, and applied himself to the recruiting his troops, and the like business of the war; and it was not long before he paid the Imperialists with interest.

I returned to Frankfort-au-Main after this action, which happened the 17th of August 1634; but the progress of the Imperialists was so great that there was no staying at Frankfort. The chancellor Oxenstiern removed to Magdeburg, Duke Bernhard and the Landgrave marched into Alsatia, and the Imperialists carried all before them for all the rest of the campaign. They took Philipsburg by surprise; they took Augsburg by famine, Spire and Treves by sieges, taking the Elector prisoner. But this success did one piece of service to the Swedes, that it brought the French into the war on their side, for the Elector of Treves was their confederate. The French gave the conduct of the war to Duke Bernhard. This, though the Duke of Saxony fell off, and fought against them, turned the scale so much in their favour, that they recovered their losses, and proved a terror to all Germany. The farther accounts of the war I refer to the histories of those times, which I have since read with a great deal of delight.

I confess when I saw the progress of the Imperial army, after the battle of Nördlingen, and the Duke of Saxony turning his arms against them, I thought their affairs declining; and, giving them over for lost, I left Frankfort, and came down the Rhine to Cologne, and from thence into Holland.

I came to the Hague the 8th of March 1635, having spent three years and a half in Germany, and the greatest part of it in the Swedish army.

I spent some time in Holland viewing the wonderful power of art, which I observed in the fortifications of their towns, where the very bastions stand on bottomless morasses, and yet are as firm as any in the world. There I had the opportunity of seeing the Dutch army, and their famous general, Prince Maurice. 'Tis true, the men behaved themselves well enough in action, when they were put to it, but the prince's way of beating his enemies without fighting, was so unlike the gallantry of my royal instructor, that it had no manner of relish with me. Our way in Germany was always to seek out the enemy and fight him; and, give the Imperialists their due, they were seldom hard to be found, but were as free of their flesh as we were.

Whereas Prince Maurice would lie in a camp till he starved half his men, if by lying there he could but starve two-thirds of his enemies; so that indeed the war in Holland had more of fatigues and hardships in it, and ours had more of fighting and blows. Hasty marches, long and unwholesome encampments, winter parties, counter-marching, dodging and entrenching, were the exercises of his men, and oftentimes killed him more men with hunger, cold and diseases, than he could do with fighting. Not that it required less courage, but rather more, for a soldier had at any time rather die in the field a la coup de mousquet, than be starved with hunger, or frozen to death in the trenches.

Nor do I think I lessen the reputation of that great general; for 'tis most certain he ruined the Spaniard more by spinning the war thus out in length, than he could possibly have done by a swift conquest. For had he, Gustavus-like, with a torrent of victory dislodged the Spaniard of all the twelve provinces in five years, whereas he was forty years a-beating them out of seven, he had left them rich and strong at home, and able to keep them in constant apprehensions of a return of his power. Whereas, by the long continuance of the war, he so broke the very heart of the Spanish monarchy, so absolutely and irrecoverably impoverished them, that they have ever since languished of the disease, till they are fallen from the most powerful, to be the most despicable nation in the world.

The prodigious charge the King of Spain was at in losing the seven provinces, broke the very spirit of the nation; and that so much, that all the wealth of their Peruvian mountains have not been able to retrieve it; King Philip having often declared that war, besides his Armada for invading England, had cost him 370,000,000 of ducats, and 4,000,000 of the best soldiers in Europe; whereof, by an unreasonable Spanish obstinacy, above 60,000 lost their lives before Ostend, a town not worth a sixth part either of the blood or money it cost in a siege of three years; and which at last he had never taken, but that Prince Maurice thought it not worth the charge of defending it any longer.

However, I say, their way of fighting in Holland did not relish with me at all. The prince lay a long time before a little fort called Schenkenschanz, which the Spaniard took by surprise, and I thought he might have taken it much sooner. Perhaps it might be my mistake, but I fancied my hero, the King of Sweden, would have carried it sword in hand, in half the time.

However it was, I did not like it; so in the latter end of the year I came to the Hague, and took shipping for England, where I arrived, to the great satisfaction of my father and all my friends. My father was then in London, and carried me to kiss the king's hand. His Majesty was pleased to receive me very well, and to say a great many very obliging things to my father upon my account.

I spent my time very retired from court, for I was almost wholly in the country; and it being so much different from my genius, which hankered after a warmer sport than hunting among our Welsh mountains, I could not but be peeping in all the foreign accounts from Germany, to see who and who was together. There I could never hear of a battle, and the Germans being beaten, but I began to wish myself there. But when an account came of the progress of John Baner, the Swedish general in Saxony, and of the constant victories he had there over the Saxons, I could no longer contain myself, but told my father this life was very disagreeable to me; that I lost my time here, and might to much more advantage go into Germany, where I was sure I might make my fortune upon my own terms; that, as young as I was, I might have been a general officer by this time, if I had not laid down my commission; that General Baner, or the Marshal Horn, had either of them so much respect for me, that I was sure I might have anything of them; and that if he pleased to give me leave, I would go for Germany again. My father was very unwilling to let me go, but seeing me uneasy, told me that, if I was resolved, he would oblige me to stay no longer in England than the next spring, and I should have his consent.

The winter following began to look very unpleasant upon us in England, and my father used often to sigh at it; and would tell me sometimes he was afraid we should have no need to send Englishmen to fight in Germany.

The cloud that seemed to threaten most was from Scotland. My father, who had made himself master of the arguments on both sides, used to be often saying he feared there was some about the king who exasperated him too much against the Scots, and drove things too high. For my part, I confess I did not much trouble my head with the cause; but all my fear was they would not fall out, and we should have no fighting. I have often reflected since, that I ought to have known better, that had seen how the most flourishing provinces of Germany were reduced to the most miserable condition that ever any country in the world was, by the ravagings of soldiers, and the calamities of war.

How much soever I was to blame, yet so it was, I had a secret joy at the news of the king's raising an army, and nothing could have withheld me from appearing in it; but my eagerness was anticipated by an express the king sent to my father, to know if his son was in England; and my father having ordered me to carry the answer myself, I waited upon his Majesty with the messenger. The king received me with his usual kindness, and asked me if I was willing to serve him against the Scots?

I answered, I was ready to serve him against any that his Majesty thought fit to account his enemies, and should count it an honour to receive his commands. Hereupon his Majesty offered me a commission. I told him, I supposed there would not be much time for raising of men; that if his Majesty pleased I would be at the rendezvous with as many gentlemen as I could get together, to serve his Majesty as volunteers.

The truth is, I found all the regiments of horse the king designed to raise were but two as regiments; the rest of the horse were such as the nobility raised in their several countries, and commanded them themselves; and, as I had commanded a regiment of horse abroad, it looked a little odd to serve with a single troop at home; and the king took the thing presently. "Indeed 'twill be a volunteer war," said the king, "for the Northern gentry have sent me an account of above 4000 horse they have already." I bowed, and told his Majesty I was glad to hear his subjects were forward to serve him. So taking his Majesty's orders to be at York by the end of March, I returned to my father.

65

My father was very glad I had not taken a commission, for I know not from what kind of emulation between the western and northern gentry. The gentlemen of our side were not very forward in the service; their loyalty to the king in the succeeding times made it appear it was not for any disaffection to his Majesty's interest or person, or to the cause; but this, however, made it difficult for me when I came home to get any gentlemen of quality to serve with me, so that I presented myself to his Majesty only as a volunteer, with eight gentlemen and about thirty-six countrymen well mounted and armed.

And as it proved, these were enough, for this expedition ended in an accommodation with the Scots; and they not advancing so much as to their own borders, we never came to any action. But the armies lay in the counties of Northumberland and Durham, ate up the country, and spent the king a vast sum of money; and so this war ended, a pacification was made, and both sides returned.

The truth is, I never saw such a despicable appearance of men in arms to begin a war in my life; whether it was that I had seen so many braver armies abroad that prejudiced me against them, or that it really was so; for to me they seemed little better than a rabble met together to devour, rather than fight for their king and country. There was indeed a great appearance of gentlemen, and those of extraordinary quality; but their garb, their equipages, and their mien, did not look like war; their troops were filled with footmen and servants, and wretchedly armed, God wot. I believe I might say, without vanity, one regiment of Finland horse would have made sport at beating them all. There were such crowds of parsons (for this was a Church war in particular) that the camp and court was full of them; and the king was so eternally besieged with clergymen of one sort or another, that it gave offence to the chief of the nobility.

As was the appearance, so was the service. The army marched to the borders, and the headquarter was at Berwick-upon-Tweed; but the Scots never appeared, no, not so much as their scouts; whereupon the king called a council of war, and there it was resolved to send the Earl of Holland with a party of horse into Scotland, to learn some news of the enemy. And truly the first news he brought us was, that finding their army encamped about Coldingham, fifteen miles from Berwick, as soon as he appeared, the Scots drew out a party to charge him, upon which most of his men halted--I don't say run away, but 'twas next door to it--for they could not be persuaded to fire their pistols, and wheel of like soldiers, but retreated in such a disorderly and shameful manner, that had the enemy but had either the courage or conduct to have followed them, it must have certainly ended in the ruin of the whole party. [Footnote 1: Upon the breach of the match between the King of England and the Infanta of Spain; and particularly upon the old quarrel of the King of Bohemia and the Palatinate.]

THE SECOND PART

I confess, when I went into arms at the beginning of this war, I never troubled myself to examine sides: I was glad to hear the drums beat for soldiers, as if I had been a mere Swiss, that had not cared which side went up or down, so I had my pay. I went as eagerly and blindly about my business, as the meanest wretch that 'listed in the army; nor had I the least compassionate thought for the miseries of my native country, till after the fight at Edgehill. I had known as much, and perhaps more than most in the army, what it was to have an enemy ranging in the bowels of a kingdom; I had seen the most flourishing provinces of Germany reduced to perfect deserts, and the voracious Crabats, with inhuman barbarity, quenching the fires of the plundered villages with the blood of the inhabitants. Whether this had hardened me against the natural tenderness which I afterwards found return upon me, or not, I cannot tell; but I reflected upon myself afterwards with a great deal of trouble, for the unconcernedness of my temper at the approaching ruin of my native country.

I was in the first army at York, as I have already noted, and, I must confess, had the least diversion there that ever I found in an army in my life. For when I was in Germany with the King of Sweden, we used to see the king with the general officers every morning on horseback viewing his men, his artillery, his horses, and always something going forward. Here we saw nothing but courtiers and clergymen, bishops and parsons, as busy as if the direction of the war had been in them. The king was seldom seen among us, and never without some of them always about him. Those few of us that had seen the wars, and would have made a short end of this for him, began to be very uneasy; and particularly a certain nobleman took the freedom to tell the king that the clergy would certainly ruin the expedition. The case was this: he would have had the king have immediately marched into Scotland, and put the matter to the trial of a battle; and he urged it every day. And the king finding his reasons very good, would often be of his opinion; but next morning he would be of another mind.

This gentleman was a man of conduct enough, and of unquestioned courage, and afterwards lost his life for the king. He saw we had an army of young stout fellows numerous enough; and though they had not yet seen much service, he was for bringing them to action, that the Scots might not have time to strengthen themselves, nor they have time by idleness and sotting, the bane of soldiers, to make themselves unfit for anything.

I was one morning in company with this gentleman; and as he was a warm man, and eager in his discourse, "A pox of these priests," says he, "'tis for them the king has raised this army, and put his friends to a vast charge; and now we are come, they won't let us fight."

But I was afterwards convinced the clergy saw further into the matter than we did. They saw the Scots had a better army than we had--bold and ready, commanded by brave officers-- and they foresaw that if we fought we should be beaten, and if beaten, they were undone. And 'twas very true, we had all been ruined if we had engaged.

It is true when we came to the pacification which followed, I confess I was of the same mind the gentleman had been of; for we had better have fought and been beaten than have made so dishonourable a treaty without striking a stroke. This pacification seems to me to have laid the scheme of all the blood and confusion which followed in the Civil War. For whatever the king and his friends might pretend to do by talking big, the Scots saw he was to be bullied into anything, and that when it came to the push the courtiers never cared to bring it to blows. I have little or nothing to say as to action in this mock expedition. The king was persuaded at last to march to Berwick; and, as I have said already, a party of horse went out to learn news of the Scots, and as soon as they saw them, ran away from them bravely.

This made the Scots so insolent that, whereas before they lay encamped behind a river, and never showed themselves, in a sort of modest deference to their king, which was the pretence of not being aggressors or invaders, only arming in their own defence, now, having been invaded by the English troops entering Scotland, they had what they wanted. And to show it was not fear that retained them before, but policy, now they came up in parties to our very gates, braving and facing us every day.

I had, with more curiosity than discretion, put myself as a volunteer at the head of one of our parties of horse, under my Lord Holland, when they went out to discover the enemy; they went, they said, to see what the Scots were a-doing.

We had not marched far, but our scouts brought word they had discovered some horse, but could not come up to them, because a river parted them. At the heels of these came another party of our men upon the spur to us, and said the enemy was behind, which might be true for aught we knew; but it was so far behind that nobody could see them, and yet the country was plain and open for above a mile before us. Hereupon we made a halt, and, indeed, I was afraid it would have been an odd sort of a halt, for our men began to look one upon another, as they do in like cases, when they are going to break; and when the scouts came galloping in the men were in such disorder, that had but one man broke away, I am satisfied they had all run for it.

I found my Lord Holland did not perceive it; but after the first surprise was a little over I told my lord what I had observed, and that unless some course was immediately taken they would all run at the first sight of the enemy. I found he was much concerned at it, and began to consult what course to take to prevent it. I confess 'tis a hard question how to make men stand and face an enemy, when fear has possessed their minds with an inclination to run away. But I'll give that honour to the memory of that noble gentleman, who, though his experience in matters of war was small, having never been in much service, yet his courage made amends for it; for I daresay he would not have turned his horse from an army of enemies, nor have saved his life at the price of running away for it.

My lord soon saw, as well as I, the fright the men were in, after I had given him a hint of it; and to encourage them, rode through their ranks and spoke cheerfully to them, and used what arguments he thought proper to settle their minds. I remembered a saying which I heard old Marshal Gustavus Horn speak in Germany, "If you find your men falter, or in doubt, never suffer them to halt, but keep them advancing; for while they are going forward, it keeps up their courage."

As soon as I could get opportunity to speak to him, I gave him this as my opinion. "That's very well," says my lord, "but I am studying," says he, "to post them so as that they can't run if they would; and if they stand but once to face the enemy, I don't fear them afterwards."

While we were discoursing thus, word was brought that several parties of the enemies were seen on the farther side of the river, upon which my lord gave the word to march; and as we were marching on, my lord calls out a lieutenant who had been an old soldier, with only five troopers whom he had most confidence in, and having given him his lesson, he sends him away. In a quarter of an hour one of the five troopers comes back galloping and hallooing, and tells us his lieutenant had, with his small party, beaten a party of twenty of the enemy's horse over the river, and had secured the pass, and desired my lord would march up to him immediately.

Tis a strange thing that men's spirits should be subjected to such sudden changes, and capable of so much alteration from shadows of things. They were for running before they saw the enemy, now they are in haste to be led on, and but that in raw men we are obliged to bear with anything, the disorder in both was intolerable. The story was a premeditated sham, and not a word of truth in it, invented to raise their spirits, and cheat them out of their cowardly phlegmatic apprehensions, and my lord had his end in it; for they were all on fire to fall on. And I am persuaded, had they been led immediately into a battle begun to their hands, they would have laid about them like furies; for there is nothing like victory to flush a young soldier. Thus, while the humour was high, and the fermentation lasted, away we marched, and, passing one of their great commons, which they call moors, we came to the river, as he called it, where our lieutenant was posted with his four men; 'twas a little brook fordable with ease, and, leaving a guard at the pass, we advanced to the top of a small ascent, from whence we had a fair view of the Scots army, as they lay behind another river larger than the former.

Our men were posted well enough, behind a small enclosure, with a narrow lane in their front. And my lord had caused his dragoons to be placed in the front to line the hedges; and in this posture he stood viewing the enemy at a distance. The Scots, who had some intelligence of our coming, drew out three small parties, and sent them by different ways to observe our number; and, forming a fourth party, which I guessed to be about 600 horse, advanced to the top of the plain, and drew up to face us, but never offered to attack us.

One of the small parties, making about 100 men, one third foot, passes upon our flank in view, but out of reach; and, as they marched, shouted at us, which our men, better pleased with that work than with fighting, readily enough answered, and would fain have fired at them for the pleasure of making a noise, for they were too far off to hit them.

I observed that these parties had always some foot with them; and yet if the horse galloped, or pushed on ever so forward, the foot were as forward as they, which was an extraordinary advantage.

Gustavus Adolphus, that king of soldiers, was the first that I have ever observed found the advantage of mixing small bodies of musketeers among his horse; and, had he had such nimble strong fellows as these, he would have prized them above all the rest of his men. These were those they call Highlanders. They would run on foot with their arms and all their accoutrements, and keep very good order too, and yet keep pace with the horse, let them go at what rate they would. When I saw the foot thus interlined among the horse, together with the way of ordering their flying parties, it presently occurred to my mind that here was some of our old Scots come home out of Germany that had the ordering of matters, and if so, I knew we were not a match for them.

Thus we stood facing the enemy till our scouts brought us word the whole Scots army was in motion, and in full march to attack us; and, though it was not true, and the fear of our men doubled every object, yet 'twas thought convenient to make our retreat. The whole matter was that the scouts having informed them what they could of our strength, the 600 were ordered to march towards us, and three regiments of foot were drawn out to support the horse.

I know not whether they would have ventured to attack us, at least before their foot had come up; but whether they would have put it to the hazard or no, we were resolved not to hazard the trial, so we drew down to the pass. And, as retreating looks something like running away, especially when an enemy is at hand, our men had much ado to make their retreat pass for a march, and not a flight; and, by their often looking behind them, anybody might know what they would have done if they had been pressed.

I confess, I was heartily ashamed when the Scots, coming up to the place where we had been posted, stood and shouted at us. I would have persuaded my lord to have charged them, and he would have done it with all his heart, but he saw it was not practicable; so we stood at gaze with them above two hours, by which time their foot were come up to them, and yet they did not offer to attack us. I never was so ashamed of myself in my life; we were all dispirited. The Scots gentlemen would come out single, within shot of our post, which in a time of war is always accounted a challenge to any single gentleman, to come out and exchange a pistol with them, and nobody would stir; at last our old lieutenant rides out to meet a Scotchman that came pickeering on his quarter. This lieutenant was a brave and a strong fellow, had been a soldier in the Low Countries; and though he was not of any quality, only a mere soldier, had his preferment for his conduct. He gallops bravely up to his adversary, and exchanging their pistols, the lieutenant's horse happened to be killed. The Scotchman very generously dismounts, and engages him with his sword, and fairly masters him, and carries him away prisoner; and I think this horse was all the blood was shed in that war.

The lieutenant's name thus conquered was English, and as he was a very stout old soldier, the disgrace of it broke his heart. The Scotchman, indeed, used him very generously; for he treated him in the camp very courteously, gave him another horse, and set him at liberty, gratis. But the man laid it so to heart, that he never would appear in the army, but went home to his own country and died.

I had enough of party-making, and was quite sick with indignation at the cowardice of the men; and my lord was in as great a fret as I, but there was no remedy. We durst not go about to retreat, for we should have been in such confusion that the enemy must have discovered it; so my lord resolved to keep the post, if possible, and send to the king for some foot. Then were our men ready to fight with one another who should be the messenger; and at last when a lieutenant with twenty dragoons was despatched, he told us afterwards he found himself an hundred strong before he was gotten a mile from the place.

In short, as soon as ever the day declined, and the dusk of the evening began to shelter the designs of the men, they dropped away from us one by one; and at last in such numbers, that if we had stayed till the morning, we had not had fifty men left; out of 1200 horse and dragoons.

When I saw how it was, consulting with some of the officers, we all went to my Lord Holland, and pressed him to retreat, before the enemy should discern the flight of our men; so he drew us off, and we came to the camp the next morning, in the shamefullest condition that ever poor men could do. And this was the end of the worst expedition ever I made in my life. To fight and be beaten is a casualty common to a soldier, and I have since had enough of it; but to run away at the sight of an enemy, and neither strike or be stricken, this is the very shame of the profession, and no man that has done it ought to show his face again in the field, unless disadvantages of place or number make it tolerable, neither of which was our case.

My Lord Holland made another march a few days after, in hopes to retrieve this miscarriage; but I had enough of it, so I kept in my quarters. And though his men did not desert him as before, yet upon the appearance of the enemy they did not think fit to fight, and came off with but little more honour than they did before.

There was no need to go out to seek the enemy after this, for they came, as I have noted, and pitched in sight of us, and their parties came up every day to the very out-works of Berwick, but nobody cared to meddle with them.

And in this posture things stood when the pacification was agreed on by both parties, which, like a short truce, only gave both sides breath to prepare for a new war more ridiculously managed than the former. When the treaty was so near a conclusion as that conversation was admitted on both sides, I went over to the Scotch camp to satisfy my curiosity, as many of our English officers did also.

I confess the soldiers made a very uncouth figure, especially the Highlanders. The oddness and barbarity of their garb and arms seemed to have something in it remarkable.

They were generally tall swinging fellows; their swords were extravagantly, and, I think, insignificantly broad, and they carried great wooden targets, large enough to cover the upper part of their bodies. Their dress was as antique as the rest; a cap on their heads, called by them a bonnet, long hanging sleeves behind, and their doublet, breeches, and stockings of a stuff they called plaid, striped across red and yellow, with short cloaks of the same. These fellows looked, when drawn out, like a regiment of merry-andrews, ready for Bartholomew Fair. They are in companies all of a name, and therefore call one another only by their Christian names, as Jemmy, Jocky, that is, John, and Sawny, that is, Alexander, and the like. And they scorn to be commanded but by one of their own clan or family. They are all gentlemen, and proud enough to be kings. The meanest fellow among them is as tenacious of his honour as the best nobleman in the country, and they will fight and cut one another's throats for every trifling affront.

But to their own clans or lairds, they are the willingest and most obedient fellows in nature. Give them their due, were their skill in exercises and discipline proportioned to their courage, they would make the bravest soldiers in the world. They are large bodies, and prodigiously strong; and two qualities they have above other nations, viz., hardy to endure hunger, cold, and hardships, and wonderfully swift of foot. The latter is such an advantage in the field that I know none like it; for if they conquer, no enemy can escape them, and if they run, even the horse can hardly overtake them. These were some of them, who, as I observed before, went out in parties with their horse.

There were three or four thousand of these in the Scots army, armed only with swords and targets; and in their belts some of them had a pistol, but no muskets at that time among them.

But there were also a great many regiments of disciplined men, who, by their carrying their arms, looked as if they understood their business, and by their faces, that they durst see an enemy.

I had not been half-an-hour in their camp after the ceremony of giving our names, and passing their out-guards and main-guard was over, but I was saluted by several of my acquaintance; and in particular, by one who led the Scotch volunteers at the taking the castle of

Oppenheim, of which I have given an account. They used me with all the respect they thought due to me, on account of old affairs, gave me the word, and a sergeant waited upon me whenever I pleased to go abroad.

I continued twelve or fourteen days among them, till the pacification was concluded; and they were ordered to march home. They spoke very respectfully of the king, but I found were exasperated to the last degree at Archbishop Laud and the English bishops, for endeavouring to impose the Common Prayer Book upon them; and they always talked with the utmost contempt of our soldiers and army. I always waived the discourse about the clergy, and the occasion of the war, but I could not but be too sensible what they said of our men was true; and by this I perceived they had an universal intelligence from among us, both of what we were doing, and what sort of people we were that were doing it; and they were mighty desirous of coming to blows with us. I had an invitation from their general, but I declined it, lest I should give offence. I found they accepted the pacification as a thing not likely to hold, or that they did not design should hold; and that they were resolved to keep their forces on foot, notwithstanding the agreement. Their whole army was full of brave officers, men of as much experience and conduct as any in the world; and all men who know anything of the war, know good officers presently make a good army.

Things being thus huddled up, the English came back to York, where the army separated, and the Scots went home to increase theirs; for I easily foresaw that peace was the farthest thing from their thoughts.

The next year the flame broke out again. The king draws his forces down into the north, as before, and expresses were sent to all the gentlemen that had commands to be at the place by the 15th of July. As I had accepted of no command in the army, so I had no inclination at all to go, for I foresaw there would be nothing but disgrace attend it. My father, observing such an alteration in my usual forwardness, asked me one day what was the matter, that I who used to be so forward to go into the army, and so eager to run abroad to fight, now showed no inclination to appear when the service of the king and country called me to it? I told him I had as much zeal as ever for the king's service, and for the country too: but he knew a soldier could not abide to be beaten; and being from thence a little more inquisitive, I told him the observations I had made in the Scots army, and the people I had conversed with there. "And, sir," says I, "assure yourself, if the king offers to fight them, he will be beaten; and I don't love to engage when my judgment tells me beforehand I shall be worsted." And as I had foreseen, it came to pass; for the Scots resolving to proceed, never stood upon the ceremony of aggression, as before, but on the 20th of August they entered England with their army.

However, as my father desired, I went to the king's army, which was then at York, but not gotten all together. The king himself was at London, but upon this news takes post for the army, and advancing a part of his forces, he posted the Lord Conway and Sir Jacob Astley, with a brigade of foot and some horse, at Newburn, upon the river Tyne, to keep the Scots from passing that river.

The Scots could have passed the Tyne without fighting; but to let us see that they were able to force their passage, they fall upon his body of men and notwithstanding all the advantages of the place, they beat them from the post, took their baggage and two pieces of cannon, with some prisoners. Sir Jacob Astley made what resistance he could, but the Scots charged with so much fury, and being also overpowered, he was soon put into confusion. Immediately the Scots made themselves masters of Newcastle, and the next day of Durham, and laid those two counties under intolerable contributions.

Now was the king absolutely ruined; for among his own people the discontents before were so plain, that had the clergy had any forecast, they would never have embroiled him with the Scots, till he had fully brought matters to an understanding at home. But the case was thus: the king, by the good husbandry of Bishop Juxon, his treasurer, had a million of ready money in his treasury, and upon that account, having no need of a Parliament, had not called one in twelve years; and perhaps had never called another, if he had not by this unhappy circumstance been reduced to a necessity of it; for now this ready money was spent in two foolish expeditions, and his army appeared in a condition not fit to engage the Scots. The detachment under Sir Jacob Astley, which were of the flower of his men, had been routed at Newburn, and the enemy had possession of two entire counties.

All men blamed Laud for prompting the king to provoke the Scots, a headstrong nation, and zealous for their own way of worship; and Laud himself found too late the consequences of it, both to the whole cause and to himself; for the Scots, whose native temper is not easily to forgive an injury, pursued him by their party in England, and never gave it over till they laid his head on the block.

The ruined country now clamoured in his Majesty's ears with daily petitions, and the gentry of other neighbouring counties cry out for peace and Parliament. The king, embarrassed with these difficulties, and quite empty of money, calls a great council of the nobility at York, and demands their advice, which any one could have told him before would be to call a Parliament.

I cannot, without regret, look back upon the misfortune of the king, who, as he was one of the best princes in his personal conduct that ever reigned in England, had yet some of the greatest unhappinesses in his conduct as a king, that ever prince had, and the whole course of his life demonstrated it.

1. An impolitic honesty. His enemies called it obstinacy; but as I was perfectly acquainted with his temper, I cannot but think it was his judgment, when he thought he was in the right, to adhere to it as a duty though against his interest.

2. Too much compliance when he was complying. No man but himself would have denied what at some times he denied, and have granted what at other times he granted; and this uncertainty of counsel proceeded from two things.

1. The heat of the clergy, to whom he was exceedingly devoted, and for whom, indeed, he ruined himself.

2. The wisdom of his nobility.

Thus when the counsel of his priests prevailed, all was fire and fury; the Scots were rebels, and must be subdued, and the Parliament's demands were to be rejected as exorbitant. But whenever the king's judgment was led by the grave and steady advice of his nobility and counsellors, he was always inclined by them to temperate his measures between the two extremes. And had he gone on in such a temper, he had never met with the misfortunes which afterward attended him, or had so many thousands of his friends lost their lives and fortunes in his service.

I am sure we that knew what it was to fight for him, and that loved him better than any of the clergy could pretend to, have had many a consultation how to bring over our master from so espousing their interest, as to ruin himself for it; but 'twas in vain.

I took this interval when I sat still and only looked on, to make these remarks, because I remember the best friends the king had were at this time of that opinion, that 'twas an unaccountable piece of indiscretion, to commence a quarrel with the Scots, a poor and obstinate people, for a ceremony and book of Church discipline, at a time when the king stood but upon indifferent terms with his people at home.

The consequence was, it put arms into the hands of his subjects to rebel against him; it embroiled him with his Parliament in England, to whom he was fain to stoop in a fatal and unusual manner to get money, all his own being spent, and so to buy off the Scots whom he could not beat off.

I cannot but give one instance of the unaccountable politics of his ministers. If they overruled this unhappy king to it, with design to exhaust and impoverish him, they were the worst of traitors; if not, the grossest of fools. They prompted the king to equip a fleet against the Scots, and to put on board it 5000 land men. Had this been all, the design had been good, that while the king had faced the army upon the borders, these 5000, landing in the Firth of Edinburgh, might have put that whole nation into disorder. But in order to this, they advised the king to lay out his money in fitting out the biggest ships he had, and the "Royal Sovereign," the biggest ship the world had ever seen, which cost him no less than £100,000, was now built, and fitted out for this voyage.

This was the most incongruous and ridiculous advice that could be given, and made us all believe we were betrayed, though we knew not by whom. To fit out ships of 100 guns to invade Scotland, which had not one man-of-war in the world, nor any open confederacy with any prince or state that had any fleet, 'twas a most ridiculous thing. An hundred sail of Newcastle colliers, to carry the men with their stores and provisions, and ten frigates of 40 guns each, had been as good a fleet as reason and the nature of the thing could have made tolerable.

Thus things were carried on, till the king, beggared by the mismanagement of his counsels, and beaten by the Scots, was driven to the necessity of calling a Parliament in England.

It is not my design to enter into the feuds and brangles of this Parliament. I have noted, by observations of their mistakes, who brought the king to this happy necessity of calling them.

His Majesty had tried Parliaments upon several occasions before, but never found himself so much embroiled with them but he could send them home, and there was an end of it; but as he could not avoid calling these, so they took care to put him out of a condition to dismiss them.

The Scots army was now quartered upon the English. The counties, the gentry, and the assembly of lords at York, petitioned for a Parliament.

74

The Scots presented their demands to the king, in which it was observed that matters were concerted between them and a party in England; and I confess when I saw that, I began to think the king in an ill case; for as the Scots pretended grievances, we thought, the king redressing those grievances, they could ask no more; and therefore all men advised the king to grant their full demands. And whereas the king had not money to supply the Scots in their march home, I know there were several meetings of gentlemen with a design to advance considerable sums of money to the king to set him free, and in order to reinstate his Majesty, as before. Not that we ever advised the king to rule without a Parliament, but we were very desirous of putting him out of the necessity of calling them, at least just then. But the eighth article of the Scots' demands expressly required, that an English Parliament might be called to remove all obstructions of commerce, and to settle peace, religion, and liberty; and in another article they tell the king, the 24th of September being the time his Majesty appointed for the meeting of the peers, will make it too long ere the Parliament meet. And in another, that a Parliament was the only way of settling peace, and bring them to his Majesty's obedience.

When we saw this in the army, 'twas time to look about. Everybody perceived that the Scots army would call an English Parliament; and whatever aversion the king had to it, we all saw he would be obliged to comply with it; and now they all began to see their error, who advised the king to this Scotch war.

While these things were transacting, the assembly of the peers meet at York, and by their advice a treaty was begun with the Scots. I had the honour to be sent with the first message which was in writing.

I brought it, attended by a trumpet and a guard of 500 horse, to the Scots quarters. I was stopped at Darlington, and my errand being known, General Leslie sent a Scots major and fifty horses to receive me, but would let neither my trumpet or guard set foot within their quarters. In this manner I was conducted to audience in the chapter-house at Durham, where a committee of Scots lords who attended the army received me very courteously, and gave me their answer in writing also.

'Twas in this answer that they showed, at least to me, their design of embroiling the king with his English subjects; they discoursed very freely with me, and did not order me to withdraw when they debated their private opinions. They drew up several answers but did not like them; at last they gave me one which I did not receive, I thought it was too insolent to be borne with. As near as I can remember it was thus: The commissioners of Scotland attending the service in the army, do refuse any treaty in the city of York. One of the commissioners who treated me with more distinction than the rest, and discoursed freely with me, gave me an opportunity to speak more freely of this than I expected.

I told them if they would return to his Majesty an answer fit for me to carry, or if they would say they would not treat at all, I would deliver such a message. But I entreated them to consider the answer was to their sovereign, and to whom they made a great profession of duty and respect, and at least they ought to give their reasons why they declined a treaty at York, and to name some other place, or humbly to desire his Majesty to name some other place; but to send word they would not treat at York, I could deliver no such message, for when put into English it would signify they would not treat at all.

I used a great many reasons and arguments with them on this head, and at last with some difficulty obtained of them to give the reason, which was the Earl of Strafford's having the chief command at York, whom they declared their mortal enemy, he having declared them rebels in Ireland.

With this answer I returned. I could make no observations in the short time I was with them, for as I stayed but one night, so I was guarded as a close prisoner all the while. I saw several of their officers whom I knew, but they durst not speak to me, and if they would have ventured, my guard would not have permitted them.

In this manner I was conducted out of their quarters to my own party again, and having delivered my message to the king and told his Majesty the circumstances, I saw the king receive the account of the haughty behaviour of the Scots with some regret; however, it was his Majesty's time now to bear, and therefore the Scots were complied with, and the treaty appointed at Ripon; where, after much debate, several preliminary articles were agreed on, as a cessation of arms, quarters, and bounds to the armies, subsistence to the Scots army, and the residue of the demands was referred to a treaty at London, &c. We were all amazed at the treaty, and I cannot but remember we used to wish much rather we had been suffered to fight; for though we had been worsted at first, the power and strength of the king's interest, which was not yet tried, must, in fine, have been too strong for the Scots, whereas now we saw the king was for complying with anything, and all his friends would be ruined.

I confess I had nothing to fear, and so was not much concerned, but our predictions soon came to pass, for no sooner was this Parliament called but abundance of those who had embroiled their king with his people of both kingdoms, like the disciples when their Master was betrayed to the Jews, forsook him and fled; and now Parliament tyranny began to succeed Church tyranny, and we soldiers were glad to see it at first. The bishops trembled, the judges went to gaol, the officers of the customs were laid hold on; and the Parliament began to lay their fingers on the great ones, particularly Archbishop Laud and the Earl of Strafford. We had no great concern for the first, but the last was a man of so much conduct and gallantry, and so beloved by the soldiers and principal gentry of England, that everybody was touched with his misfortune.

The Parliament now grew mad in their turn, and as the prosperity of any party is the time to show their discretion, the Parliament showed they knew as little where to stop as other people. The king was not in a condition to deny anything, and nothing could be demanded but they pushed it. They attainted the Earl of Strafford, and thereby made the king cut off his right hand to save his left, and yet not save it neither. They obtained another bill to empower them to sit during their own pleasure, and after them, triennial Parliaments to meet, whether the king call them or no; and granting this completed his Majesty's ruin.

Had the House only regulated the abuses of the court, punished evil counsellors, and restored Parliaments to their original and just powers, all had been well, and the king, though he had been more than mortified, had yet reaped the benefit of future peace; for now the Scots were sent home, after having eaten up two countries, and received a prodigious sum of money to boot. And the king, though too late, goes in person to Edinburgh, and grants them all they could desire, and more than they asked; but in England, the desires of ours were unbounded, and drove at all extremes.

They drew out the bishops from sitting in the House, made a protestation equivalent to the Scotch Covenant, and this done, print their remonstrance. This so provoked the king, that he resolves upon seizing some of the members, and in an ill hour enters the House in person to take them. Thus one imprudent thing on one hand produced another of the other hand, till the king was obliged to leave them to themselves, for fear of being mobbed into something or other unworthy of himself.

These proceedings began to alarm the gentry and nobility of England; for, however willing we were to have evil counsellors removed, and the government return to a settled and legal course, according to the happy constitution of this nation, and might have been forward enough to have owned the king had been misled, and imposed upon to do things which he had rather had not been done, yet it did not follow, that all the powers and prerogatives of the crown should devolve upon the Parliament, and the king in a manner be deposed, or else sacrificed to the fury of the rabble.

The heats of the House running them thus to all extremes, and at last to take from the king the power of the militia, which indeed was all that was left to make him anything of a king, put the king upon opposing force with force; and thus the flame of civil war began.

However backward I was in engaging in the second year's expedition against the Scots, I was as forward now, for I waited on the king at York, where a gallant company of gentlemen as ever were seen in England, engaged themselves to enter into his service; and here some of us formed ourselves into troops for the guard of his person.

The king having been waited upon by the gentry of Yorkshire, and having told them his resolution of erecting his royal standard, and received from them hearty assurances of support, dismisses them, and marches to Hull, where lay the train of artillery, and all the arms and ammunition belonging to the northern army which had been disbanded. But here the Parliament had been beforehand with his Majesty, so that when he came to Hull, he found the gates shut, and Sir John Hotham, the governor, upon the walls, though with a great deal of seeming humility and protestations of loyalty to his person, yet with a positive denial to admit any of the king's attendants into the town. If his Majesty pleased to enter the town in person with any reasonable number of his household, he would submit, but would not be prevailed on to receive the king as he would be received, with his forces, though those forces were then but very few.

The king was exceedingly provoked at this repulse, and indeed it was a great surprise to us all, for certainly never prince began a war against the whole strength of his kingdom under the circumstances that he was in. He had not a garrison, or a company of soldiers in his pay, not a stand of arms, or a barrel of powder, a musket, cannon or mortar, not a ship of all the fleet, or money in his treasury to procure them; whereas the Parliament had all his navy, and ordnance, stores, magazines, arms, ammunition, and revenue in their keeping. And this I take to be another defect of the king's counsel, and a sad instance of the distraction of his affairs, that when he saw how all things were going to wreck, as it was impossible but he should see it, and 'tis plain he did see it, that he should not long enough before it came to extremities secure the navy, magazines, and stores of war, in the hands of his trusty servants, that would have been sure to have preserved them for his use, at a time when he wanted them.

It cannot be supposed but the gentry of England, who generally preserved their loyalty for their royal master, and at last heartily showed it, were exceedingly discouraged at first when they saw the Parliament had all the means of making war in their own hands, and the king was naked and destitute either of arms or ammunition, or money to procure them. Not but that the king, by extraordinary application, recovered the disorder the want of these things had thrown him into, and supplied himself with all things needful.

But my observation was this, had his Majesty had the magazines, navy, and forts in his own hand, the gentry, who wanted but the prospect of something to encourage them, had come in at first, and the Parliament, being unprovided, would have been presently reduced to reason. But this was it that balked the gentry of Yorkshire, who went home again, giving the king good promises, but never appeared for him, till by raising a good army in Shropshire and Wales, he marched towards London, and they saw there was a prospect of their being supported.

In this condition the king erected his standard at Nottingham, 22nd August 1642, and I confess, I had very melancholy apprehensions of the king's affairs, for the appearance to the royal standard was but small. The affront the king had met with at Hull, had balked and dispirited the northern gentry, and the king's affairs looked with a very dismal aspect. We had expresses from London of the prodigious success of the Parliament levies, how their men came in faster than they could entertain them, and that arms were delivered out to whole companies listed together, and the like. And all this while the king had not got together a thousand foot, and had no arms for them neither. When the king saw this, he immediately despatches five several messengers, whereof one went to the Marquis of Worcester into Wales; one went to the queen, then at Windsor; one to the Duke of Newcastle, then Marquis of Newcastle, into the north; one into Scotland; and one into France, where the queen soon after arrived to raise money, and buy arms, and to get what assistance she could among her own friends. Nor was her Majesty idle, for she sent over several ships laden with arms and ammunition, with a fine train of artillery, and a great many very good officers; and though one of the first fell into the hands of the Parliament, with three hundred barrels of powder and some arms, and one hundred and fifty gentlemen, yet most of the gentlemen found means, one way or other, to get to us, and most of the ships the queen freighted arrived; and at last her Majesty came herself, and brought an extraordinary supply both of men, money, arms, &c., with which she joined the king's forces under the Earl of Newcastle in the north.

Finding his Majesty thus bestirring himself to muster his friends together, I asked him if he thought it might not be for his Majesty's service to let me go among my friends, and his loyal subjects about Shrewsbury? "Yes," says the king, smiling, "I intend you shall, and I design to go with you myself." I did not understand what the king meant then, and did not think it good manners to inquire, but the next day I found all things disposed for a march, and the king on horseback by eight of the clock; when calling me to him, he told me I should go before, and let my father and all my friends know he would be at Shrewsbury the Saturday following. I left my equipages, and taking post with only one servant, was at my father's the next morning by break of day. My father was not surprised at the news of the king's coming at all, for, it seems, he, together with the royal gentry of those parts, had sent particularly to give the king an invitation to move that way, which I was not made privy to, with an account what encouragement they had there in the endeavours made for his interest. In short, the whole country was entirely for the king, and such was the universal joy the people showed when the news of his Majesty's coming down was positively known, that all manner of business was laid aside, and the whole body of the people seemed to be resolved upon the war.

As this gave a new face to the king's affairs, so I must own it filled me with joy; for I was astonished before, when I considered what the king and his friends were like to be exposed to. The news of the proceedings of the Parliament, and their powerful preparations, were now no more terrible; the king came at the time appointed, and having lain at my father's house one night, entered Shrewsbury in the morning. The acclamations of the people, the concourse of the nobility and gentry about his person, and the crowds which now came every day into the standard, were incredible.

The loyalty of the English gentry was not only worth notice, but the power of the gentry is extraordinary visible in this matter. The king, in about six weeks' time, which was the most of his stay at Shrewsbury, was supplied with money, arms, ammunition, and a train of artillery, and listed a body of an army upwards of 20,000 men.

His Majesty seeing the general alacrity of his people, immediately issued out commissions, and formed regiments of horse and foot; and having some experienced officers about him, together with about sixteen who came from France, with a ship loaded with arms and some field-pieces which came very seasonably into the Severn, the men were exercised, regularly disciplined, and quartered, and now we began to look like soldiers. My father had raised a regiment of horse at his own charge, and completed them, and the king gave out arms to them from the supplies which I mentioned came from abroad. Another party of horse, all brave stout fellows, and well mounted, came in from Lancashire, and the Earl of Derby at the head of them. The Welshmen came in by droves; and so great was the concourse of people, that the king began to think of marching, and gave the command, as well as the trust of regulating the army, to the brave Earl of Lindsey, as general of the foot. The Parliament general being the Earl of Essex, two braver men, or two better officers, were not in the kingdom; they had both been old soldiers, and had served together as volunteers in the Low Country wars, under Prince Maurice. They had been comrades and companions abroad, and now came to face one another as enemies in the field.

Such was the expedition used by the king and his friends, in the levies of this first army, that notwithstanding the wonderful expedition the Parliament made, the king was in the field before them; and now the gentry in other parts of the nation bestirred themselves, and seized upon, and garrisoned several considerable places, for the king. In the north, the Earl of Newcastle not only garrisoned the most considerable places, but even the general possession of the north was for the king, excepting Hull, and some few places, which the old Lord Fairfax had taken up for the Parliament. On the other hand, entire Cornwall and most of the western counties were the king's. The Parliament had their chief interest in the south and eastern part of England, as Kent, Surrey, and, Sussex, Essex, Suffolk, Norfolk, Cambridge, Bedford, Huntingdon, Hertford, Buckinghamshire, and the other midland counties. These were called, or some of them at least, the associated counties, and felt little of the war, other than the charges; but the main support of the Parliament was the city of London.

The king made the seat of his court at Oxford, which he caused to be regularly fortified. The Lord Say had been here, and had possession of the city for the enemy, and was debating about fortifying it, but came to no resolution, which was a very great over-sight in them; the situation of the place, and the importance of it, on many accounts, to the city of London, considered; and they would have retrieved this error afterwards, but then 'twas too late; for the king made it the headquarter, and received great supplies and assistance from the wealth of the colleges, and the plenty of the neighbouring country. Abingdon, Wallingford, Basing, and Reading, were all garrisoned and fortified as outworks to defend this as the centre. And thus all England became the theatre of blood, and war was spread into every corner of the country, though as yet there was no stroke struck. I had no command in this army. My father led his own regiment, and, old as he was, would not leave his royal master, and my elder brother stayed at home to support the family. As for me, I rode a volunteer in the royal troop of guards, which may very well deserve the title of a royal troop, for it was composed of young gentlemen, sons of the nobility, and some of the prime gentry of the nation, and I think not a person of so mean a birth or fortune as myself. We reckoned in this troop two and thirty lords, or who came afterwards to be such, and eight and thirty of younger sons of the nobility, five French noblemen, and all the rest gentlemen of very good families and estates.

And that I may give the due to their personal valour, many of this troop lived afterwards to have regiments and troops under their command in the service of the king, many of them lost their lives for him, and most of them their estates. Nor did they behave unworthy of themselves in their first showing their faces to the enemy, as shall be mentioned in its place.

While the king remained at Shrewsbury, his loyal friends bestirred themselves in several parts of the kingdom. Goring had secured Portsmouth, but being young in matters of war, and not in time relieved, though the Marquis of Hertford was marching to relieve him, yet he was obliged to quit the place, and shipped himself for Holland, from whence he returned with relief for the king, and afterwards did very good service upon all occasions, and so effectually cleared himself of the scandal the hasty surrender of Portsmouth had brought upon his courage.

The chief power of the king's forces lay in three places, in Cornwall, in Yorkshire, and at Shrewsbury. In Cornwall, Sir Ralph Hopton, afterwards Lord Hopton, Sir Bevil Grenvile, and Sir Nicholas Slanning secured all the country, and afterwards spread themselves over Devonshire and Somersetshire, took Exeter from the Parliament, fortified Bridgewater and Barnstaple, and beat Sir William Waller at the battle of Roundway Down, as I shall touch at more particularly when I come to recite the part of my own travels that way.

In the north, The Marquis of Newcastle secured all the country, garrisoned York, Scarborough, Carlisle, Newcastle, Pomfret, Leeds, and all the considerable places, and took the field with a very good army, though afterwards he proved more unsuccessful than the rest, having the whole power of a kingdom at his back, the Scots coming in with an army to the assistance of the Parliament, which, indeed, was the general turn of the scale of the war; for had it not been for this Scots army, the king had most certainly reduced the Parliament, at least to good terms of peace, in two years' time.

The king was the third article. His force at Shrewsbury I have noted already. The alacrity of the gentry filled him with hopes, and all his army with vigour, and the 8th of October 1642, his Majesty gave orders to march. The Earl of Essex had spent above a month after his leaving London (for he went thence the 9th of September) in modelling and drawing together his forces; his rendezvous was at St Albans, from whence he marched to Northampton, Coventry, and Warwick, and leaving garrisons in them, he comes on to Worcester. Being thus advanced, he possesses Oxford, as I noted before, Banbury, Bristol, Gloucester, and Worcester, out of all which places, except Gloucester, we drove him back to London in a very little while.

Sir John Byron had raised a very good party of 500 horse, most gentlemen, for the king, and had possessed Oxford; but on the approach of the Lord Say quitted it, being now but an open town, and retreated to Worcester, from whence, on the approach of Essex's army, he retreated to the king.

And now all things grew ripe for action, both parties having secured their posts, and settled their schemes of the war, taken their posts and places as their measures and opportunities directed. The field was next in their eye, and the soldiers began to inquire when they should fight, for as yet there had been little or no blood drawn; and 'twas not long before they had enough of it; for, I believe, I may challenge all the historians in Europe to tell me of any war in the world where, in the space of four years, there were so many pitched battles, sieges, fights, and skirmishes, as in this war. We never encamped or entrenched, never fortified the avenues to our posts, or lay fenced with rivers and defiles; here was no leaguers in the field, as at the story of Nuremberg, neither had our soldiers any tents, or what they call heavy baggage. 'Twas the general maxim of this war, "Where is the enemy? let us go and fight them," or, on the other hand, if the enemy was coming, "What was to be done?" "Why, what should be done? Draw out into the fields and fight them." I cannot say 'twas the prudence of the parties, and had the king fought less he had gained more. And I shall remark several times when the eagerness of fighting was the worst counsel, and proved our loss. This benefit, however, happened in general to the country, that it made a quick, though a bloody, end of the war, which otherwise had lasted till it might have ruined the whole nation.

On the 10th of October the king's army was in full march, his Majesty, generalissimo, the Earl of Lindsey, general of the foot, Prince Rupert, general of the horse; and the first action in the field was by Prince Rupert and Sir John Byron. Sir John had brought his body of 500 horse, as I noted already, from Oxford to Worcester; the Lord Say, with a strong party, being in the neighbourhood of Oxford, and expected in the town, Colonel Sandys, a hot man, and who had more courage than judgment, advances with about 1500 horse and dragoons, with design to beat Sir John Byron out of Worcester, and take post there for the Parliament.

The king had notice that the Earl of Essex designed for Worcester, and Prince Rupert was ordered to advance with a body of horse and dragoons to face the enemy, and bring off Sir John Byron. This his Majesty did to amuse the Earl of Essex, that he might expect him that way; whereas the king's design was to get between the Earl of Essex's army and the city of London; and his Majesty's end was doubly answered, for he not only drew Essex on to Worcester, where he spent more time than he needed, but he beat the party into the bargain. I went volunteer in this party, and rode in my father's regiment; for though we really expected not to see the enemy, yet I was tired with lying still. We came to Worcester just as notice was brought to Sir John Byron, that a party of the enemy was on their march for Worcester, upon which the prince immediately consulting what was to be done, resolves to march the next morning and fight them.

The enemy, who lay at Pershore, about eight miles from Worcester, and, as I believe, had no notice of our march, came on very confidently in the morning, and found us fairly drawn up to receive them. I must confess this was the bluntest, downright way of making war that ever was seen. The enemy, who, in all the little knowledge I had of war, ought to have discovered our numbers, and guessed by our posture what our design was, might easily have informed themselves that we intended to attack them, and so might have secured the advantage of a bridge in their front; but without any regard to these methods of policy, they came on at all hazards. Upon this notice, my father proposed to the prince to halt for them, and suffer ourselves to be attacked, since we found them willing to give us the advantage. The prince approved of the advice, so we halted within view of a bridge, leaving space enough on our front for about half the number of their forces to pass and draw up; and at the bridge was posted about fifty dragoons, with orders to retire as soon as the enemy advanced, as if they had been afraid. On the right of the road was a ditch, and a very high bank behind, where we had placed 300 dragoons, with orders to lie flat on their faces till the enemy had passed the bridge, and to let fly among them as soon as our trumpets sounded a charge. Nobody but Colonel Sandys would have been caught in such a snare, for he might easily have seen that when he was over the bridge there was not room enough for him to fight in. But the Lord of hosts was so much in their mouths, for that was the word for that day, that they took little heed how to conduct the host of the Lord to their own advantage.

As we expected, they appeared, beat our dragoons from the bridge, and passed it. We stood firm in one line with a reserve, and expected a charge, but Colonel Sandys, showing a great deal more judgment than we thought he was master of, extends himself to the left, finding the ground too strait, and began to form his men with a great deal of readiness and skill, for by this time he saw our number was greater than he expected. The prince perceiving it, and foreseeing that the stratagem of the dragoons would be frustrated by this, immediately charges with the horse, and the dragoons at the same time standing upon their feet, poured in their shot upon those that were passing the bridge. This surprise put them into such disorder, that we had but little work with them. For though Colonel Sandys with the troops next him sustained the shock very well, and behaved themselves gallantly enough, yet the confusion beginning in their rear, those that had not yet passed the bridge were kept back by the fire of the dragoons, and the rest were easily cut in pieces. Colonel Sandys was mortally wounded and taken prisoner, and the crowd was so great to get back, that many pushed into the water, and were rather smothered than drowned. Some of them who never came into the fight, were so frighted, that they never looked behind them till they came to Pershore, and, as we were afterwards informed, the lifeguards of the general who had quartered in the town, left it in disorder enough, expecting us at the heels of their men.

If our business had been to keep the Parliament army from coming to Worcester, we had a very good opportunity to have secured the bridge at Pershore; but our design lay another way, as I have said, and the king was for drawing Essex on to the Severn, in hopes to get behind him, which fell out accordingly.

Essex, spurred by this affront in the infancy of their affairs, advances the next day, and came to Pershore time enough to be at the funeral of some of his men; and from thence he advances to Worcester.

We marched back to Worcester extremely pleased with the good success of our first attack, and our men were so flushed with this little victory that it put vigour into the whole army. The enemy lost about 3000 men, and we carried away near 150 prisoners, with 500 horses, some standards and arms, and among the prisoners their colonel; but he died a little after of his wounds. Upon the approach of the enemy, Worcester was quitted, and the forces marched back to join the king's army, which lay then at Bridgnorth, Ludlow, and thereabout. As the king expected, it fell out; Essex found so much work at Worcester to settle Parliament quarters, and secure Bristol, Gloucester, and Hereford, that it gave the king a full day's march of him. So the king, having the start of him, moves towards London; and Essex, nettled to be both beaten in fight and outdone in conduct, decamps, and follows the king.

The Parliament, and the Londoners too, were in a strange consternation at this mistake of their general; and had the king, whose great misfortune was always to follow precipitant advices,--had the king, I say, pushed on his first design, which he had formed with very good reason, and for which he had been dodging with Essex eight or ten days, viz., of marching directly to London, where he had a very great interest, and where his friends were not yet oppressed and impoverished, as they were afterwards, he had turned the scale of his affairs. And every man expected it; for the members began to shift for themselves, expresses were sent on the heels of one another to the Earl of Essex to hasten after the king, and, if possible, to bring him to a battle. Some of these letters fell into our hands, and we might easily discover that the Parliament were in the last confusion at the thoughts of our coming to London. Besides this, the city was in a worse fright than the House, and the great moving men began to go out of town. In short, they expected us, and we expected to come, but Providence for our ruin had otherwise determined it.

Essex, upon news of the king's march, and upon receipt of the Parliament's letters, makes long marches after us, and on the 23rd of October reaches the village of Kineton, in Warwickshire. The king was almost as far as Banbury, and there calls a council of war. Some of the old officers that foresaw the advantage the king had, the concern the city was in, and the vast addition, both to the reputation of his forces and the increase of his interest, it would be if the king could gain that point, urged the king to march on to London. Prince Rupert and the fresh colonels pressed for fighting, told the king it dispirited their men to march with the enemy at their heels; that the Parliament army was inferior to him by 6000 men, and fatigued with hasty marching; that as their orders were to fight, he had nothing to do but to post himself to advantage, and receive them to their destruction; that the action near Worcester had let them know how easy it was to deal with a rash enemy; and that 'twas a dishonour for him, whose forces were so much superior, to be pursued by his subjects in rebellion. These and the like arguments prevailed with the king to alter his wiser measures and resolve to fight. Nor was this all; when a resolution of fighting was taken, that part of the advice which they who were for fighting gave, as a reason for their opinion, was forgot, and instead of halting and posting ourselves to advantage till the enemy came up, we were ordered to march back and meet them.

Nay, so eager was the prince for fighting, that when, from the top of Edgehill, the enemy's army was descried in the bottom between them and the village of Kineton, and that the enemy had bid us defiance, by discharging three cannons, we accepted the challenge, and answering with two shots from our army, we must needs forsake the advantages of the hills, which they must have mounted under the command of our cannon, and march down to them into the plain. I confess, I thought here was a great deal more gallantry than discretion; for it was plainly taking an advantage out of our own hands, and putting it into the hands of the enemy. An enemy that must fight, may always be fought with to advantage. My old hero, the glorious Gustavus Adolphus, was as forward to fight as any man of true valour mixed with any policy need to be, or ought to be; but he used to say, "An enemy reduced to a necessity of fighting is half beaten."

Tis true, we were all but young in the war; the soldiers hot and forward, and eagerly desired to come to hands with the enemy. But I take the more notice of it here, because the king in this acted against his own measures; for it was the king himself had laid the design of getting the start of Essex, and marching to London. His friends had invited him thither, and expected him, and suffered deeply for the omission; and yet he gave way to these hasty counsels, and suffered his judgment to be overruled by majority of voices; an error, I say, the King of Sweden was never guilty of. For if all the officers at a council of war were of a different opinion, yet unless their reasons mastered his judgment, their votes never altered his measures. But this was the error of our good, but unfortunate master, three times in this war, and particularly in two of the greatest battles of the time, viz., this of Edgehill, and that of Naseby.

The resolution for fighting being published in the army, gave an universal joy to the soldiers, who expressed an extraordinary ardour for fighting. I remember my father talking with me about it, asked me what I thought of the approaching battle. I told him I thought the king had done very well; for at that time I did not consult the extent of the design, and had a mighty mind, like other rash people, to see it brought to a day, which made me answer my father as I did. "But," said I, "sir, I doubt there will be but indifferent doings on both sides, between two armies both made up of fresh men, that have never seen any service." My father minded little what I spoke of that; but when I seemed pleased that the king had resolved to fight, he looked angrily at me, and told me he was sorry I could see no farther into things. "I tell you," says he hastily, "if the king should kill and take prisoners this whole army, general and all, the Parliament will have the victory; for we have lost more by slipping this opportunity of getting into London, than we shall ever get by ten battles." I saw enough of this afterwards to convince me of the weight of what my father said, and so did the king too; but it was then too late. Advantages slipped in war are never recovered.

We were now in a full march to fight the Earl of Essex. It was on Sunday morning the 24th of October 1642, fair weather overhead, but the ground very heavy and dirty. As soon as we came to the top of Edgehill, we discovered their whole army. They were not drawn up, having had two miles to march that morning, but they were very busy forming their lines, and posting the regiments as they came up. Some of their horse were exceedingly fatigued, having marched forty-eight hours together; and had they been suffered to follow us three or four days' march farther, several of their regiments of horse would have been quite ruined, and their foot would have been rendered unserviceable for the present. But we had no patience.

As soon as our whole army was come to the top of the hill, we were drawn up in order of battle. The king's army made a very fine appearance; and indeed they were a body of gallant men as ever appeared in the field, and as well furnished at all points; the horse exceedingly well accoutred, being most of them gentlemen and volunteers, some whole regiments serving without pay; their horses very good and fit for service as could be desired.

The whole army were not above 18,000 men, and the enemy not 1000 over or under, though we had been told they were not above 12,000; but they had been reinforced with 4000 men from Northampton. The king was with the general, the Earl of Lindsey, in the main battle; Prince Rupert commanded the right wing, and the Marquis of Hertford, the Lord Willoughby, and several other very good officers the left.

The signal of battle being given with two cannon shots, we marched in order of battalia down the hill, being drawn up in two lines with bodies of reserve; the enemy advanced to meet us much in the same form, with this difference only, that they had placed their cannon on their right, and the king had placed ours in the centre, before, or rather between two great brigades of foot. Their cannon began with us first, and did some mischief among the dragoons of our left wing; but our officers, perceiving the shot took the men and missed the horses, ordered all to alight, and every man leading his horse, to advance in the same order; and this saved our men, for most of the enemy's shot flew over their heads. Our cannon made a terrible execution upon their foot for a quarter of an hour, and put them into great confusion, till the general obliged them to halt, and changed the posture of his front, marching round a small rising ground by which he avoided the fury of our artillery.

By this time the wings were engaged, the king having given the signal of battle, and ordered the right wing to fall on. Prince Rupert, who, as is said, commanded that wing, fell on with such fury, and pushed the left wing of the Parliament army so effectually, that in a moment he filled all with terror and confusion. Commissary-General Ramsey, a Scotsman, a Low Country Soldier, and an experienced officer, commanded their left wing, and though he did all that an expert soldier, and a brave commander could do, yet 'twas to no purpose; his lines were immediately broken, and all overwhelmed in a trice. Two regiments of foot, whether as part of the left wing, or on the left of the main body, I know not, were disordered by their own horse, and rather trampled to death by the horses, than beaten by our men; but they were so entirely broken and disordered, that I do not remember that ever they made one volley upon our men; for their own horse running away, and falling foul on these foot, were so vigorously followed by our men, that the foot never had a moment to rally or look behind them. The point of the left wing of horse were not so soon broken as the rest, and three regiments of them stood firm for some time. The dexterous officers of the other regiments taking the opportunity, rallied a great many of their scattered men behind them, and pieced in some troops with those regiments; but after two or three charges, which a brigade of our second line, following the prince, made upon them, they also were broken with the rest.

I remember that at the great battle of Leipsic, the right wing of the Imperialists having fallen in upon the Saxons with like fury to this, bore down all before them, and beat the Saxons quite out of the field; upon which the soldiers cried, "Victoria, let us follow." "No, no," said the old General Tilly, "let them go, but let us beat the Swedes too, and then all's our own." Had Prince Rupert taken this method, and instead of following the fugitives, who were dispersed so effectually that two regiments would have secured them from rallying--I say, had he fallen in upon the foot, or wheeled to the left, and fallen in upon the rear of the enemy's right wing of horse, or returned to the assistance of the left wing of our horse, we had gained the most absolute and complete victory that could be; nor had 1000 men of the enemy's army got off. But this prince, who was full of fire, and pleased to see the rout of an enemy, pursued them quite to the town of Kineton, where indeed he killed abundance of their men, and some time also was lost in plundering the baggage.

But in the meantime, the glory and advantage of the day was lost to the king, for the right wing of the Parliament horse could not be so broken. Sir William Balfour made a desperate charge upon the point of the king's left, and had it not been for two regiments of dragoons who were planted in the reserve, had routed the whole wing, for he broke through the first line, and staggered the second, who advanced to their assistance, but was so warmly received by those dragoons, who came seasonably in, and gave their first fire on horseback, that his fury was checked, and having lost a great many men, was forced to wheel about to his own men; and had the king had but three regiments of horse at hand to have charged him, he had been routed. The rest of this wing kept their ground, and received the first fury of the enemy with great firmness; after which, advancing in their turn, they were at once masters of the Earl of Essex's cannon. And here we lost another advantage; for if any foot had been at hand to support these horse, they had carried off the cannon, or turned it upon the main battle of the enemy's foot, but the foot were otherwise engaged. The horse on this side fought with great obstinacy and variety of success a great while. Sir Philip Stapleton, who commanded the guards of the Earl of Essex, being engaged with a party of our Shrewsbury cavaliers, as we called them, was once in a fair way to have been cut off by a brigade of our foot, who, being advanced to fall on upon the Parliament's main body, flanked Sir Philip's horse in their way, and facing to the left, so furiously charged him with their pikes, that he was obliged to retire in great disorder, and with the loss of a great many men and horses.

All this while the foot on both sides were desperately engaged, and coming close up to the teeth of one another with the clubbed musket and push of pike, fought with great resolution, and a terrible slaughter on both sides, giving no quarter for a great while; and they continued to do thus, till, as if they were tired, and out of wind, either party seemed willing enough to leave off, and take breath. Those which suffered most were that brigade which had charged Sir William Stapleton's horse, who being bravely engaged in the front with the enemy's foot, were, on the sudden, charged again in front and flank by Sir William Balfour's horse and disordered, after a very desperate defence. Here the king's standard was taken, the standard-bearer, Sir Edward Verney, being killed; but it was rescued again by Captain Smith, and brought to the king the same night, for which the king knighted the captain.

This brigade of foot had fought all the day, and had not been broken at last, if any horse had been at hand to support them. The field began to be now clear; both armies stood, as it were, gazing at one another, only the king, having rallied his foot, seemed inclined to renew the charge, and began to cannonade them, which they could not return, most of their cannon being nailed while they were in our possession, and all the cannoniers killed or fled; and our gunners did execution upon Sir William Balfour's troops for a good while.

My father's regiment being in the right with the prince, I saw little of the fight but the rout of the enemy's left, and we had as full a victory there as we could desire, but spent too much time in it. We killed about 2000 men in that part of the action, and having totally dispersed them, and plundered their baggage, began to think of our fellows when 'twas too late to help them. We returned, however, victorious to the king, just as the battle was over. The king asked the prince what news? He told him he could give his Majesty a good account of the enemy's horse. "Ay, by G--d," says a gentleman that stood by me, "and of their carts too." That word was spoken with such a sense of the misfortune, and made such an impression on the whole army, that it occasioned some ill blood afterwards among us; and but that the king took up the business, it had been of ill consequence, for some person who had heard the gentleman speak it, informed the prince who it was, and the prince resenting it, spoke something about it in the hearing of the party when the king was present. The gentleman, not at all surprised, told his Highness openly he had said the words; and though he owned he had no disrespect for his Highness, yet he could not but say, if it had not been so, the enemy's army had been better beaten. The prince replied something very disobliging; upon which the gentleman came up to the king, and kneeling, humbly besought his Majesty to accept of his commission, and to give him leave to tell the prince, that whenever his Highness pleased, he was ready to give him satisfaction. The prince was exceedingly provoked, and as he was very passionate, began to talk very oddly, and without all government of himself. The gentleman, as bold as he, but much calmer preserved his temper, but maintained his quarrel; and the king was so concerned, that he was very much out of humour with the prince about it. However, his Majesty, upon consideration, soon ended the dispute, by laying his commands on them both to speak no more of it for that day; and refusing the commission from the colonel, for he was no less, sent for them both next morning in private, and made them friends again. But to return to our story. We came back to the king timely enough to put the Earl of Essex's men out of all humour of renewing the fight, and as I observed before, both parties stood gazing at one another, and our cannon playing upon them obliged Sir William Balfour's horse to wheel off in some disorder, but they returned us none again, which, as we afterwards understood, was, as I said before, for want of both powder and gunners, for the cannoniers and firemen were killed, or had quitted their train in the fight, when our horse had possession of their artillery; and as they had spiked up some of the cannon, so they had carried away fifteen carriages of powder.

Night coming on, ended all discourse of more fighting, and the king drew off and marched towards the hills. I know no other token of victory which the enemy had than their lying in the field of battle all night, which they did for no other reason than that, having lost their baggage and provisions, they had nowhere to go, and which we did not, because we had good quarters at hand.

The number of prisoners and of the slain were not very unequal; the enemy lost more men, we most of quality. Six thousand men on both sides were killed on the spot, whereof, when our rolls were examined, we missed 2500. We lost our brave general the old Earl of Lindsey, who was wounded and taken prisoner, and died of his wounds; Sir Edward Stradling, Colonel Lundsford, prisoners; and Sir Edward Verney and a great many gentlemen of quality slain. On the other hand, we carried off Colonel Essex, Colonel Ramsey, and the Lord St John, who also died of his wounds; we took five ammunition waggons full of powder, and brought off about 500 horse in the defeat of the left wing, with eighteen standards and colours, and lost seventeen.

The slaughter of the left wing was so great, and the flight so effectual, that several of the officers rid clear away, coasting round, and got to London, where they reported that the Parliament army was entirely defeated--all lost, killed, or taken, as if none but them were left alive to carry the news. This filled them with consternation for a while, but when other messengers followed, all was restored to quiet again, and the Parliament cried up their victory and sufficiently mocked God and their general with their public thanks for it. Truly, as the fight was a deliverance to them, they were in the right to give thanks for it; but as to its being a victory, neither side had much to boast of, and they less a great deal than we had.

I got no hurt in this fight, and indeed we of the right wing had but little fighting; I think I had discharged my pistols but once, and my carabine twice, for we had more fatigue than fight; the enemy fled, and we had little to do but to follow and kill those we could overtake. I spoiled a good horse, and got a better from the enemy in his room, and came home weary enough. My father lost his horse, and in the fall was bruised in his thigh by another horse treading on him, which disabled him for some time, and at his request, by his Majesty's consent, I commanded the regiment in his absence.

The enemy received a recruit of 4000 men the next morning; if they had not, I believe they had gone back towards Worcester; but, encouraged by that reinforcement, they called a council of war, and had a long debate whether they could attack us again; but notwithstanding their great victory, they durst not attempt it, though this addition of strength made them superior to us by 3000 men.

The king indeed expected, that when these troops joined them they would advance, and we were preparing to receive them at a village called Aynho, where the headquarters continued three or four days; and had they really esteemed the first day's work a victory, as they called it, they would have done it, but they thought not good to venture, but march away to Warwick, and from thence to Coventry. The king, to urge them to venture upon him, and come to a second battle, sits down before Banbury, and takes both town and castle; and two entire regiments of foot, and one troop of horse, quit the Parliament service, and take up their arms for the king. This was done almost before their faces, which was a better proof of a victory on our side, than any they could pretend to. From Banbury we marched to Oxford; and now all men saw the Parliament had made a great mistake, for they were not always in the right any more than we, to leave Oxford without a garrison. The king caused new regular works to be drawn round it, and seven royal bastions with ravelins and out-works, a double ditch, counterscarp, and covered way; all which, added to the advantage of its situation, made it a formidable place, and from this time it became our place of arms, and the centre of affairs on the king's side.

If the Parliament had the honour of the field, the king reaped the fruits of the victory; for all this part of the country submitted to him. Essex's army made the best of their way to London, and were but in an ill condition when they came there, especially their horse.

The Parliament, sensible of this, and receiving daily accounts of the progress we made, began to cool a little in their temper, abated of their first rage, and voted an address for peace; and sent to the king to let him know they were desirous to prevent the effusion of more blood, and to bring things to an accommodation, or, as they called it, a right understanding.

I was now, by the king's particular favour, summoned to the councils of war, my father continuing absent and ill; and now I began to think of the real grounds, and which was more, of the fatal issue of this war. I say, I now began it; for I cannot say that I ever rightly stated matters in my own mind before, though I had been enough used to blood, and to see the destruction of people, sacking of towns, and plundering the country; yet 'twas in Germany, and among strangers; but I found a strange, secret and unaccountable sadness upon my spirits, to see this acting in my own native country. It grieved me to the heart, even in the rout of our enemies, to see the slaughter of them; and even in the fight, to hear a man cry for quarter in English, moved me to a compassion which I had never been used to; nay, sometimes it looked to me as if some of my own men had been beaten; and when I heard a soldier cry, "O God, I am shot," I looked behind me to see which of my own troop was fallen. Here I saw myself at the cutting of the throats of my friends; and indeed some of my near relations. My old comrades and fellow-soldiers in Germany were some with us, some against us, as their opinions happened to differ in religion. For my part, I confess I had not much religion in me, at that time; but I thought religion rightly practised on both sides would have made us all better friends; and therefore sometimes I began to think, that both the bishops of our side, and the preachers on theirs, made religion rather the pretence than the cause of the war. And from those thoughts I vigorously argued it at the council of war against marching to Brentford, while the address for a treaty of peace from the Parliament was in hand: for I was for taking the Parliament by the handle which they had given us, and entering into a negotiation, with the advantage of its being at their own request.

I thought the king had now in his hands an opportunity to make an honourable peace; for this battle of Edgehill, as much as they boasted of the victory to hearten up their friends, had sorely weakened their army, and discouraged their party too, which in effect was worse as to their army. The horse were particularly in an ill case, and the foot greatly diminished, and the remainder very sickly; but besides this, the Parliament were greatly alarmed at the progress we made afterward; and still fearing the king's surprising them, had sent for the Earl of Essex to London, to defend them; by which the country was, as it were, defeated and abandoned, and left to be plundered; our parties overrun all places at pleasure. All this while I considered, that whatever the soldiers of fortune meant by the war, our desires were to suppress the exorbitant power of a party, to establish our king in his just and legal rights; but not with a design to destroy the constitution of government, and the being of Parliament. And therefore I thought now was the time for peace, and there were a great many worthy gentlemen in the army of my mind; and, had our master had ears to hear us, the war might have had an end here.

This address for peace was received by the king at Maidenhead, whither this army was now advanced, and his Majesty returned answer by Sir Peter Killegrew, that he desired nothing more, and would not be wanting on his part. Upon this the Parliament name commissioners, and his Majesty excepting against Sir John Evelyn, they left him out, and sent others; and desired the king to appoint his residence near London, where the commissioners might wait upon him. Accordingly the king appointed Windsor for the place of treaty, and desired the treaty might be hastened.

And thus all things looked with a favourable aspect, when one unlucky action knocked it all on the head, and filled both parties with more implacable animosities than they had before, and all hopes of peace vanished.

During this progress of the king's armies, we were always abroad with the horse ravaging the country, and plundering the Roundheads. Prince Rupert, a most active vigilant party man, and I must own, fitter for such than for a general, was never lying still, and I seldom stayed behind; for our regiment being very well mounted, he would always send for us, if he had any extraordinary design in hand.

One time in particular he had a design upon Aylesbury, the capital of Buckinghamshire; indeed our view at first was rather to beat the enemy out of town and demolish their works, and perhaps raise some contributions on the rich country round it, than to garrison the place, and keep it; for we wanted no more garrisons, being masters of the field.

The prince had 2500 horse with him in this expedition, but no foot; the town had some foot raised in the country by Mr Hampden, and two regiments of country militia, whom we made light of, but we found they stood to their tackle better than well enough. We came very early to the town, and thought they had no notice of us; but some false brother had given them the alarm, and we found them all in arms, the hedges without the town lined with musketeers, on that side in particular where they expected us, and two regiments of foot drawn up in view to support them, with some horse in the rear of all.

The prince, willing, however, to do something, caused some of his horse to alight, and serve as dragoons; and having broken a way into the enclosures, the horse beat the foot from behind the hedges, while the rest who were alighted charged them in the lane which leads to the town. Here they had cast up some works, and fired from their lines very regularly, considering them as militia only, the governor encouraging them by his example; so that finding without some foot there would be no good to be done, we gave it over, and drew off; and so Aylesbury escaped a scouring for that time.

I cannot deny but these flying parties of horse committed great spoil among the country people; and sometimes the prince gave a liberty to some cruelties which were not at all for the king's interest; because it being still upon our own country, and the king's own subjects, whom in all his declarations he protested to be careful of, it seemed to contradict all those protestations and declarations, and served to aggravate and exasperate the common people; and the king's enemies made all the advantages of it that was possible, by crying out of twice as many extravagancies as were committed.

'Tis true, the king, who naturally abhorred such things, could not restrain his men, no, nor his generals, so absolutely as he would have done. The war, on his side, was very much _à la_ volunteer; many gentlemen served him at their own charge, and some paid whole regiments themselves: sometimes also the king's affairs were straiter than ordinary, and his men were not very well paid, and this obliged him to wink at their excursions upon the country, though he did not approve of them. And yet I must own, that in those parts of England where the war was hottest, there never was seen that ruin and depopulation, murders, and barbarities, which I have seen even among Protestant armies abroad, in Germany and other foreign parts of the world. And if the Parliament people had seen those things abroad, as I had, they would not have complained.

The most I have seen was plundering the towns for provisions, drinking up their beer, and turning our horses into their fields, or stacks of corn; and sometimes the soldiers would be a little rude with the wenches; but alas! what was this to Count Tilly's ravages in Saxony? Or what was our taking of Leicester by storm, where they cried out of our barbarities, to the sacking of New Brandenburg, or the taking of Magdeburg? In Leicester, of 7000 or 8000 people in the town, 300 were killed; in Magdeburg, of 25,000 scarce 2700 were left, and the whole town burnt to ashes. I myself have seen seventeen or eighteen villages on fire in a day, and the people driven away from their dwellings, like herds of cattle. I do not instance these greater barbarities to justify lesser actions, which are nevertheless irregular; but I do say, that circumstances considered, this war was managed with as much humanity on both sides as could be expected, especially also considering the animosity of parties. But to return to the prince: he had not always the same success in these enterprises, for sometimes we came short home. And I cannot omit one pleasant adventure which happened to a party of ours, in one of these excursions into Buckinghamshire. The major of our regiment was soundly beaten by a party, which, as I may say, was led by a woman; and, if I had not rescued him, I know not but he had been taken prisoner by a woman. It seems our men had besieged some fortified house about Oxfordshire, towards Thame, and the house being defended by the lady in her husband's absence, she had yielded the house upon a capitulation; one of the articles of which was, to march out with all her servants, soldiers, and goods, and to be conveyed to Thame. Whether she thought to have gone no farther, or that she reckoned herself safe there, I know not; but my major, with two troops of horse, meets with this lady and her party, about five miles from Thame, as we were coming back from our defeated attack of Aylesbury.

We reckoned ourselves in an enemy's country, and had lived a little at large, or at discretion, as 'tis called abroad; and these two troops, with the major, were returning to our detachment from a little village, where, at the farmer's house, they had met with some liquor, and truly some of his men were so drunk they could but just sit upon their horses. The major himself was not much better, and the whole body were but in a sorry condition to fight. Upon the road they meet this party; the lady having no design of fighting, and being, as she thought, under the protection of the articles, sounds a parley, and desired to speak with the officer. The major, as drunk as he was, could tell her, that by the articles she was to be assured no farther than Thame, and being now five miles beyond it, she was a fair enemy, and therefore demanded to render themselves prisoners. The lady seemed surprised, but being sensible she was in the wrong, offered to compound for her goods, and would have given him £300, and I think seven or eight horses. The major would certainly have taken it, if he had not been drunk; but he refused it, and gave threatening words to her, blustering in language which he thought proper to fright a woman, viz., that he would cut them all to pieces, and give no quarter, and the like.

The lady, who had been more used to the smell of powder than he imagined, called some of her servants to her, and, consulting with them what to do, they all unanimously encouraged her to let them fight; told her it was plain that the commander was drunk, and all that were with him were rather worse than he, and hardly able to sit their horses; and that therefore one bold charge would put them all into confusion. In a word, she consented, and, as she was a woman, they desired her to secure herself among the waggons; but she refused, and told them bravely she would take her fate with them. In short, she boldly bade my major defiance, and that he might do his worst, since she had offered him fair, and he had refused it; her mind was altered now, and she would give him nothing, and bade his officer that parleyed longer with her be gone; so the parley ended. After this she gave him fair leave to go back to his men; but before he could tell his tale to them she was at his heels with all her men, and gave him such a home charge as put his men into disorder, and, being too drunk to rally, they were knocked down before they knew what to do with themselves, and in a few minutes more they took to a plain flight. But what was still worse, the men, being some of them very drunk, when they came to run for their lives fell over one another, and tumbled over their horses, and made such work that a troop of women might have beaten them all. In this pickle, with the enemy at his heels, I came in with him, hearing the noise. When I appeared the pursuers retreated, and, seeing what a condition my people were in, and not knowing the strength of the enemy, I contented myself with bringing them off without pursuing the other; nor could I ever hear positively who this female captain was. We lost seventeen or eighteen of our men, and about thirty horses; but when the particulars of the story was told us, our major was so laughed at by the whole army, and laughed at everywhere, that he was ashamed to show himself for a week or a fortnight after.

But to return to the king: his Majesty, as I observed, was at Maidenhead addressed by the Parliament for peace, and Windsor being appointed for the place of treaty, the van of his army lay at Colebrook. In the meantime, whether it were true or only a pretence, but it was reported the Parliament general had sent a body of his troops, with a train of artillery, to Hammersmith, in order to fall upon some part of our army, or to take some advanced post, which was to the prejudice of our men; whereupon the king ordered the army to march, and, by the favour of a thick mist, came within half a mile of Brentford before he was discovered. There were two regiments of foot, and about 600 horse into the town, of the enemy's best troops; these taking the alarm, posted themselves on the bridge at the west end of the town. The king attacked them with a select detachment of his best infantry, and they defended themselves with incredible obstinacy. I must own I never saw raw men, for they could not have been in arms above four months, act like them in my life. In short, there was no forcing these men, for, though two whole brigades of our foot, backed by our horse, made five several attacks upon them they could not break them, and we lost a great many brave men in that action. At last, seeing the obstinacy of these men, a party of horse was ordered to go round from Osterley; and, entering the town on the north side, where, though the horse made some resistance, it was not considerable, the town was presently taken. I led my regiment through an enclosure, and came into the town nearer to the bridge than the rest, by which means I got first into the town; but I had this loss by my expedition, that the foot charged me before the body was come up, and poured in their shot very furiously. My men were but in an ill case, and would not have stood much longer, if the rest of the horse coming up the lane had not found them other employment. When the horse were thus entered, they immediately dispersed the enemy's horse, who fled away towards London, and falling in sword in hand upon the rear of the foot, who were engaged at the bridge, they were all cut in pieces, except about 200, who, scorning to ask quarter, desperately threw themselves into the river of Thames, where they were most of them drowned.

The Parliament and their party made a great outcry at this attempt--that it was base and treacherous while in a treaty of peace; and that the king, having amused them with hearkening to a treaty, designed to have seized upon their train of artillery first, and, after that, to have surprised both the city of London and the Parliament. And I have observed since, that our historians note this action as contrary to the laws of honour and treaties, though as there was no cessation of arms agreed on, nothing is more contrary to the laws of war than to suggest it.

That it was a very unhappy thing to the king and whole nation, as it broke off the hopes of peace, and was the occasion of bringing the Scots army in upon us, I readily acknowledge, but that there was anything dishonourable in it, I cannot allow. For though the Parliament had addressed to the king for peace, and such steps were taken in it as before, yet, as I have said, there was no proposals made on either side for a cessation of arms, and all the world must allow, that in such cases the war goes on in the field, while the peace goes on in the cabinet. And if the war goes on, admit the king had designed to surprise the city or Parliament, or all of them, it had been no more than the custom of war allows, and what they would have done by him if they could. The treaty of Westphalia, or peace of Munster, which ended the bloody wars of Germany, was a precedent for this. That treaty was actually negotiating seven years, and yet the war went on with all the vigour and rancour imaginable, even to the last. Nay, the very time after the conclusion of it, but before the news could be brought to the army, did he that was afterwards King of Sweden, Carolus Gustavus, take the city of Prague by surprise, and therein an inestimable booty. Besides, all the wars of Europe are full of examples of this kind, and therefore I cannot see any reason to blame the king for this action as to the fairness of it. Indeed, as to the policy of it, I can say little; but the case was this. The king had a gallant army, flushed with success, and things hitherto had gone on very prosperously, both with his own army and elsewhere; he had above 35,000 men in his own army, including his garrison left at Banbury, Shrewsbury, Worcester, Oxford, Wallingford, Abingdon, Reading, and places adjacent.

On the other hand, the Parliament army came back to London in but a very sorry condition;[1] for what with their loss in their victory, as they called it, at Edgehill, their sickness, and a hasty march to London, they were very much diminished, though at London they soon recruited them again. And this prosperity of the king's affairs might encourage him to strike this blow, thinking to bring the Parliament to the better terms by the apprehensions of the superior strength of the king's forces.

But, however it was, the success did not equally answer the king's expectation. The vigorous defence the troops posted at Brentford made as above, gave the Earl of Essex opportunity, with extraordinary application, to draw his forces out to Turnham Green. And the exceeding alacrity of the enemy was such, that their whole army appeared with them, making together an army of 24,000 men, drawn up in view of our forces by eight o'clock the next morning. The city regiments were placed between the regular troops, and all together offered us battle, but we were not in a condition to accept it. The king indeed was sometimes of the mind to charge them, and once or twice ordered parties to advance to begin to skirmish, but upon better advice altered his mind, and indeed it was the wisest counsel to defer the fighting at that time. The Parliament generals were as unfixed in their resolutions, on the other side, as the king; sometimes they sent out parties, and then called them back again. One strong party of near 3000 men marched off towards Acton, with orders to amuse us on that side, but were countermanded. Indeed, I was of the opinion we might have ventured the battle, for though the Parliament's army were more numerous, yet the city trained bands, which made up 4000 of their foot, were not much esteemed, and the king was a great deal stronger in horse than they. But the main reason that hindered the engagement, was want of ammunition, which the king having duly weighed, he caused the carriages and cannon to draw off first, and then the foot, the horse continuing to force the enemy till all was clear gone; and then we drew off too and marched to Kingston, and the next day to Reading.

Now the king saw his mistake in not continuing his march for London, instead of facing about to fight the enemy at Edgehill. And all the honour we had gained in so many successful enterprises lay buried in this shameful retreat from an army of citizens' wives; for truly that appearance at Turnham Green was gay, but not great. There was as many lookers-on as actors. The crowds of ladies, apprentices, and mob was so great, that when the parties of our army advanced, and as they thought, to charge, the coaches, horsemen, and crowd, that cluttered away to be out of harm's way, looked little better than a rout. And I was persuaded a good home charge from our horse would have sent their whole army after them. But so it was, that this crowd of an army was to triumph over us, and they did it, for all the kingdom was carefully informed how their dreadful looks had frightened us away.

Upon our retreat, the Parliament resent this attack, which they call treacherous, and vote no accommodation; but they considered of it afterwards, and sent six commissioners to the king with propositions. But the change of the scene of action changed the terms of peace, and now they made terms like conquerors, petition him to desert his army, and return to the Parliament, and the like. Had his Majesty, at the head of his army, with the full reputation they had before, and in the ebb of their affairs, rested at Windsor, and commenced a treaty, they had certainly made more reasonable proposals; but now the scabbard seemed to be thrown away on both sides.

The rest of the winter was spent in strengthening parties and places, also in fruitless treaties of peace, messages, remonstrances, and paper war on both sides, and no action remarkable happened anywhere that I remember. Yet the king gained ground everywhere, and his forces in the north increased under the Earl of Newcastle; also my Lord Goring, then only called Colonel Goring, arrived from Holland, bringing three ships laden with arms and ammunition, and notice that the queen was following with more. Goring brought 4000 barrels of gunpowder, and 20,000 small arms; all which came very seasonably, for the king was in great want of them, especially the powder. Upon this recruit the Earl of Newcastle draws down to York, and being above 16,000 strong, made Sir Thomas Fairfax give ground, and retreat to Hull.

Whoever lay still, Prince Rupert was always abroad, and I chose to go out with his Highness as often as I had opportunity, for hitherto he was always successful. About this time the prince being at Oxford, I gave him intelligence of a party of the enemy who lived a little at large, too much for good soldiers, about Cirencester. The prince, glad of the news, resolved to attack them, and though it was a wet season, and the ways exceeding bad, being in February, yet we marched all night in the dark, which occasioned the loss of some horses and men too, in sloughs and holes, which the darkness of the night had suffered them to fall into. We were a very strong party, being about 3000 horse and dragoons, and coming to Cirencester very early in the morning, to our great satisfaction the enemy were perfectly surprised, not having the least notice of our march, which answered our end more ways than one. However, the Earl of Stamford's regiment made some resistance; but the town having no works to defend it, saving a slight breastwork at the entrance of the road, with a turnpike, our dragoons alighted, and forcing their way over the bellies of Stamford's foot, they beat them from their defence, and followed them at their heels into the town. Stamford's regiment was entirely cut in pieces, and several others, to the number of about 800 men, and the town entered without any other resistance. We took 1200 prisoners, 3000 arms, and the county magazine, which at that time was considerable; for there was about 120 barrels of powder, and all things in proportion.

I received the first hurt I got in this war at this action, for having followed the dragoons and brought my regiment within the barricado which they had gained, a musket bullet struck my horse just in the head, and that so effectually that he fell down as dead as a stone all at once. The fall plunged me into a puddle of water and daubed me; and my man having brought me another horse and cleaned me a little, I was just getting up, when another bullet struck me on my left hand, which I had just clapped on the horse's main to lift myself into the saddle. The blow broke one of my fingers, and bruised my hand very much; and it proved a very painful hurt to me. For the present I did not much concern myself about it, but made my man tie it up close in my handkerchief, and led up my men to the market-place, where we had a very smart brush with some musketeers who were posted in the churchyard; but our dragoons soon beat them out there, and the whole town was then our own. We made no stay here, but marched back with all our booty to Oxford, for we knew the enemy were very strong at Gloucester, and that way.

Much about the same time, the Earl of Northampton, with a strong party, set upon Lichfield, and took the town, but could not take the Close; but they beat a body of 4000 men coming to the relief of the town, under Sir John Gell, of Derbyshire, and Sir William Brereton, of Cheshire, and killing 600 of them, dispersed the rest.

Our second campaign now began to open; the king marched from Oxford to relieve Reading, which was besieged by the Parliament forces; but General Fielding, Lieutenant-Governor, Sir Arthur Ashton being wounded, surrendered to Essex before the king could come up; for which he was tried by martial law, and condemned to die, but the king forbore to execute the sentence. This was the first town we had lost in the war, for still the success of the king's affairs was very encouraging. This bad news, however, was overbalanced by an account brought the king at the same time, by an express from York, that the queen had landed in the north, and had brought over a great magazine of arms and ammunition, besides some men. Some time after this her Majesty, marching southward to meet the king, joined the army near Edgehill, where the first battle was fought. She brought the king 3000 foot, 1500 horse and dragoons, six pieces of cannon, 1500 barrels of powder, 12,000 small arms.

During this prosperity of the king's affairs his armies increased mightily in the western counties also. Sir William Waller, indeed, commanded for the Parliament in those parts too, and particularly in Dorsetshire, Hampshire, and Berkshire, where he carried on their cause but too fast; but farther west, Sir Nicholas Slanning, Sir Ralph Hopton, and Sir Bevil Grenvile had extended the king's quarters from Cornwall through Devonshire, and into Somersetshire, where they took Exeter, Barnstaple, and Bideford; and the first of these they fortified very well, making it a place of arms for the west, and afterwards it was the residence of the queen.

At last, the famous Sir William Waller and the king's forces met, and came to a pitched battle, where Sir William lost all his honour again. This was at Roundway Down in Wiltshire. Waller had engaged our Cornish army at Lansdown, and in a very obstinate fight had the better of them, and made them retreat to the Devizes. Sir William Hopton, however, having a good body of foot untouched, sent expresses and messengers one in the neck of another to the king for some horse, and the king being in great concern for that army, who were composed of the flower of the Cornish men, commanded me to march with all possible secrecy, as well as expedition, with 1200 horse and dragoons from Oxford, to join them. We set out in the depth of the night, to avoid, if possible, any intelligence being given of our route, and soon joined with the Cornish army, when it was as soon resolved to give battle to Waller; and, give him his due, he was as forward to fight as we. As it is easy to meet when both sides are willing to be found, Sir William Waller met us upon Roundway Down, where we had a fair field on both sides, and room enough to draw up our horse. In a word, there was little ceremony to the work; the armies joined, and we charged his horse with so much resolution, that they quickly fled, and quitted the field; for we over-matched him in horse, and this was the entire destruction of their army. For the infantry, which outnumbered ours by 1500, were now at our mercy; some faint resistance they made, just enough to give us occasion to break into their ranks with our horse, where we gave time to our foot to defeat others that stood to their work, upon which they began to disband, and run every way they could; but our horse having surrounded them, we made a fearful havoc of them.

We lost not about 200 men in this action; Waller lost about 4000 killed and taken, and as many dispersed that never returned to their colours. Those of foot that escaped got into Bristol, and Waller, with the poor remains of his routed regiments, got to London; so that it is plain some ran east, and some ran west, that is to say, they fled every way they could.

My going with this detachment prevented my being at the siege of Bristol, which Prince Rupert attacked much about the same time, and it surrendered in three days. The Parliament questioned Colonel Nathaniel Fiennes, the governor, and had him tried as a coward by a court-martial, and condemned to die, but suspended the execution also, as the king did the governor of Reading. I have often heard Prince Rupert say, they did Colonel Fiennes wrong in that affair; and that if the colonel would have summoned him, he would have demanded a passport of the Parliament, and have come up and convinced the court that Colonel Fiennes had not misbehaved himself, and that he had not a sufficient garrison to defend a city of that extent; having not above 1200 men in the town, excepting some of Waller's runaways, most of whom were unfit for service, and without arms; and that the citizens in general being disaffected to him, and ready on the first occasion to open the gates to the king's forces, it was impossible for him to have kept the city. "And when I had farther informed them," said the prince, "of the measures I had taken for a general assault the next day, I am confident I should have convinced them that I had taken the city by storm, if he had not surrendered." The king's affairs were now in a very good posture, and three armies in the north, west, and in the centre, counted in the musters about 70,000 men besides small garrisons and parties abroad. Several of the lords, and more of the commons, began to fall off from the Parliament, and make their peace with the king; and the affairs of the Parliament began to look very ill. The city of London was their inexhaustible support and magazine, both for men, money, and all things necessary; and whenever their army was out of order, the clergy of their party in but one Sunday or two, would preach the young citizens out of their shops, the labourers from their masters, into the army, and recruit them on a sudden. And all this was still owing to the omission I first observed, of not marching to London, when it might have been so easily effected.

We had now another, or a fairer opportunity, than before, but as ill use was made of it. The king, as I have observed, was in a very good posture; he had three large armies roving at large over the kingdom. The Cornish army, victorious and numerous, had beaten Waller, secured and fortified Exeter, which the queen had made her residence, and was there delivered of a daughter, the Princess Henrietta Maria, afterwards Duchess of Orleans, and mother of the Duchess Dowager of Savoy, commonly known in the French style by the title of Madam Royal. They had secured Salisbury, Sherborne Castle, Weymouth, Winchester, and Basing-house, and commanded the whole country, except Bridgewater and Taunton, Plymouth and Lynn; all which places they held blocked up. The king was also entirely master of all Wales, Monmouthshire, Cheshire, Shropshire, Staffordshire, Worcestershire, Oxfordshire, Berkshire, and all the towns from Windsor up the Thames to Cirencester, except Reading and Henley; and of the whole Severn, except Gloucester.

The Earl of Newcastle had garrisons in every strong place in the north, from Berwick-upon-Tweed to Boston in Lincolnshire, and

Newark-upon-Trent, Hull only excepted, whither the Lord Fairfax and his son Sir Thomas were retreated, their troops being routed and broken, Sir Thomas Fairfax his baggage, with his lady and servants taken prisoners, and himself hardly scaping. And now a great council of war was held in the king's quarters, what enterprise to go upon; and it happened to be the very same day when the Parliament were in a serious debate what should become of them, and whose help they should seek. And indeed they had cause for it; and had our counsels been as ready and well-grounded as theirs, we had put an end to the war in a month's time.

In this council the king proposed the marching to London, to put an end to the Parliament and encourage his friends and loyal subjects in Kent, who were ready to rise for him; and showed us letters from the Earl of Newcastle, wherein he offered to join his Majesty with a detachment of 4000 horse, and 8000 foot, if his Majesty thought fit to march southward, and yet leave forces sufficient to guard the north from any invasion. I confess, when I saw the scheme the king had himself drawn for this attempt, I felt an unusual satisfaction in my mind, from the hopes that he might bring this war to some tolerable end; for I professed myself on all occasions heartily weary with fighting with friends, brothers, neighbours, and acquaintance, and I made no question but this motion of the king's would effectually bring the Parliament to reason.

All men seemed to like the enterprise but the Earl of Worcester, who, on particular views for securing the country behind, as he called it, proposed the taking in the town of Gloucester and Hereford first. He made a long speech of the danger of leaving Massey, an active bold fellow, with a strong party in the heart of all the king's quarters, ready on all occasions to sally out and surprise the neighbouring garrisons, as he had done Sudley Castle and others; and of the ease and freedom to all those western parts to have them fully cleared of the enemy. Interest presently backs this advice, and all those gentlemen whose estates lay that way, or whose friends lived about Worcester, Shrewsbury, Bridgnorth, or the borders, and who, as they said, had heard the frequent wishes of the country to have the city of Gloucester reduced, fell in with this advice, alleging the consequence it was for the commerce of the country to have the navigation of the Severn free, which was only interrupted by this one town from the sea up to Shrewsbury, &c. I opposed this, and so did several others. Prince Rupert was vehemently against it; and we both offered, with the troops of the country, to keep Gloucester blocked up during the king's march for London, so that Massey should not be able to stir.

This proposal made the Earl of Worcester's party more eager for the siege than before, for they had no mind to a blockade which would leave the country to maintain the troops all the summer; and of all men the prince did not please them, for, he having no extraordinary character for discipline, his company was not much desired even by our friends. Thus, in an ill hour, 'twas resolved to sit down before Gloucester. The king had a gallant army of 28,000 men whereof 11,000 horse, the finest body of gentlemen that ever I saw together in my life; their horses without comparison, and their equipages the finest and the best in the world, and their persons Englishmen, which, I think, is enough to say of them.

According to the resolution taken in the council of war, the army marched westward, and sat down before Gloucester the beginning of August. There we spent a month to the least purpose that ever army did. Our men received frequent affronts from the desperate sallies of an inconsiderable enemy. I cannot forbear reflecting on the misfortunes of this siege. Our men were strangely dispirited in all the assaults they gave upon the place; there was something looked like disaster and mismanagement, and our men went on with an ill will and no resolution. The king despised the place, and thinking to carry it sword in hand, made no regular approaches, and the garrison, being desperate, made therefore the greater slaughter. In this work our horse, who were so numerous and so fine, had no employment. Two thousand horse had been enough for this business, and the enemy had no garrison or party within forty miles of us, so that we had nothing to do but look on with infinite regret upon the losses of our foot.

The enemy made frequent and desperate sallies, in one of which I had my share. I was posted upon a parade, or place of arms, with part of my regiment, and part of Colonel Goring's regiment of horse, in order to support a body of foot, who were ordered to storm the point of a breastwork which the enemy had raised to defend one of the avenues to the town. The foot were beat off with loss, as they always were; and Massey, the governor, not content to have beaten them from his works, sallies out with near 400 men, and falling in upon the foot as they were rallying under the cover of our horse, we put ourselves in the best posture we could to receive them. As Massey did not expect, I suppose, to engage with any horse, he had no pikes with him, which encouraged us to treat him the more rudely; but as to desperate men danger is no danger, when he found he must clear his hands of us, before he could despatch the foot, he faces up to us, fires but one volley of his small shot, and fell to battering us with the stocks of their muskets in such a manner that one would have thought they had been madmen.

We at first despised this way of clubbing us, and charging through them, laid a great many of them upon the ground, and in repeating our charge, trampled more of them under our horses' feet; and wheeling thus continually, beat them off from our foot, who were just upon the point of disbanding. Upon this they charged us again with their fire, and at one volley killed thirty-three or thirty-four men and horses; and had they had pikes with them, I know not what we should have done with them. But at last charging through them again, we divided them; one part of them being hemmed in between us and our own foot, were cut in pieces to a man; the rest as I understood afterwards, retreated into the town, having lost 300 of their men.

In this last charge I received a rude blow from a stout fellow on foot with the butt end of his musket which perfectly stunned me, and fetched me off from my horse; and had not some near me took care of me, I had been trod to death by our own men. But the fellow being immediately killed, and my friends finding me alive, had taken me up, and carried me off some distance, where I came to myself again after some time, but knew little of what I did or said that night. This was the reason why I say I afterwards understood the enemy retreated; for I saw no more what they did then, nor indeed was I well of this blow for all the rest of the summer, but had frequent pains in my head, dizzinesses and swimming, that gave me some fears the blow had injured the skull; but it wore off again, nor did it at all hinder my attending my charge. This action, I think, was the only one that looked like a defeat given the enemy at this siege. We killed them near 300 men, as I have said, and lost about sixty of our troopers.

All this time, while the king was harassing and weakening the best army he ever saw together during the whole war, the Parliament generals, or rather preachers, were recruiting theirs; for the preachers were better than drummers to raise volunteers, zealously exhorting the London dames to part with their husbands, and the city to send some of their trained bands to join the army for the relief of Gloucester; and now they began to advance towards us.

The king hearing of the advance of Essex's army, who by this time was come to Aylesbury, had summoned what forces he had within call, to join him; and accordingly he received 3000 foot from Somersetshire; and having battered the town for thirty-six hours, and made a fair breach, resolves upon an assault, if possible, to carry the town before the enemy came up. The assault was begun about seven in the evening, and the men boldly mounted the breach; but after a very obstinate and bloody dispute, were beaten out again by the besieged with great loss.

Being thus often repulsed, and the Earl of Essex's army approaching, the king calls a council of war, and proposed to fight Essex's army. The officers of the horse were for fighting; and without doubt we were superior to him both in number and goodness of our horse, but the foot were not in an equal condition; and the colonels of foot representing to the king the weakness of their regiments, and how their men had been balked and disheartened at this cursed siege, the graver counsel prevailed, and it was resolved to raise the siege, and retreat towards Bristol, till the army was recruited. Pursuant to this resolution, the 5th of September, the king, having before sent away his heavy cannon and baggage, raised the siege, and marched to Berkeley Castle. The Earl of Essex came the next day to Birdlip Hills; and understanding by messengers from Colonel Massey, that the siege was raised, sends a recruit of 2500 men into the city, and followed us himself with a great body of horse. This body of horse showed themselves to us once in a large field fit to have entertained them in; and our scouts having assured us they were not above 4000, and had no foot with them, the king ordered a detachment of about the same number to face them. I desired his Majesty to let us have two regiments of dragoons with us, which was then 800 men in a regiment, lest there might be some dragoons among the enemy; which the king granted, and accordingly we marched, and drew up in view of them. They stood their ground, having, as they supposed, some advantage of the manner they were posted in, and expected we would charge them. The king, who did us the honour to command this party, finding they would not stir, calls me to him, and ordered me with the dragoons, and my own regiment, to take a circuit round by a village to a certain lane, where in their retreat they must have passed, and which opened to a small common on the flank; with orders, if they engaged, to advance and charge them in the flank. I marched immediately; but though the country about there was almost all enclosures, yet there scouts were so vigilant, that they discovered me, and gave notice to the body; upon which their whole party moved to the left, as if they intended to charge me, before the king with his body of horse could come. But the king was too vigilant to be circumvented so; and therefore his Majesty perceiving this, sends away three regiments of horse to second me, and a messenger before them, to order me to halt, and expect the enemy, for that he would follow with the whole body.

But before this order reached me, I had halted for some time; for finding myself discovered, and not judging it safe to be entirely cut off from the main body, I stopped at the village, and causing my dragoons to alight, and line a thick hedge on my left, I drew up my horse just at the entrance into the village opening to a common. The enemy came up on the trot to charge me, but were saluted with a terrible fire from the dragoons out of the hedge, which killed them near 100 men. This being a perfect surprise to them, they halted, and just at that moment they received orders from their main body to retreat; the king at the same time appearing upon some heights in their rear, which obliged them to think of retreating, or coming to a general battle, which was none of their design. I had no occasion to follow them, not being in a condition to attack the whole body; but the dragoons coming out into the common, gave them another volley at a distance, which reached them effectually, for it killed about twenty of them, and wounded more; but they drew off, and never fired a shot at us, fearing to be enclosed between two parties, and so marched away to their general's quarters, leaving ten or twelve more of their fellows killed, and about 180 horses. Our men, after the country fashion, gave them a shout at parting, to let them see we knew they were afraid of us.

However, this relieving of Gloucester raised the spirits as well as the reputation of the Parliament forces, and was a great defeat to us; and from this time things began to look with a melancholy aspect, for the prosperous condition of the king's affairs began to decline. The opportunities he had let slip were never to be recovered, and the Parliament, in their former extremity, having voted an invitation to the Scots to march to their assistance, we had now new enemies to encounter; and, indeed, there began the ruin of his Majesty's affairs, for the Earl of Newcastle, not able to defend himself against the Scots on his rear, the Earl of Manchester in his front, and Sir Thomas Fairfax on his flank, was everywhere routed and defeated, and his forces obliged to quit the field to the enemy.

About this time it was that we first began to hear of one Oliver Cromwell, who, like a little cloud, rose out of the east, and spread first into the north, till it shed down a flood that overwhelmed the three kingdoms.

He first was a private captain of horse, but now commanded a regiment whom he armed _cap-à-pie à la cuirassier_; and, joining with the Earl of Manchester, the first action we heard of him that made him anything famous was about Grantham, where, with only his own regiment, he defeated twenty-four troops of horse and dragoons of the king's forces; then, at Gainsborough, with two regiments, his own of horse and one of dragoons, where he defeated near 3000 of the Earl of Newcastle's men, killed Lieutenant-General Cavendish, brother to the Earl of Devonshire, who commanded them, and relieved Gainsborough; and though the whole army came in to the rescue, he made good his retreat to Lincoln with little loss; and the next week he defeated Sir John Henderson at Winceby, near Horncastle, with sixteen regiments of horse and dragoons, himself having not half that number; killed the Lord Widdrington, Sir Ingram Hopton, and several gentlemen of quality. Thus this firebrand of war began to blaze, and he soon grew a terror to the north; for victory attended him like a page of honour, and he was scarce ever known to be beaten during the whole war.

Now we began to reflect again on the misfortune of our master's counsels. Had we marched to London, instead of besieging Gloucester, we had finished the war with a stroke. The Parliament's army was in a most despicable condition, and had never been recruited, had we not given them a month's time, which we lingered away at this fatal town of Gloucester.

But 'twas too late to reflect; we were a disheartened army, but we were not beaten yet, nor broken. We had a large country to recruit in, and we lost no time but raised men apace. In the meantime his Majesty, after a short stay at Bristol, makes back again towards Oxford with a part of the foot and all the horse.

At Cirencester we had a brush again with Essex; that town owed us a shrewd turn for having handled them coarsely enough before, when Prince Rupert seized the county magazine.

I happened to be in the town that night with Sir Nicholas Crisp, whose regiment of horse quartered there with Colonel Spencer and some foot; my own regiment was gone before to Oxford. About ten at night, a party of Essex's men beat up our quarters by surprise, just as we had served them before. They fell in with us, just as people were going to bed, and having beaten the out-guards, were gotten into the middle of the town before our men could get on horseback. Sir Nicholas Crisp, hearing the alarm, gets up, and with some of his clothes on, and some off, comes into my chamber. "We are all undone," says he, "the Roundheads are upon us." We had but little time to consult, but being in one of the principal inns in the town, we presently ordered the gates of the inn to be shut, and sent to all the inns where our men were quartered to do the like, with orders, if they had any back-doors, or ways to get out, to come to us. By this means, however, we got so much time as to get on horseback, and so many of our men came to us by back ways, that we had near 300 horse in the yards and places behind the house. And now we began to think of breaking out by a lane which led from the back side of the inn, but a new accident determined us another, though a worse way.

The enemy being entered, and our men cooped up in the yards of the inns, Colonel Spencer, the other colonel, whose regiment of horse lay also in the town, had got on horseback before us, and engaged with the enemy, but being overpowered, retreated fighting, and sends to Sir Nicholas Crisp for help. Sir Nicholas, moved to see the distress of his friend, turning to me, says he, "What can we do for him?" I told him I thought 'twas time to help him, if possible; upon which, opening the inn gates, we sallied out in very good order, about 300 horse. And several of the troops from other parts of the town joining us, we recovered Colonel Spencer, and charging home, beat back the enemy to their main body. But finding their foot drawn up in the churchyard, and several detachments moving to charge us, we retreated in as good order as we could. They did not think fit to pursue us, but they took all the carriages which were under the convoy of this party, and laden with provisions and ammunition, and above 500 of our horse, the foot shifted away as well as they could. Thus we made off in a shattered condition towards Farringdon, and so to Oxford, and I was very glad my regiment was not there.

We had small rest at Oxford, or indeed anywhere else; for the king was marched from thence, and we followed him. I was something uneasy at my absence from my regiment, and did not know how the king might resent it, which caused me to ride after them with all expedition. But the armies were engaged that very day at Newbury, and I came in too late. I had not behaved myself so as to be suspected of a wilful shunning the action; but a colonel of a regiment ought to avoid absence from his regiment in time of fight, be the excuse never so just, as carefully as he would a surprise in his quarters. The truth is, 'twas an error of my own, and owing to two day's stay I made at the Bath, where I met with some ladies who were my relations.

And this is far from being an excuse; for if the king had been a Gustavus Adolphus, I had certainly received a check for it.

This fight was very obstinate, and could our horse have come to action as freely as the foot, the Parliament army had suffered much more; for we had here a much better body of horse than they, and we never failed beating them where the weight of the work lay upon the horse.

Here the city train-bands, of which there was two regiments, and whom we used to despise, fought very well. They lost one of their colonels, and several officers in the action; and I heard our men say, they behaved themselves as well as any forces the Parliament had.

The Parliament cried victory here too, as they always did; and indeed where the foot were concerned they had some advantage; but our horse defeated them evidently. The king drew up his army in battalia, in person, and faced them all the next day, inviting them to renew the fight; but they had no stomach to come on again.

It was a kind of a hedge fight, for neither army was drawn out in the field; if it had, 'twould never have held from six in the morning to ten at night.

But they fought for advantages; sometimes one side had the better, sometimes another. They fought twice through the town, in at one end, and out at the other; and in the hedges and lanes, with exceeding fury. The king lost the most men, his foot having suffered for want of the succour of their horse, who on two several occasions could not come at them. But the Parliament foot suffered also, and two regiments were entirely cut in pieces, and the king kept the field.

Essex, the Parliament general, had the pillage of the dead, and left us to bury them; for while we stood all day to our arms, having given them a fair field to fight us in, their camp rabble stripped the dead bodies, and they not daring to venture a second engagement with us, marched away towards London.

The king lost in this action the Earls of Carnarvon and Sunderland, the Lord Falkland, a French marquis and some very gallant officers, and about 1200 men. The Earl of Carnarvon was brought into an inn in Newbury, where the king came to see him. He had just life enough to speak to his Majesty, and died in his presence. The king was exceedingly concerned for him, and was observed to shed tears at the sight of it. We were indeed all of us troubled for the loss of so brave a gentleman, but the concern our royal master discovered, moved us more than ordinary. Everybody endeavoured to have the king out of the room, but he would not stir from the bedside, till he saw all hopes of life was gone.

The indefatigable industry of the king, his servants and friends, continually to supply and recruit his forces, and to harass and fatigue the enemy, was such, that we should still have given a good account of the war had the Scots stood neuter. But bad news came every day out of the north; as for other places, parties were always in action. Sir William Waller and Sir Ralph Hopton beat one another by turns; and Sir Ralph had extended the king's quarters from Launceston in Cornwall, to Farnham in Surrey, where he gave Sir William Waller a rub, and drove him into the castle. But in the north, the storm grew thick, the Scots advanced to the borders, and entered England in confederacy with the Parliament, against their king; for which the Parliament requited them afterwards as they deserved.

Had it not been for this Scotch army, the Parliament had easily been reduced to terms of peace; but after this they never made any proposals fit for the king to receive. Want of success before had made them differ among themselves. Essex and Waller could never agree; the Earl of Manchester and the Lord Willoughby differed to the highest degree; and the king's affairs went never the worse for it. But this storm in the north ruined us all; for the Scots prevailed in Yorkshire, and being joined with Fairfax, Manchester, and Cromwell, carried all before them; so that the king was obliged to send Prince Rupert, with a body of 4000 horse, to the assistance of the Earl of Newcastle, where that prince finished the destruction of the king's interest, by the rashest and unaccountablest action in the world, of which I shall speak in its place.

Another action of the king's, though in itself no greater a cause of offence than the calling the Scots into the nation, gave great offence in general, and even the king's own friends disliked it; and was carefully improved by his enemies to the disadvantage of the king, and of his cause. The rebels in Ireland had, ever since the bloody massacre of the Protestants, maintained a war against the English, and the Earl of Ormond was general and governor for the king. The king, finding his affairs pinch him at home, sends orders to the Earl of Ormond to consent to a cessation of arms with the rebels, and to ship over certain of his regiments hither to his Majesty's assistance. 'Tis true, the Irish had deserved to be very ill treated by the English; but while the Parliament pressed the king with a cruel and unnatural war at home, and called in an army out of Scotland to support their quarrel with their king, I could never be convinced, that it was such a dishonourable action for the king to suspend the correction of his Irish rebels till he was in a capacity to do it with safety to himself; or to delay any farther assistance to preserve himself at home; and the troops he recalled being his own, it was no breach of his honour to make use of them, since he now wanted them for his own security against those who fought against him at home.

But the king was persuaded to make one step farther, and that, I confess, was unpleasing to us all; and some of his best and most faithful servants took the freedom to speak plainly to him of it; and that was bringing some regiments of the Irish themselves over. This cast, as we thought, an odium upon our whole nation, being some of those very wretches who had dipped their hands in the innocent blood of the Protestants, and, with unheard-of butcheries, had massacred so many thousands of English in cool blood.

Abundance of gentlemen forsook the king upon this score; and seeing they could not brook the fighting in conjunction with this wicked generation, came into the declaration of the Parliament, and making composition for their estates, lived retired lives all the rest of war, or went abroad.

But as exigences and necessities oblige us to do things which at other times we would not do, and is, as to man, some excuse for such things; so I cannot but think the guilt and dishonour of such an action must lie, very much of it, at least, at their doors, who drove the king to these necessities and distresses, by calling in an army of his own subjects whom he had not injured, but had complied with them in everything, to make war upon him without any provocation. As to the quarrel between the king and his Parliament, there may something be said on both sides; and the king saw cause himself to disown and dislike some things he had done, which the Parliament objected against, such as levying money without consent of Parliament, infractions on their privileges, and the like. Here, I say, was some room for an argument at least, and concessions on both sides were needful to come to a peace. But for the Scots, all their demands had been answered, all their grievances had been redressed, they had made articles with their sovereign, and he had performed those articles; their capital enemy Episcopacy was abolished; they had not one thing to demand of the king which he had not granted.

And therefore they had no more cause to take up arms against their sovereign than they had against the Grand Seignior. But it must for ever lie against them as a brand of infamy, and as a reproach on their whole nation that, purchased by the Parliament's money, they sold their honesty, and rebelled against their king for hire; and it was not many years before, as I have said already, they were fully paid the wages of their unrighteousness, and chastised for their treachery by the very same people whom they thus basely assisted. Then they would have retrieved it, if it had not been too late.

But I could not but accuse this age of injustice and partiality, who while they reproached the king for his cessation of arms with the Irish rebels, and not prosecuting them with the utmost severity, though he was constrained by the necessities of the war to do it, could yet, at the same time, justify the Scots taking up arms in a quarrel they had no concern in, and against their own king, with whom they had articled and capitulated, and who had so punctually complied with all their demands, that they had no claim upon him, no grievances to be redressed, no oppression to cry out of, nor could ask anything of him which he had not granted.

But as no action in the world is so vile, but the actors can cover with some specious pretence, so the Scots now passing into England publish a declaration to justify their assisting the Parliament. To which I shall only say, in my opinion, it was no justification at all; for admit the Parliament's quarrel had been never so just, it could not be just in them to aid them, because 'twas against their own king too, to whom they had sworn allegiance, or at least had crowned him, and thereby had recognised his authority. For if maladministration be, according to Prynne's doctrine, or according to their own Buchanan, a sufficient reason for subjects to take up arms against their prince, the breach of his coronation oath being supposed to dissolve the oath of allegiance, which however I cannot believe; yet this can never be extended to make it lawful, that because a king of England may, by maladministration, discharge the subjects of England from their allegiance, that therefore the subjects of Scotland may take up arms against the King of Scotland, he having not infringed the compact of government as to them, and they having nothing to complain of for themselves. Thus I thought their own arguments were against them, and Heaven seemed to concur with it; for although they did carry the cause for the English rebels, yet the most of them left their bones here in the quarrel.

But what signifies reason to the drum and the trumpet! The Parliament had the supreme argument with those men, viz., the money; and having accordingly advanced a good round sum, upon payment of this (for the Scots would not stir a foot without it) they entered England on the 15th of January 1643[-4], with an army of 12,000 men, under the command of old Leslie, now Earl of Leven, an old soldier of great experience, having been bred to arms from a youth in the service of the Prince of Orange.

The Scots were no sooner entered England but they were joined by all the friends to the Parliament party in the north; and first, Colonel Grey, brother to the Lord Grey, joined them with a regiment of horse, and several out of Westmoreland and Cumberland, and so they advanced to Newcastle, which they summon to surrender. The Earl of Newcastle, who rather saw than was able to prevent this storm, was in Newcastle, and did his best to defend it; but the Scots, increased by this time to above 20,000, lay close siege to the place, which was but meanly fortified, and having repulsed the garrison upon several sallies, and pressing the place very close, after a siege of twelve days, or thereabouts, they enter the town sword in hand. The Earl of Newcastle got away, and afterwards gathered what forces together he could, but [was] not strong enough to hinder the Scots from advancing to Durham, which he quitted to them, nor to hinder the conjunction of the Scots with the forces of Fairfax, Manchester, and Cromwell. Whereupon the earl, seeing all things thus going to wreck, he sends his horse away, and retreats with his foot into York, making all necessary preparations for a vigorous defence there, in case he should be attacked, which he was pretty sure of, as indeed afterwards happened. York was in a very good posture of defence, the fortifications very regular, and exceeding strong; well furnished with provisions, and had now a garrison of 12,000 men in it. The governor under the Earl of Newcastle was Sir Thomas Glemham, a good soldier, and a gentleman brave enough.

The Scots, as I have said, having taken Durham, Tynemouth Castle, and Sunderland, and being joined by Sir Thomas Fairfax, who had taken Selby, resolve, with their united strength, to besiege York; but when they came to view the city, and saw a plan of the works, and had intelligence of the strength of the garrison, they sent expresses to Manchester and Cromwell for help, who came on, and joined them with 9000, making together about 30,000 men, rather more than less.

Now had the Earl of Newcastle's repeated messengers convinced the king that it was absolutely necessary to send some forces to his assistance, or else all would be lost in the north. Whereupon Prince Rupert was detached, with orders first to go into Lancashire and relieve Lathom House, defended by the brave Countess of Derby, and then, taking all the forces he could collect in Cheshire, Lancashire, and Yorkshire, to march to relieve York.

The prince marched from Oxford with but three regiments of horse and one of dragoons, making in all about 2800 men. The colonels of horse were Colonel Charles Goring, the Lord Byron, and myself; the dragoons were of Colonel Smith. In our march we were joined by a regiment of horse from Banbury, one of dragoons from Bristol, and three regiments of horse from Chester, so that when we came into Lancashire we were about 5000 horse and dragoons. These horse we received from Chester were those who, having been at the siege of Nantwich, were obliged to raise the siege by Sir Thomas Fairfax; and the foot having yielded, the horse made good their retreat to Chester, being about 2000, of whom three regiments now joined us. We received also 2000 foot from West Chester, and 2000 more out of Wales, and with this strength we entered Lancashire. We had not much time to spend, and a great deal of work to do.

Bolton and Liverpool felt the first fury of our prince; at Bolton, indeed, he had some provocation, for here we were like to be beaten off. When first the prince came to the town, he sent a summons to demand the town for the king, but received no answer but from their guns, commanding the messenger to keep off at his peril. They had raised some works about the town, and having by their intelligence learnt that we had no artillery, and were only a flying party (so they called us), they contemned the summons, and showed themselves upon their ramparts, ready for us. The prince was resolved to humble them, if possible, and takes up his quarters close to the town. In the evening he orders me to advance with one regiment of dragoons and my horse, to bring them off, if occasion was, and to post myself as near as possible I could to the lines, yet so as not to be discovered; and at the same time, having concluded what part of the works to fall upon, he draws up his men on two other sides, as if he would storm them there; and, on a signal, I was to begin the real assault on my side with my dragoons.

I had got so near the town with my dragoons, making them creep upon their bellies a great way, that we could hear the soldiers talk on the walls, when the prince, believing one regiment would be too few, sends me word that he had ordered a regiment of foot to help, and that I should not discover myself till they were come up to me. This broke our measures, for the march of this regiment was discovered by the enemy, and they took the alarm. Upon this I sent to the prince, to desire he would put off the storm for that night, and I would answer for it the next day; but the prince was impatient, and sent orders we should fall on as soon as the foot came up to us. The foot marched out of the way, missed us, and fell in with a road that leads to another part of the town; and being not able to find us, make an attack upon the town themselves; but the defendants, being ready for them, received them very warmly, and beat them off with great loss.

I was at a loss now what to do; for hearing the guns, and by the noise knowing it was an assault upon the town, I was very uneasy to have my share in it; but as I had learnt under the King of Sweden punctually to adhere to the execution of orders, and my orders being to lie still till the foot came up with me, I would not stir if I had been sure to have done never so much service; but, however, to satisfy myself, I sent to the prince to let him know that I continued in the same place expecting the foot, and none being yet come, I desired farther orders. The prince was a little amazed at this, and finding there must be some mistake, came galloping away in the dark to the place and drew off the men, which was no hard matter, for they were willing enough to give it over.

As for me, the prince ordered me to come off so privately as not to be discovered, if possible, which I effectually did; and so we were balked for that night. The next day the prince fell on upon another quarter with three regiments of foot, but was beaten off with loss, and the like a third time. At last the prince resolved to carry it, doubled his numbers, and, renewing the attack with fresh men, the foot entered the town over their works, killing in the first heat of the action all that came in their way; some of the foot at the same time letting in the horse, and so the town was entirely won. There was about 600 of the enemy killed, and we lost above 400 in all, which was owing to the foolish mistakes we made. Our men got some plunder here, which the Parliament made a great noise about; but it was their due, and they bought it dear enough.

Liverpool did not cost us so much, nor did we get so much by it, the people having sent their women and children and best goods on board the ships in the road; and as we had no boats to board them with, we could not get at them. Here, as at Bolton, the town and fort was taken by storm, and the garrison were many of them cut in pieces, which, by the way, was their own faults.

Our next step was Lathom House, which the Countess of Derby had gallantly defended above eighteen weeks against the Parliament forces; and this lady not only encouraged her men by her cheerful and noble maintenance of them, but by examples of her own undaunted spirit, exposing herself upon the walls in the midst of the enemy's shot, would be with her men in the greatest dangers; and she well deserved our care of her person, for the enemy were prepared to use her very rudely if she fell into their hands.

Upon our approach the enemy drew off, and the prince not only effectually relieved this vigorous lady, but left her a good quantity of all sorts of ammunition, three great guns, 500 arms, and 200 men, commanded by a major, as her extraordinary guard.

Here the way being now opened, and our success answering our expectation, several bodies of foot came in to us from Westmoreland and from Cumberland; and here it was that the prince found means to surprise the town of Newcastle-upon-Tyne, which was recovered for the king by the management of the mayor of the town, and some loyal gentlemen of the county, and a garrison placed there again for the king.

But our main design being the relief of York, the prince advanced that way apace, his army still increasing; and being joined by the Lord Goring from Richmondshire with 4000 horse, which were the same the Earl of Newcastle had sent away when he threw himself into York with the infantry, we were now 18,000 effective men, whereof 10,000 horse and dragoons; so the prince, full of hopes, and his men in good heart, boldly marched directly for York.

The Scots, as much surprised at the taking of Newcastle as at the coming of their enemy, began to inquire which way they should get home, if they should be beaten; and calling a council of war, they all agreed to raise the siege. The prince, who drew with him a great train of carriages charged with provision and ammunition for the relief of the city, like a wary general, kept at a distance from the enemy, and fetching a great compass about, brings all safe into the city, and enters into York himself with all his army.

No action of this whole war had gained the prince so much honour, or the king's affairs so much advantage, as this, had the prince but had the power to have restrained his courage after this, and checked his fatal eagerness for fighting. Here was a siege raised, the reputation of the enemy justly stirred, a city relieved, and furnished with all things necessary in the face of an army superior in a number by near 10,000 men, and commanded by a triumvirate of Generals Leven, Fairfax, and Manchester. Had the prince but remembered the proceeding of the great Duke of Parma at the relief of Paris, he would have seen the relieving the city was his business; 'twas the enemy's business to fight if possible, 'twas his to avoid it; for, having delivered the city, and put the disgrace of raising the siege upon the enemy, he had nothing further to do but to have waited till he had seen what course the enemy would take, and taken his further measures from their motion.

But the prince, a continual friend to precipitant counsels, would hear no advice. I entreated him not to put it to the hazard; I told him that he ought to consider if he lost the day he lost the kingdom, and took the crown off from the king's head. I put him in mind that it was impossible those three generals should continue long together; and that if they did, they would not agree long in their counsels, which would be as well for us as their separating. 'Twas plain Manchester and Cromwell must return to the associated counties, who would not suffer them to stay, for fear the king should attempt them. That he could subsist well enough, having York city and river at his back; but the Scots would eat up the country, make themselves odious, and dwindle away to nothing, if he would but hold them at bay a little. Other general officers were of the same mind; but all I could say, or they either, to a man deaf to anything but his own courage, signified nothing. He would draw out and fight; there was no persuading him to the contrary, unless a man would run the risk of being upbraided with being a coward, and afraid of the work. The enemy's army lay on a large common, called Marston Moor, doubtful what to do. Some were for fighting the prince, the Scots were against it, being uneasy at having the garrison of Newcastle at their backs; but the prince brought their councils of war to a result, for he let them know they must fight him, whether they would or no; for the prince being, as before, 18,000 men, and the Earl of Newcastle having joined him with 8000 foot out of the city, were marched in quest of the enemy, had entered the moor in view of their army, and began to draw up in order of battle; but the night coming on, the armies only viewed each other at a distance for that time. We lay all night upon our arms, and with the first of the day were in order of battle; the enemy was getting ready, but part of Manchester's men were not in the field, but lay about three miles off, and made a hasty march to come up.

The prince's army was exceedingly well managed; he himself commanded the left wing, the Earl of Newcastle the right wing; and the Lord Goring, as general of the foot, assisted by Major-General Porter and Sir Charles Lucas, led the main battle. I had prevailed with the prince according to the method of the King of Sweden, to place some small bodies of musketeers in the intervals of his horse, in the left wing, but could not prevail upon the Earl of Newcastle to do it in the right, which he afterwards repented. In this posture we stood facing the enemy expecting they would advance to us, which at last they did; and the prince began the day by saluting them with his artillery, which, being placed very well, galled them terribly for a quarter of an hour. They could not shift their front, so they advanced the hastier to get within our great guns, and consequently out of their danger, which brought the fight the sooner on.

The enemy's army was thus ordered; Sir Thomas Fairfax had the right wing, in which was the Scots horse, and the horse of his own and his father's army; Cromwell led the left wing, with his own and the Earl of Manchester's horse, and the three generals, Leslie, old Fairfax, and Manchester, led the main battle.

The prince, with our left wing, fell on first, and, with his usual fury, broke like a clap of thunder into the right wing of the Scots horse, led by Sir Thomas Fairfax, and, as nothing could stand in his way, he broke through and through them, and entirely routed them, pursuing them quite out of the field. Sir Thomas Fairfax, with a regiment of lances, and about 500 of his own horse, made good the ground for some time; but our musketeers, which, as I said, were such an unlooked-for sort of an article in a fight among the horse, that those lances, which otherwise were brave fellows, were mowed down with their shot, and all was put into confusion. Sir Thomas Fairfax was wounded in the face, his brother killed, and a great slaughter was made of the Scots, to whom I confess we showed no favour at all. While this was doing on our left, the Lord Goring with the main battle charged the enemy's foot; and particularly one brigade commanded by Major-General Porter, being mostly pikemen, not regarding the fire of the enemy, charged with that fury in a close body of pikes, that they overturned all that came in their way, and breaking into the middle of the enemy's foot, filled all with terror and confusion, insomuch that the three generals, thinking all had been lost, fled, and quitted the field.

But matters went not so well with that always unfortunate gentleman the Earl of Newcastle and our right wing of horse; for Cromwell charged the Earl of Newcastle with a powerful body of horse. And though the earl, and those about him, did what men could do, and behaved themselves with all possible gallantry, yet there was no withstanding Cromwell's horse, but, like Prince Rupert, they bore down all before them. And now the victory was wrung out of our hands by our own gross miscarriage; for the prince, as 'twas his custom, too eager in the chase of the enemy, was gone and could not be heard of. The foot in the centre, the right wing of the horse being routed by Cromwell, was left, and without the guard of his horse; Cromwell having routed the Earl of Newcastle, and beaten him quite out of the field, and Sir Thomas Fairfax rallying his dispersed troops, they fall all together upon the foot. General Lord Goring, like himself, fought like a lion, but, forsaken of his horse, was hemmed in on all sides, and overthrown; and an hour after this, the prince returning, too late to recover his friends, was obliged with the rest to quit the field to conquerors.

This was a fatal day to the king's affairs, and the risk too much for any man in his wits to run; we lost 4000 men on the spot, 3000 prisoners, among whom was Sir Charles Lucas, Major-General Porter, Major-General Tilyard, and about 170 gentlemen of quality. We lost all our baggage, twenty-five pieces of cannon, 3000 carriages, 150 barrels of powder, 10,000 arms. The prince got into York with the Earl of Newcastle, and a great many gentlemen; and 7000 or 8000 of the men, as well horse as foot.

I had but very coarse treatment in this fight; for returning with the prince from the pursuit of the right wing, and finding all lost, I halted with some other officers, to consider what to do. At first we were for making our retreat in a body, and might have done so well enough, if we had known what had happened, before we saw ourselves in the middle of the enemy; for Sir

Thomas Fairfax, who had got together his scattered troops, and joined by some of the left wing, knowing who we were, charged us with great fury. 'Twas not a time to think of anything but getting away, or dying upon the spot; the prince kept on in the front, and Sir Thomas Fairfax by this charge cut off about three regiments of us from our body; but bending his main strength at the prince, left us, as it were, behind him, in the middle of the field of battle. We took this for the only opportunity we could have to get off, and joining together, we made across the place of battle in as good order as we could, with our carabines presented. In this posture we passed by several bodies of the enemy's foot, who stood with their pikes charged to keep us off; but they had no occasion, for we had no design to meddle with them, but to get from them.

Thus we made a swift march, and thought ourselves pretty secure; but our work was not done yet, for on a sudden we saw ourselves under a necessity of fighting our way through a great body of Manchester's horse, who came galloping upon us over the moor. They had, as we suppose, been pursuing some of our broken troops which were fled before, and seeing us, they gave us a home charge. We received them as well as we could, but pushed to get through them, which at last we did with a considerable loss to them.

However, we lost so many men, either killed or separated from us (for all could not follow the same way), that of our three regiments we could not be above 400 horse together when we got quite clear, and these were mixed men, some of one troop and regiment, some of another. Not that I believe many of us were killed in the last attack, for we had plainly the better of the enemy, but our design being to get off, some shifted for themselves one way and some another, in the best manner they could, and as their several fortunes guided them. Four hundred more of this body, as I afterwards understood, having broke through the enemy's body another way, kept together, and got into Pontefract Castle, and 300 more made northward and to Skipton, where the prince afterwards fetched them off.

These few of us that were left together, with whom I was, being now pretty clear of pursuit, halted, and began to inquire who and who we were, and what we should do; and on a short debate, I proposed we should make to the first garrison of the king's that we could recover, and that we should keep together, lest the country people should insult us upon the roads. With this resolution we pushed on westward for Lancashire, but our misfortunes were not yet at an end. We travelled very hard, and got to a village upon the river Wharfe, near Wetherby. At Wetherby there was a bridge, but we understood that a party from Leeds had secured the town and the post, in order to stop the flying Cavaliers, and that 'twould be very hard to get through there, though, as we understood afterwards, there were no soldiers there but a guard of the townsmen. In this pickle we consulted what course to take. To stay where we were till morning, we all concluded, would not be safe. Some advised to take the stream with our horses, but the river, which is deep, and the current strong, seemed to bid us have a care what we did of that kind, especially in the night. We resolved therefore to refresh ourselves and our horses, which indeed is more than we did, and go on till we might come to a ford or bridge, where we might get over. Some guides we had, but they either were foolish or false, for after we had rode eight or nine miles, they plunged us into a river at a place they called a ford, but 'twas a very ill one, for most of our horses swam, and seven or eight were lost, but we saved the men. However, we got all over.

We made bold with our first convenience to trespass upon the country for a few horses, where we could find them, to remount our men whose horses were drowned, and continued our march. But being obliged to refresh ourselves at a small village on the edge of Bramham Moor, we found the country alarmed by our taking some horses, and we were no sooner got on horseback in the morning, and entering on the moor, but we understood we were pursued by some troops of horse. There was no remedy but we must pass this moor; and though our horses were exceedingly tired, yet we pressed on upon a round trot, and recovered an enclosed country on the other side, where we halted. And here, necessity putting us upon it, we were obliged to look out for more horses, for several of our men were dismounted, and others' horses disabled by carrying double, those who lost their horses getting up behind them. But we were supplied by our enemies against their will. The enemy followed us over the moor, and we having a woody enclosed country about us, where we were, I observed by their moving, they had lost sight of us; upon which I proposed concealing ourselves till we might judge of their numbers. We did so, and lying close in a wood, they passed hastily by us, without skirting or searching the wood, which was what on another occasion they would not have done. I found they were not above 150 horse, and considering, that to let them go before us, would be to alarm the country, and stop our design, I thought, since we might be able to deal with them, we should not meet with a better place for it, and told the rest of our officers my mind, which all our party presently (for we had not time for a long debate) agreed to.

Immediately upon this I caused two men to fire their pistols in the wood, at two different places, as far asunder as I could. This I did to give them an alarm, and amuse them; for being in the lane, they would otherwise have got through before we had been ready, and I resolved to engage them there, as soon as 'twas possible. After this alarm, we rushed out of the wood, with about a hundred horse, and charged them on the flank in a broad lane, the wood being on their right. Our passage into the lane being narrow, gave us some difficulty in our getting out; but the surprise of the charge did our work; for the enemy, thinking we had been a mile or two before, had not the least thoughts of this onset, till they heard us in the wood, and then they who were before could not come back. We broke into the lane just in the middle of them, and by that means divided them; and facing to the left, charged the rear. First our dismounted men, which were near fifty, lined the edge of the wood, and fired with their carabines upon those which were before, so warmly, that they put them into a great disorder. Meanwhile fifty more of our horse from the farther part of the wood showed themselves in the lane upon their front. This put them of the foremost party into a great perplexity, and they began to face about, to fall upon us who were engaged in the rear. But their facing about in a lane where there was no room to wheel, as one who understands the manner of wheeling a troop of horse must imagine, put them into a great disorder. Our party in the head of the lane taking the advantage of this mistake of the enemy, charged in upon them, and routed them entirely. Some found means to break into the enclosures on the other side of the lane, and get away. About thirty were killed, and about twenty-five made prisoners, and forty very good horses were taken; all this while not a man of ours was lost, and not above seven or eight wounded. Those in the rear behaved themselves better, for they stood our charge with a great deal of resolution, and all we could do could not break them; but at last our men who had fired on foot through the hedges at the other party, coming to do the like here, there was no standing it any longer. The rear of them faced about and retreated out of the lane, and drew up in the open field to receive and rally their fellows. We killed about seventeen of them, and followed them to the end of the lane, but had no mind to have any more fighting than needs must, our condition at that time not making it proper, the towns round us being all in the enemy's hands, and the country but indifferently pleased with us; however, we stood facing them till they thought fit to march away. Thus we were supplied with horses enough to remount our men, and pursued our first design of getting into Lancashire. As for our prisoners, we let them off on foot.

But the country being by this time alarmed, and the rout of our army everywhere known, we foresaw abundance of difficulties before us; we were not strong enough to venture into any great towns, and we were too many to be concealed in small ones. Upon this we resolved to halt in a great wood about three miles beyond the place where we had the last skirmish, and sent our scouts to discover the country, and learn what they could, either of the enemy or of our friends.

Anybody may suppose we had but indifferent quarters here, either for ourselves or for our horses; but, however, we made shift to lie here two days and one night. In the interim I took upon me, with two more, to go to Leeds to learn some news; we were disguised like country ploughmen; the clothes we got at a farmer's house, which for that particular occasion we plundered; and I cannot say no blood was shed in a manner too rash, and which I could not have done at another time; but our case was desperate, and the people too surly, and shot at us out of the window, wounded one man and shot a horse, which we counted as great a loss to us as a man, for our safety depended upon our horses. Here we got clothes of all sorts, enough for both sexes, and thus dressing myself up _au paysan,_ with a white cap on my head, and a fork on my shoulder, and one of my comrades in the farmer's wife's russet gown and petticoat, like a woman, the other with an old crutch like a lame man, and all mounted on such horses as we had taken the day before from the country, away we go to Leeds by three several ways, and agreed to meet upon the bridge. My pretended country woman acted her part to the life, though the party was a gentleman of good quality, of the Earl of Worcester's family; and the cripple did as well as he but I thought myself very awkward in my dress, which made me very shy, especially among the soldiers. We passed their sentinels and guards at Leeds unobserved, and put up our horses at several houses in the town, from whence we went up and down to make our remarks. My cripple was the fittest to go among the soldiers, because there was less danger of being pressed. There he informed himself of the matters of war, particularly that the enemy sat down again to the siege of York; that flying parties were in pursuit of the Cavaliers; and there he heard that 500 horse of the Lord Manchester's men had followed a party of Cavaliers over Bramham Moor, and that entering a lane, the Cavaliers, who were 1000 strong, fell upon them, and killed them all but about fifty. This, though it was a lie, was very pleasant to us to hear, knowing it was our party because of the other part of the story, which was thus: That the Cavaliers had taken possession of such a wood, where they rallied all the troops of their flying army; that they had plundered the country as they came, taking all the horses they could get; that they had plundered Goodman Thomson's house, which was the farmer I mentioned, and killed man, woman, and child; and that they were about 2000 strong.

My other friend in woman's clothes got among the good wives at an inn, where she set up her horse, and there she heard the same sad and dreadful tidings; and that this party was so strong, none of the neighbouring garrisons durst stir out; but that they had sent expresses to York, for a party of horse to come to their assistance.

I walked up and down the town, but fancied myself so ill disguised, and so easy to be known, that I cared not to talk with anybody. We met at the bridge exactly at our time, and compared our intelligence, found it answered our end of coming, and that we had nothing to do but to get back to our men; but my cripple told me, he would not stir till he bought some victuals so away he hops with his crutch, and buys four or five great pieces of bacon, as many of hung beef, and two or three loaves; and borrowing a sack at the inn (which I suppose he never restored), he loads his horse, and getting a large leather bottle, he filled that of aqua-vitae instead of small beer; my woman comrade did the like. I was uneasy in my mind, and took no care bu to get out of the town; however, we all came off well enough; but 'twas well for me that I had no provisions with me, as you will hear presently.

We came, as I said, into the town by several ways, and so we went out; but about three miles from the town we met again exactly where we had agreed. I being about a quarter of a mile from the rest, I meets three country fellows on horseback; one had a long pole on his shoulder, another a fork, the third no weapon at all, that I saw. I gave them the road very orderly, being habited like one of their brethren; but one of them stopping short at me, and looking earnestly calls out, "Hark thee, friend," says he, in a broad north-country tone, "whar hast thou thilk horse?" I must confess I was in the utmost confusion at the question, neither being able to answer the question, nor to speak in his tone; so I made as if I did not hear him, and went on. "Na, but ye's not gang soa," says the boor, and comes up to me, and takes hold of the horse's bridle to stop me; at which, vexed at heart that I could not tell how to talk to him, I reached him a great knock on the pate with my fork, and fetched him off of his horse, and then began to mend my pace. The other clowns, though it seems they knew not what the fellow wanted, pursued me, and finding they had better heels than I, I saw there was no remedy but to make use of my hands, and faced about.

The first that came up with me was he that had no weapons, so I thought I might parley with him, and speaking as country-like as I could, I asked him what he wanted? "Thou'st knaw that soon," says Yorkshire, "and ise but come at thee." "Then keep awa', man," said I, "or ise brain thee." By this time the third man came up, and the parley ended; for he gave me no words, but laid at me with his long pole, and that with such fury, that I began to be doubtful of him. I was loth to shoot the fellow, though I had pistols under my grey frock, as well for that the noise of a pistol might bring more people in, the village being on our rear, and also because I could not imagine what the fellow meant, or would have. But at last, finding he would be too many for me with that long weapon, and a hardy strong fellow, I threw myself off my horse, and running in with him, stabbed my fork into his horse. The horse being wounded, staggered awhile, and then fell down, and the booby had not the sense to get down in time, but fell with him. Upon which, giving him a knock or two with my fork, I secured him. The other, by this time, had furnished himself with a great stick out of a hedge, and before I was disengaged from the last fellow, gave me two such blows, that if the last had not missed my head and hit me on the shoulder, I had ended the fight and my life together. 'Twas time to look about me now, for this was a madman. I defended myself with my fork, but 'twould not do. At last, in short, I was forced to pistol him and get on horseback again, and with all the speed I could make, get away to the wood to our men.

If my two fellow-spies had not been behind, I had never known what was the meaning of this quarrel of the three countrymen, but my cripple had all the particulars. For he being behind us, as I have already observed, when he came up to the first fellow who began the fray, he found him beginning to come to himself. So he gets off, and pretends to help him, and sets him up upon his breech, and being a very merry fellow, talked to him: "Well, and what's the matter now?" says he to him. "Ah, wae's me," says the fellow, "I is killed." "Not quite, mon," says the cripple. "Oh, that's a fau thief," says he, and thus they parleyed. My cripple got him on's feet, and gave him a dram of his aqua-vitae bottle, and made much of him, in order to know what was the occasion of the quarrel. Our disguised woman pitied the fellow too, and together they set him up again upon his horse, and then he told him that that fellow was got upon one of his brother's horses who lived at Wetherby. They said the Cavaliers stole him, but 'twas like such rogues. No mischief could be done in the country, but 'twas the poor Cavaliers must bear the

111

blame, and the like, and thus they jogged on till they came to the place where the other two lay. The first fellow they assisted as they had done t'other, and gave him a dram out of the leather bottle, but the last fellow was past their care, so they came away. For when they understood that 'twas my horse they claimed, they began to be afraid that their own horses might be known too, and then they had been betrayed in a worse pickle than I, and must have been forced to have done some mischief or other to have got away.

I had sent out two troopers to fetch them off, if there was any occasion; but their stay was not long and the two troopers saw them at a distance coming towards us, so they returned.

I had enough of going for a spy, and my companions had enough of staying in the wood for other intelligences agreed with ours, and all concurred in this, that it was time to be going; however, this use we made of it, that while the country thought us so strong we were in the less danger of being attacked, though in the more of being observed; but all this while we heard nothing of our friends till the next day. We heard Prince Rupert, with about 1000 horse, was at Skipton, and from thence marched away to Westmoreland.

We concluded now we had two or three days' time good; for, since messengers were sent to York for a party to suppress us, we must have at least two days' march of them, and therefore all concluded we were to make the best of our way. Early in the morning, therefore, we decamped from those dull quarters; and as we marched through a village we found the people very civil to us, and the women cried out, "God bless them, 'tis pity the Roundheads should make such work with such brave men," and the like. Finding we were among our friends, we resolved to halt a little and refresh ourselves; and, indeed, the people were very kind to us, gave us victuals and drink, and took care of our horses. It happened to be my lot to stop at a house where the good woman took a great deal of pains to provide for us; but I observed the good man walked about with a cap upon his head, and very much out of order. I took no great notice of it, being very sleepy, and having asked my landlady to let me have a bed, I lay down and slept heartily. When I waked I found my landlord on another bed groaning very heavily. When I came downstairs, I found my cripple talking with my landlady; he was now out of his disguise, but we called him cripple still; and the other, who put on the woman's clothes, we called Goody Thompson. As soon as he saw me, he called me out, "Do you know," says he, "the man of the house you are quartered in?" "No, not I," says I. "No; so I believe, nor they you," says he; "if they did, the good wife would not have made you a posset, and fetched a white loaf for you." "What do you mean?" says I. "Have you seen the man?" says he. "Seen him," says I; "yes, and heard him too; the man's sick, and groans so heavily," says I, "that I could not lie upon the bed any longer for him." "Why, this is the poor man," says he, "that you knocked down with your fork yesterday, and I have had all the story out yonder at the next door." I confess it grieved me to have been forced to treat one so roughly who was one of our friends, but to make some amends, we contrived to give the poor man his brother's horse; and my cripple told him a formal story, that he believed the horse was taken away from the fellow by some of our men, and if he knew him again, if 'twas his friend's horse, he should have him. The man came down upon the news, and I caused six or seven horses, which were taken at the same time, to be shown him; he immediately chose the right; so I gave him the horse, and we pretended a great deal of sorrow for the man's hurt, and that we had not knocked the fellow on the head as well as took away the horse. The man was so overjoyed at the revenge he thought was taken on the fellow, that we heard him groan no more.

We ventured to stay all day at this town and the next night, and got guides to lead us to Blackstone Edge, a ridge of mountains which part this side of Yorkshire from Lancashire. Early in the morning we marched, and kept our scouts very carefully out every way, who brought us no news for this day.

We kept on all night, and made our horses do penance for that little rest they had, and the next morning we passed the hills and got into Lancashire, to a town called Littlebrough, and from thence to Rochdale, a little market town. And now we thought ourselves safe as to the pursuit of enemies from the side of York. Our design was to get to Bolton, but all the county was full of the enemy in flying parties, and how to get to Bolton we knew not.

At last we resolved to send a messenger to Bolton; but he came back and told us he had with lurking and hiding tried all the ways that he thought possible, but to no purpose, for he could not get into the town. We sent another, and he never returned, and some time after we understood he was taken by the enemy. At last one got into the town, but brought us word they were tired out with constant alarms, had been strictly blocked up, and every day expected a siege, and therefore advised us either to go northward where Prince Rupert and the Lord Goring ranged at liberty, or to get over Warrington Bridge, and so secure our retreat to Chester.

This double direction divided our opinions. I was for getting into Chester, both to recruit myself with horses and with money, both which I wanted, and to get refreshment, which we all wanted; but the major part of our men were for the north. First they said there was their general, and 'twas their duty to the cause, and the king's interest obliged us to go where we could do best service; and there was their friends, and every man might hear some news of his own regiment, for we belonged to several regiments. Besides, all the towns to the left of us were possessed by Sir William Brereton, Warrington, and Northwich, garrisoned by the enemy, and a strong party at Manchester, so that 'twas very likely we should be beaten and dispersed before we could get to Chester. These reasons, and especially the last, determined us for the north, and we had resolved to march the next morning, when other intelligence brought us to more speedy resolutions.

We kept our scouts continually abroad to bring us intelligence of the enemy, whom we expected on our backs, and also to keep an eye upon the country; for, as we lived upon them something at large, they were ready enough to do us any ill turn, as it lay in their power.

The first messenger that came to us was from our friends at Bolton, to inform us that they were preparing at Manchester to attack us. One of our parties had been as far as Stockport, on the edge of Cheshire, and was pursued by a party of the enemy, but got off by the help of the night. Thus, all things looked black to the south, we had resolved to march northward in the morning, when one of our scouts from the side of Manchester, assured us Sir Thomas Middleton, with some of the Parliament forces and the country troops, making above 1200 men, were on the march to attack us, and would certainly beat up our quarters that night. Upon this advice we resolved to be gone; and, getting all things in readiness, we began to march about two hours before night. And having gotten a trusty fellow for a guide, a fellow that we found was a friend to our side, he put a project into my head which saved us all for that time; and that was, to give out in the village that we were marched to Yorkshire, resolving to get into Pontefract Castle; and accordingly he leads us out of the town the same way we came in, and, taking a boy with him, he sends the boy back just at night, and bade him say he saw us go up the hills at Blackstone Edge; and it happened very well, for this party were so sure of us, that they had placed 400 men on the road to the northward to intercept our retreat that way, and had left no way for us, as they thought, to get away but back again.

About ten o'clock at night, they assaulted our quarters, but found we were gone; and being informed which way, they followed upon the spur, and travelling all night, being moonlight, they found themselves the next day about fifteen miles east, just out of their way. For we had, by the help of our guide, turned short at the foot of the hills, and through blind untrodden paths, and with difficulty enough, by noon the next day had reached almost twenty-five miles north, near a town called Clitheroe. Here we halted in the open field, and sent out our people to see how things were in the country.

This part of the country, almost unpassable, and walled round with hills, was indifferent quiet, and we got some refreshment for ourselves, but very little horse-meat, and so went on. But we had not marched far before we found ourselves discovered, and the 400 horse sent to lie in wait for us as before, having understood which way we went, followed us hard; and by letters to some of their friends at Preston, we found we were beset again.

Our guide began now to be out of his knowledge, and our scouts brought us word, the enemy's horse was posted before us, and we knew they were in our rear. In this exigence, we resolved to divide our small body, and so amusing them, at least one might get off, if the other miscarried. I took about eighty horse with me, among which were all that I had of our own regiment, amounting to above thirty-two, and took the hills towards Yorkshire. Here we met with such unpassable hills, vast moors, rocks, and stonyways, as lamed all our horses and tired our men; and some times I was ready to think we should never be able to get over them, till our horses failing, and jackboots being but indifferent things to travel in, we might be starved before we should find any road, or towns; for guide we had none, but a boy who knew but little, and would cry when we asked him any questions. I believe neither men nor horses ever passed in some places where we went, and for twenty hours we saw not a town nor a house, excepting sometimes from the top of the mountains, at a vast distance. I am persuaded we might have encamped here, if we had had provisions, till the war had been over, and have met with no disturbance; and I have often wondered since, how we got into such horrible places, as much as how we got out. That which was worse to us than all the rest, was, that we knew not where we were going, nor what part of the country we should come into, when we came out of those desolate crags. At last, after a terrible fatigue, we began to see the western parts of Yorkshire, some few villages, and the country at a distance looked a little like England, for I thought before it looked like old Brennus Hill, which the Grisons call "the grandfather of the Alps." We got some relief in the villages, which indeed some of us had so much need of, that they were hardly able to sit their horses, and others were forced to help them off, they were so faint. I never felt so much of the power of hunger in my life, for having not eaten in thirty hours, I was as ravenous as a hound; and if I had had a piece of horse-flesh, I believe I should not have had patience to have staid dressing it, but have fallen upon it raw, and have eaten it as greedily as a Tartar. However I ate very cautiously, having often seen the danger of men's eating heartily after long fasting.

Our next care was to inquire our way. Halifax, they told us, was on our right. There we durst not think of going. Skipton was before us, and there we knew not how it was, for a body of 3000 horse, sent out by the enemy in pursuit of Prince Rupert, had been there but two days before, and the country people could not tell us whether they were gone, or no. And Manchester's horse, which were sent out after our party, were then at Halifax, in quest of us, and afterwards marched into Cheshire. In this distress we would have hired a guide, but none of the country people would go with us, for the Roundheads would hang them, they said, when they came there. Upon this I called a fellow to me, "Hark ye, friend," says I, "dost thee know the way so as to bring us into Westmoreland, and not keep the great road from York?" "Ay, merry," says he, "I ken the ways weel enou!" "And you would go and guide us," said I, "but that you are afraid the Roundheads will hang you?" "Indeed would I," says the fellow. "Why then," says I, "thou hadst as good be hanged by a Cavalier as a Roundhead, for if thou wilt not go, I'll hang thee just now." "Na, and ye serve me soa," says the fellow, "Ise ene gang with ye, for I care not for hanging; and ye'll get me a good horse, Ise gang and be one of ye, for I'll nere come heame more." This pleased us still better, and we mounted the fellow, for three of our men died that night with the extreme fatigue of the last service.

Next morning, when our new trooper was mounted and clothed we hardly knew him; and this fellow led us by such ways, such wildernesses, and yet with such prudence, keeping the hills to the left, that we might have the villages to refresh ourselves, that without him, we had certainly either perished in those mountains, or fallen into the enemy's hands. We passed the great road from York so critically as to time, that from one of the hills he showed us a party of the enemy's horse who were then marching into Westmoreland. We lay still that day, finding we were not discovered by them; and our guide proved the best scout that we could have had; for he would go out ten miles at a time, and bring us in all the news of the country. Here he brought us word, that York was surrendered upon articles, and that Newcastle, which had been surprised by the king's party, was besieged by another army of Scots advanced to help their brethren.

Along the edges of those vast mountains we passed with the help of our guide, till we came into the forest of Swale; and finding ourselves perfectly concealed here, for no soldier had ever been here all the war, nor perhaps would not, if it had lasted seven years, we thought we wanted a few days' rest, at least for our horses. So we resolved to halt; and while we did so, we made some disguises, and sent out some spies into the country; but as here were no great towns, nor no post road, we got very little intelligence. We rested four days, and then marched again; and indeed having no great stock of money about us, and not very free of that we had, four days was enough for those poor places to be able to maintain us.

We thought ourselves pretty secure now; but our chief care was how to get over those terrible mountains; for having passed the great road that leads from York to Lancaster, the crags, the farther northward we looked, looked still the worse, and our business was all on the other side. Our guide told us, he would bring us out, if we would have patience, which we were obliged to, and kept on this slow march, till he brought us to Stanhope, in the country of Durham; where some of Goring's horse, and two regiments of foot, had their quarters. This was nineteen days from the battle of Marston Moor. The prince, who was then at Kendal in Westmoreland, and who had given me over as lost, when he had news of our arrival, sent an express to me, to meet him at Appleby. I went thither accordingly, and gave him an account of our journey, and there I heard the short history of the other part of our men, whom we parted from in Lancashire. They made the best of their way north; they had two resolute gentlemen who commanded; and being so closely pursued by the enemy, that they found themselves under a necessity of fighting, they halted, and faced about, expecting the charge. The boldness of the action made the officer who led the enemy's horse (which it seems were the county horse only) afraid of them; which they perceiving, taking the advantage of his fears, bravely advance, and charge them; and though they were above 200 horse, they routed them, killed about thirty or forty, got some horses, and some money, and pushed on their march night and day; but coming near Lancaster, they were so waylaid and pursued, that they agreed to separate, and shift every man for himself. Many of them fell into the enemy's hands; some were killed attempting to pass through the river Lune; some went back, six or seven got to Bolton, and about eighteen got safe to Prince Rupert.

The prince was in a better condition hereabouts than I expected; he and my Lord Goring, with the help of Sir Marmaduke Langdale, and the gentlemen of Cumberland, had gotten a body of 4000 horse, and about 6000 foot; they had retaken Newcastle, Tynemouth, Durham, Stockton, and several towns of consequence from the Scots, and might have cut them out work enough still, if that base people, resolved to engage their whole interest to ruin their sovereign, had not sent a second army of 10,000 men, under the Earl of Callander, to help their first. These came and laid siege to Newcastle, but found more vigorous resistance now than they had done before. There were in the town Sir John Morley, the Lord Crawford, Lord Reay, and Maxwell, Scots; and old soldiers, who were resolved their countrymen should buy the town very dear, if they had it; and had it not been for our disaster at Marston Moor, they had never had it; for Callander, finding he was not able to carry the town, sends to General Leven to come from the siege of York to help him.

Meantime the prince forms a very good army, and the Lord Goring, with 10,000 men, shows himself on the borders of Scotland, to try if that might not cause the Scots to recall their forces; and, I am persuaded, had he entered Scotland, the Parliament of Scotland had recalled the Earl of Callander, for they had but 5000 men left in arms to send against him; but they were loth to venture. However, this effect it had, that it called the Scots northward again, and found them work there for the rest of the summer to reduce the several towns in the bishopric of Durham.

I found with the prince the poor remains of my regiment, which, when joined with those that had been with me, could not all make up three troops, and but two captains, three lieutenants, and one cornet; the rest were dispersed, killed, or taken prisoners. However, with those, which we still called a regiment, I joined the prince, and after having done all we could on that side, the Scots being returned from York, the prince returned through Lancashire to Chester.

The enemy often appeared and alarmed us, and once fell on one of our parties, and killed us about a hundred men; but we were too many for them to pretend to fight us, so we came to Bolton, beat the troops of the enemy near Warrington, where I got a cut with a halberd in my face, and arrived at Chester the beginning of August.

The Parliament, upon their great success in the north, thinking the king's forces quite unbroken, had sent their General Essex into the west, where the king's army was commanded by Prince Maurice, Prince Rupert's elder brother, but not very strong; and the king being, as they supposed, by the absence of Prince Rupert, weakened so much as that he might be checked by Sir William Waller, who, with 4500 foot, and 1500 horse, was at that time about Winchester, having lately beaten Sir Ralph Hopton;--upon all these considerations, the Earl of Essex marches westward.

The forces in the west being too weak to oppose him, everything gave way to him, and all people expected he would besiege Exeter, where the queen was newly lying-in, and sent a trumpet to desire he would forbear the city, while she could be removed, which he did, and passed on westward, took Tiverton, Bideford, Barnstaple, Launceston, relieved Plymouth, drove Sir Richard Grenvile up into Cornwall, and followed him thither, but left Prince Maurice behind him with 4000 men about Barnstaple and Exeter.

116

The king, in the meantime, marches from Oxford into Worcester, with Waller at his heels. At Edgehill his Majesty turns upon Waller, and gave him a brush, to put him in mind of the place. The king goes on to Worcester, sends 300 horse to relieve Durley Castle, besieged by the Earl of Denby, and sending part of his forces to Bristol, returns to Oxford.

His Majesty had now firmly resolved to march into the west, not having yet any account of our misfortunes in the north. Waller and Middleton waylay the king at Cropredy Bridge. The king assaults Middleton at the bridge.

Waller's men were posted with some cannon to guard a pass. Middleton's men put a regiment of the king's foot to the rout, and pursued them.

Waller's men, willing to come in for the plunder, a thing their general had often used them to, quit their post at the pass, and their great guns, to have part in the victory. The king coming in seasonably to the relief of his men, routs Middleton, and at the same time sends a party round, who clapped in between Sir William Waller's men and their great guns, and secured the pass and the cannon too. The king took three colonels, besides other officers, and about 300 men prisoners, with eight great guns, nineteen carriages of ammunition, and killed about 200 men.

Waller lost his reputation in this fight, and was exceedingly slighted ever after, even by his own party; but especially by such as were of General Essex's party, between whom and Waller there had been jealousies and misunderstandings for some time. The king, about 8000 strong, marched on to Bristol, where Sir William Hopton joined him, and from thence he follows Essex into Cornwall. Essex still following Grenvile, the king comes to Exeter, and joining with Prince Maurice, resolves to pursue Essex; and now the Earl of Essex began to see his mistake, being cooped up between two seas, the king's army in his rear, the country his enemy, and Sir Richard Grenvile in his van.

The king, who always took the best measures when he was left to his own counsel, wisely refuses to engage, though superior in number, and much stronger in horse. Essex often drew out to fight, but the king fortifies, takes the passes and bridges, plants cannon, and secures the country to keep off provisions, and continually straitens their quarters, but would not fight.

Now Essex sends away to the Parliament for help, and they write to Waller, and Middleton, and Manchester to follow, and come up with the king in his rear; but some were too far off, and could not, as Manchester and Fairfax; others made no haste, as having no mind to it, as Waller and Middleton, and if they had, it had been too late.

At last the Earl of Essex, finding nothing to be done, and unwilling to fall into the king's hands, takes shipping, and leaves his army to shift for themselves. The horse, under Sir William Balfour, the best horse officer, and, without comparison, the bravest in all the Parliament army, advanced in small parties, as if to skirmish, but following in with the whole body, being 3500 horse, broke through, and got off. Though this was a loss to the king's victory, yet the foot were now in a condition so much the worse.

Brave old Skippon proposed to fight through with the foot and die, as he called it, like Englishmen, with sword in hand; but the rest of the officers shook their heads at it, for, being well paid, they had at present no occasion for dying.

Seeing it thus, they agreed to treat, and the king grants them conditions, upon laying down their arms, to march off free. This was too much. Had his Majesty but obliged them upon oath not to serve again for a certain time, he had done his business; but this was not thought of, so they passed free, only disarmed, the soldiers not being allowed so much as their swords. The king gained by this treaty forty pieces of cannon, all of brass, 300 barrels of gunpowder, 9000 arms, 8000 swords, match and bullet in proportion, 200 waggons, 150 colours and standards, all the bag and baggage of the army, and about 1000 of the men listed in his army. This was a complete victory without bloodshed; and had the king but secured the men from serving but for six months, it had most effectually answered the battle of Marston Moor.

As it was, it infused new life into all his Majesty's forces and friends, and retrieved his affairs very much; but especially it encouraged us in the north, who were more sensible of the blow received at Marston Moor, and of the destruction the Scots were bringing upon us all.

While I was at Chester, we had some small skirmishes with Sir William Brereton. One morning in particular Sir William drew up, and faced us, and one of our colonels of horse observing the enemy to be not, as he thought, above 200, desires leave of Prince Rupert to attack them with the like number, and accordingly he sallied out with 200 horse. I stood drawn up without the city with 800 more, ready to bring him off, if he should be put to the worst, which happened accordingly; for, not having discovered neither the country nor the enemy as he ought Sir William Brereton drew him into an ambuscade; so that before he came up with Sir William's forces, near enough to charge, he finds about 300 horse in his rear. Though he was surprised at this, yet, being a man of a ready courage, he boldly faces about with 150 of his men, leaving the other fifty to face Sir William. With this small party, he desperately charges the 300 horse in his rear, and putting them into disorder, breaks through them, and, had there been no greater force, he had cut them all in pieces. Flushed with this success, and loth to desert the fifty men he had left behind, he faces about again, and charges through them again, and with these two charges entirely routs them. Sir William Brereton finding himself a little disappointed, advances, and falls upon the fifty men just as the colonel came up to them; they fought him with a great deal of bravery, but the colonel being unfortunately killed in the first charge, the men gave way, and came flying all in confusion, with the enemy at their heels. As soon as I saw this, I advanced according to my orders, and the enemy, as soon as I appeared, gave over the pursuit. This gentleman, as I remember, was Colonel Marrow; we fetched off his body, and retreated into Chester.

The next morning the prince drew out of the city with about 1200 horse and 2000 foot and attacked Sir William Brereton in his quarters. The fight was very sharp for the time, and near 700 men, on both sides, were killed; but Sir William would not put it to a general engagement so the prince drew off, contenting himself to have insulted him in his quarters.

We now had received orders from the king to join him; but I representing to the prince the condition of my regiment, which was now 100 men, and that, being within twenty-five miles of my father's house, I might soon recruit it, my father having got some men together already, I desired leave to lie at Shrewsbury for a month, to make up my men. Accordingly, having obtained his leave, I marched to Wrexham, where in two days' time I got twenty men, and so on to Shrewsbury. I had not been here above ten days, but I received an express to come away with what recruits I had got together, Prince Rupert having positive orders to meet the king by a certain day. I had not mounted 100 men, though I had listed above 200, when these orders came but leaving my father to complete them for me, I marched with those I had and came to Oxford

The king, after the rout of the Parliament forces in the west, was marched back, took Barnstaple, Plympton, Launceston, Tiverton, and several other places, and left Plymouth besieged by Sir Richard Grenvile, met with Sir William Waller at Shaftesbury, and again at Andover, and boxed him at both places, and marched for Newbury. Here the king sent for Prince Rupert to meet him, who with 3000 horse made long marches to join him; but the Parliament having joined their three armies together, Manchester from the north, Waller and Essex (the men being clothed and armed) from the west, had attacked the king and obliged him to fight the day before the prince came up.

The king had so posted himself, as that he could not be obliged to fight but with advantage, the Parliament's forces being superior in number, and therefore, when they attacked him, he galled them with his cannon, and declining to come to a general battle, stood upon the defensive, expecting Prince Rupert with the horse.

The Parliament's forces had some advantage over our foot, and took the Earl of Cleveland prisoner. But the king, whose foot were not above one to two, drew his men under the cannon of Donnington Castle, and having secured his artillery and baggage, made a retreat with his foot in very good order, having not lost in all the fight above 300 men, and the Parliament as many. We lost five pieces of cannon and took two, having repulsed the Earl of Manchester's men on the north side of the town, with considerable loss.

The king having lodged his train of artillery and baggage in Donnington Castle, marched the next day for Oxford. There we joined him with 3000 horse and 2000 foot. Encouraged with this reinforcement, the king appears upon the hills on the north-west of Newbury, and faces the Parliament army. The Parliament having too many generals as well as soldiers, they could not agree whether they should fight or no. This was no great token of the victory they boasted of, for they were now twice our number in the whole, and their foot three for one. The king stood in battalia all day, and finding the Parliament forces had no stomach to engage him, he drew away his cannon and baggage out of Donnington Castle in view of their whole army, and marched away to Oxford.

This was such a false step of the Parliament's generals, that all the people cried shame of them. The Parliament appointed a committee to inquire into it. Cromwell accused Manchester, and he Waller, and so they laid the fault upon one another. Waller would have been glad to have charged it upon Essex, but as it happened he was not in the army, having been taken ill some days before. But as it generally is when a mistake is made, the actors fall out among themselves, so it was here. No doubt it was as false a step as that of Cornwall, to let the king fetch away his baggage and cannon in the face of three armies, and never fire a shot at them.

The king had not above 8000 foot in his army, and they above 25,000. Tis true the king had 8000 horse, a fine body, and much superior to theirs; but the foot might, with the greatest ease in the world, have prevented the removing the cannon, and in three days' time have taken the castle, with all that was in it.

Those differences produced their self-denying ordinance, and the putting by most of their old generals, as Essex, Waller, Manchester, and the like; and Sir Thomas Fairfax, a terrible man in the field, though the mildest of men out of it, was voted to have the command of all their forces, and Lambert to take the command of Sir Thomas Fairfax's troops in the north, old Skippon being Major-General.

This winter was spent on the enemy's side in modelling, as they called it, their army, and on our side in recruiting ours, and some petty excursions. Amongst the many addresses I observed one from Sussex or Surrey, complaining of the rudeness of their soldiers, from which I only observed that there were disorders among them as well as among us, only with this difference, that they, for reasons I mentioned before, were under circumstances to prevent it better than the king. But I must do the king's memory that justice, that he used all possible methods, by punishment of soldiers, charging, and sometimes entreating, the gentlemen not to suffer such disorders and such violences in their men; but it was to no purpose for his Majesty to attempt it, while his officers, generals, and great men winked at it; for the licentiousness of the soldier is supposed to be approved by the officer when it is not corrected.

The rudeness of the Parliament soldiers began from the divisions among their officers; for in many places the soldiers grew so out of all discipline and so unsufferably rude, that they, in particular, refused to march when Sir William Waller went to Weymouth. This had turned to good account for us, had these cursed Scots been out of our way, but they were the staff of the party; and now they were daily solicited to march southward, which was a very great affliction to the king and all his friends.

One booty the king got at this time, which was a very seasonable assistance to his affairs, viz., a great merchant ship, richly laden at London, and bound to the East Indies, was, by the seamen, brought into Bristol, and delivered up to the king. Some merchants in Bristol offered the king £40,000 for her, which his Majesty ordered should be accepted, reserving only thirty great guns for his own use.

The treaty at Uxbridge now was begun, and we that had been well beaten in the war heartily wished the king would come to a peace; but we all foresaw the clergy would ruin it all. The Commons were for Presbytery, and would never agree the bishops should be restored. The king was willinger to comply with anything than this, and we foresaw it would be so; from whence we used to say among ourselves, "That the clergy was resolved if there should be no bishop there should be no king."

This treaty at Uxbridge was a perfect war between the men of the gown, ours was between those of the sword; and I cannot but take notice how the lawyers, statesmen, and the clergy of every side bestirred themselves, rather to hinder than promote the peace.

There had been a treaty at Oxford some time before, where the Parliament insisting that the king should pass a bill to abolish Episcopacy, quit the militia, abandon several of his faithful servants to be exempted from pardon, and making several other most extravagant demands, nothing was done, but the treaty broke off, both parties being rather farther exasperated, than inclined to hearken to conditions.

However, soon after the success in the west, his Majesty, to let them see that victory had not puffed him up so as to make him reject the peace, sends a message to the Parliament, to put them in mind of messages of like nature which they had slighted; and to let them know, that notwithstanding he had beaten their forces, he was yet willing to hearken to a reasonable proposal for putting an end to the war.

The Parliament pretended the king, in his message, did not treat with them as a legal Parliament, and so made hesitations; but after long debates and delays they agreed to draw up propositions for peace to be sent to the king. As this message was sent to the Houses about

August, I think they made it the middle of November before they brought the propositions for peace; and, when they brought them, they had no power to enter either upon a treaty, or so much as preliminaries for a treaty, only to deliver the letter, and receive an answer.

However, such were the circumstances of affairs at this time, that the king was uneasy to see himself thus treated, and take no notice of it: the king returned an answer to the propositions, and proposed a treaty by commissioners which the Parliament appointed.

Three months more were spent in naming commissioners. There was much time spent in this treaty, but little done; the commissioners debated chiefly the article of religion, and of the militia; in the latter they were very likely to agree, in the former both sides seemed too positive. The king would by no means abandon Episcopacy nor the Parliament Presbytery; for both in their opinion were jure divino.

The commissioners finding this point hardest to adjust, went from it to that of the militia; but the time spinning out, the king's commissioners demanded longer time for the treaty; the other sent up for instructions, but the House refused to lengthen out the time.

This was thought an insolence upon the king, and gave all good people a detestation of such haughty behaviour; and thus the hopes of peace vanished, both sides prepared for war with as much eagerness as before.

The Parliament was employed at this time in what they called a-modelling their army; that is to say, that now the Independent party [was] beginning to prevail; and, as they outdid all the others in their resolution of carrying on the war to all extremities, so they were both the more vigorous and more politic party in carrying it on.

Indeed, the war was after this carried on with greater animosity than ever, and the generals pushed forward with a vigour that, as it had something in it unusual, so it told us plainly from this time, whatever they did before, they now pushed at the ruin even of the monarchy itself. All this while also the war went on, and though the Parliament had no settled army, yet their regiments and troops were always in action; and the sword was at work in every part of the kingdom.

Among an infinite number of party skirmishings and fights this winter, one happened which nearly concerned me, which was the surprise of the town and castle of Shrewsbury. Colonel Mitton, with about 1200 horse and foot, having intelligence with some people in the town, on a Sunday morning early broke into the town and took it, castle and all. The loss for the quality, more than the number, was very great to the king's affairs. They took there fifteen pieces of cannon, Prince Maurice's magazine of arms and ammunition, Prince Rupert's baggage, above fifty persons of quality and officers. There was not above eight or ten men killed on both sides, for the town was surprised, not stormed. I had a particular loss in this action; for all the men and horses my father had got together for the recruiting my regiment were here lost and dispersed, and, which was the worse, my father happening to be then in the town, was taken prisoner, and carried to Beeston Castle in Cheshire.

I was quartered all this winter at Banbury, and went little abroad; nor had we any action till the latter end of February, when I was ordered to march to Leicester with Sir Marmaduke Langdale, in order, as we thought, to raise a body of men in that county and Staffordshire to join the king.

121

We lay at Daventry one night, and continuing our march to pass the river above Northampton, that town being possessed by the enemy, we understood a party of Northampton forces were abroad, and intended to attack us. Accordingly, in the afternoon our scouts brought us word the enemy were quartered in some villages on the road to Coventry. Our commander, thinking it much better to set upon them in their quarters, than to wait for them in the field, resolves to attack them early in the morning before they were aware of it. We refreshed ourselves in the field for that day, and, getting into a great wood near the enemy, we stayed there all night, till almost break of day, without being discovered. In the morning very early we heard the enemy's trumpets sound to horse. This roused us to look abroad, and, sending out a scout, he brought us word a part of the enemy was at hand. We were vexed to be so disappointed, but finding their party small enough to be dealt with, Sir Marmaduke ordered me to charge them with 300 horse and 200 dragoons, while he at the same time entered the town. Accordingly I lay still till they came to the very skirt of the wood where I was posted, when I saluted them with a volley from my dragoons out of the wood, and immediately showed myself with my horse on their front ready to charge them. They appeared not to be surprised, and received our charge with great resolution; and, being above 400 men, they pushed me vigorously in their turn, putting my men into some disorder. In this extremity I sent to order my dragoons to charge them in the flank, which they did with great bravery, and the other still maintained the fight with desperate resolution. There was no want of courage in our men on both sides, but our dragoons had the advantage, and at last routed them, and drove them back to the village. Here Sir Marmaduke Langdale had his hands full too, for my firing had alarmed the towns adjacent, that when he came into the town he found them all in arms, and, contrary to his expectation, two regiments of foot, with about 500 horse more. As Sir Marmaduke had no foot, only horse and dragoons, this was a surprise to him; but he caused his dragoons to enter the town and charge the foot, while his horse secured the avenues of the town.

The dragoons bravely attacked the foot, and Sir Marmaduke falling in with his horse, the fight was obstinate and very bloody, when the horse that I had routed came flying into the street of the village, and my men at their heels. Immediately I left the pursuit, and fell in with all my force to the assistance of my friends, and, after an obstinate resistance, we routed the whole party; we killed about 700 men, took 350, 27 officers, 100 arms, all their baggage, and 200 horses, and continued our march to Harborough, where we halted to refresh ourselves.

Between Harborough and Leicester we met with a party of 800 dragoons of the Parliament forces. They, found themselves too few to attack us, and therefore to avoid us they had gotten into a small wood; but perceiving themselves discovered, they came boldly out, and placed themselves at the entrance into a lane, lining both sides of the hedges with their shot. We immediately attacked them, beat them from their hedges, beat them into the wood, and out of the wood again, and forced them at last to a downright run away, on foot, among the enclosures where we could not follow them, killed about 100 of them, and took 250 prisoners, with all their horses, and came that night to Leicester. When we came to Leicester, and had taken up our quarters, Sir Marmaduke Langdale sent for me to sup with him, and told me that he had a secret commission in his pocket, which his Majesty had commanded him not to open till he came to Leicester; that now he had sent for me to open it together, that we might know what it was we were to do, and to consider how to do it; so pulling out his sealed orders, we found we were to get what force we could together, and a certain number of carriages with ammunition, which the governor of Leicester was to deliver us, and a certain quantity of provision, especially corn and salt, and to relieve Newark. This town had been long besieged. The fortifications of the place together with its situation, had rendered it the strongest place in England; and, as it was the greatest pass in England, so it was of vast consequence to the king's affairs. There was in it a garrison of brave old rugged boys, fellows that, like Count Tilly's Germans, had iron faces, and they had defended themselves with extraordinary bravery a great while, but were reduced to an exceeding strait for want of provisions.

Accordingly we received the ammunition and provision, and away we went for Newark; about Melton Mowbray, Colonel Rossiter set upon us, with above 3000 men; we were about the same number, having 2500 horse, and 800 dragoons. We had some foot, but they were still at Harborough, and were ordered to come after us.

Rossiter, like a brave officer as he was, charged us with great fury, and rather outdid us in number, while we defended ourselves with all the eagerness we could, and withal gave him to understand we were not so soon to be beaten as he expected. While the fight continued doubtful, especially on our side, our people, who had charge of the carriages and provisions, began to enclose our flanks with them, as if we had been marching, which, though it was done without orders, had two very good effects, and which did us extraordinary service. First, it secured us from being charged in the flank, which Rossiter had twice attempted; and secondly, it secured our carriages from being plundered, which had spoiled our whole expedition. Being thus enclosed, we fought with great security; and though Rossiter made three desperate charges upon us; he could never break us. Our men received him with so much courage, and kept their order so well, that the enemy, finding it impossible to force us, gave it over, and left us to pursue our orders. We did not offer to chase them, but contented enough to have repulsed and beaten them off, and our business being to relieve Newark, we proceeded.

If we are to reckon by the enemy's usual method, we got the victory, because we kept the field, and had the pillage of their dead; but otherwise, neither side had any great cause to boast. We lost about 150 men, and near as many hurt; they left 170 on the spot, and carried off some. How many they had wounded we could not tell; we got seventy or eighty horses, which helped to remount some of our men that had lost theirs in the fight. We had, however, this advantage, that we were to march on immediately after this service, the enemy only to retire to their quarters, which was but hard by.

This was an injury to our wounded men, who we were after obliged to leave at Belvoir Castle, and from thence we advanced to Newark.

Our business at Newark was to relieve the place, and this we resolved to do whatever it cost, though, at the same time, we resolved not to fight unless we were forced to it. The town was rather blocked up than besieged; the garrison was strong, but ill-provided; we had sent them word of our coming to them, and our orders to relieve them, and they proposed some measures for our doing it. The chief strength of the enemy lay on the other side of the river; but they having also some notice of our design, had sent over forces to strengthen their leaguer on this side. The garrison had often surprised them by sallies, and indeed had chiefly subsisted for some time by what they brought in on this manner.

Sir Marmaduke Langdale, who was our general for the expedition, was for a general attempt to raise the siege, but I had persuaded him off of that; first, because, if we should be beaten, as might be probable, we then lost the town. Sir Marmaduke briskly replied, "A soldier ought never to suppose he shall be beaten." "But, sir," says I, "you'll get more honour by relieving the town, than by beating them. One will be a credit to your conduct, as the other will be to your courage; and if you think you can beat them, you may do it afterward, and then if you are mistaken, the town is nevertheless secured, and half your victory gained."

He was prevailed with to adhere to this advice, and accordingly we appeared before the town about two hours before night. The horse drew up before the enemy's works; the enemy drew up within their works, and seeing no foot, expected when our dragoons would dismount and attack them. They were in the right to let us attack them, because of the advantage of their batteries and works, if that had been our design; but, as we intended only to amuse them, this caution of theirs effected our design; for, while we thus faced them with our horse, two regiments of foot, which came up to us but the night before, and was all the infantry we had, with the waggons of provisions, and 500 dragoons, taking a compass clean round the town, posted themselves on the lower side of the town by the river. Upon a signal the garrison agreed on before, they sallied out at this very juncture with all the men they could spare, and dividing themselves in two parties, while one party moved to the left to meet our relief, the other party fell on upon part of that body which faced us. We kept in motion, and upon this signal advanced to their works, and our dragoons fired upon them, and the horse, wheeling and counter-marching often, kept them continually expecting to be attacked. By this means the enemy were kept employed, and our foot, with the waggons, appearing on that quarter where they were least expected, easily defeated the advanced guards and forced that post, where, entering the leaguer, the other part of the garrison, who had sallied that way, came up to them, received the waggons, and the dragoons entered with them into the town. That party which we faced on the other side of the works knew nothing of what was done till all was over; the garrison retreated in good order, and we drew off, having finished what we came for without fighting. Thus we plentifully stored the town with all things wanting, and with an addition of 500 dragoons to their garrison; after which we marched away without fighting a stroke. Our next orders were to relieve Pontefract Castle, another garrison of the king's, which had been besieged ever since a few days after the fight at Marston Moor, by the Lord Fairfax, Sir Thomas Fairfax, and other generals in their turn. By the way we were joined with 800 horse out of Derbyshire, and some foot, so many as made us about 4500 men in all.

Colonel Forbes, a Scotchman, commanded at the siege, in the absence of the Lord Fairfax. The colonel had sent to my lord for more troops, and his lordship was gathering his forces to come up to him, but he was pleased to come too late. We came up with the enemy's leaguer about the break of day, and having been discovered by their scouts, they, with more courage than discretion, drew out to meet us. We saw no reason to avoid them, being stronger in horse than they; and though we had but a few foot, we had 1000 dragoons, which helped us out. We had placed our horse and foot throughout in one line, with two reserves of horse, and between every division of horse a division of foot, only that on the extremes of our wings there were two parties of horse on each point by themselves, and the dragoons in the centre on foot. Their foot charged us home, and stood with push of pike a great while; but their horse charging our horse and musketeers, and being closed on the flanks, with those two extended troops on our wings, they were presently disordered, and fled out of the field. The foot, thus deserted, were charged on every side and broken. They retreated still fighting, and in good order for a while, but the garrison sallying upon them at the same time, and being followed close by our horse, they were scattered, entirely routed, and most of them killed. The Lord Fairfax was come with his horse as far as Ferrybridge, but the fight was over, and all he could do was to rally those that fled, and save some of their carriages, which else had fallen into our hands. We drew up our little army in order of battle the next day, expecting the Lord Fairfax would have charged us; but his lordship was so far from any such thoughts that he placed a party of dragoons, with orders to fortify the pass at Ferrybridge, to prevent our falling upon him in his retreat, which he needed not have done; for, having raised the siege of Pontefract, our business was done, we had nothing to say to him, unless we had been strong enough to stay. We lost not above thirty men in this action, and the enemy 300, with about 150 prisoners, one piece of cannon, all their ammunition, 1000 arms, and most of their baggage, and Colonel Lambert was once taken prisoner, being wounded, but got off again.

We brought no relief for the garrison, but the opportunity to furnish themselves out of the country, which they did very plentifully. The ammunition taken from the enemy was given to them, which they wanted, and was their due, for they had seized it in the sally they made, before the enemy was quite defeated.

I cannot omit taking notice on all occasions how exceeding serviceable this method was of posting musketeers in the intervals, among the horse, in all this war. I persuaded our generals to it as much as possible, and I never knew a body of horse beaten that did so: yet I had great difficulty to prevail upon our people to believe it, though it was taught me by the greatest general in the world, viz., the King of Sweden. Prince Rupert did it at the battle of Marston Moor; and had the Earl of Newcastle not been obstinate against it in his right wing, as I observed before, the day had not been lost. In discoursing this with Sir Marmaduke Langdale, I had related several examples of the serviceableness of these small bodies of firemen, and with great difficulty brought him to agree, telling him I would be answerable for the success. But after the fight, he told me plainly he saw the advantage of it, and would never fight otherwise again if he had any foot to place. So having relieved these two places, we hastened by long marches through Derbyshire, to join Prince Rupert on the edge of Shropshire and Cheshire. We found Colonel Rossiter had followed us at a distance ever since the business at Melton Mowbray, but never cared to attack us, and we found he did the like still. Our general would fain have been doing with him again, but we found him too shy. Once we laid a trap for him at Dovebridge, between Derby and Burton-upon-Trent, the body being marched two days before. Three hundred dragoons were left to guard the bridge, as if we were afraid he should fall upon us. Upon this we marched, as I said, on to Burton, and the next day, fetching a compass round, came to a village near Titbury Castle, whose name I forgot, where we lay still expecting our dragoons would be attacked. Accordingly, the colonel, strengthened with some troops of horse from Yorkshire, comes up to the bridge, and finding some dragoons posted, advances to charge them. The dragoons immediately get a-horseback, and run for it, as they were ordered. But the old lad was not to be caught so, for he halts immediately at the bridge, and would not come over till he had sent three or four flying parties abroad to discover the country. One of these parties fell into our hands, and received but coarse entertainment. Finding the plot would not take, we appeared and drew up in view of the bridge, but he would not stir. So we continued our march into Cheshire, where we joined Prince Rupert and Prince Maurice, making together a fine body, being above 8000 horse and dragoons.

This was the best and most successful expedition I was in during this war. 'Twas well concerted, and executed with as much expedition and conduct as could be desired, and the success was answerable to it. And indeed, considering the season of the year (for we set out from Oxford the latter end of February), the ways bad, and the season wet, it was a terrible march of above 200 miles, in continual action, and continually dodged and observed by a vigilant enemy, and at a time when the north was overrun by their armies, and the Scots wanting employment for their forces. Yet in less than twenty-three days we marched 200 miles, fought the enemy in open field four times, relieved one garrison besieged, and raised the siege of another, and joined our friends at last in safety.

The enemy was in great pain for Sir William Brereton and his forces, and expresses rode night and day to the Scots in the north, and to the parties in Lancashire to come to his help. The prince, who used to be rather too forward to fight than otherwise, could not be persuaded to make use of this opportunity, but loitered, if I may be allowed to say so, till the Scots, with a brigade of horse and 2000 foot, had joined him; and then 'twas not thought proper to engage them.

I took this opportunity to go to Shrewsbury to visit my father, who was a prisoner of war there, getting a pass from the enemy's governor. They allowed him the liberty of the town, and sometimes to go to his own house upon his parole, so that his confinement was not very much to his personal injury. But this, together with the charges he had been at in raising the regiment, and above £20,000 in money and plate, which at several times he had lent, or given rather to the king, had reduced our family to very ill circumstances; and now they talked of cutting down his woods.

I had a great deal of discourse with my father on this affair; and, finding him extremely concerned, I offered to go to the king and desire his leave to go to London and treat about his composition, or to render myself a prisoner in his stead, while he went up himself. In this difficulty I treated with the governor of the town, who very civilly offered me his pass to go for London, which I accepted, and, waiting on Prince Rupert, who was then at Worcester, I acquainted him with my design. The prince was unwilling I should go to London; but told me he had some prisoners of the Parliament's friends in Cumberland, and he would get an exchange for my father. I told him if he would give me his word for it I knew I might depend upon it, otherwise there was so many of the king's party in their hands, that his Majesty was tired with solicitations for exchanges, for we never had a prisoner but there was ten offers of exchanges for him. The prince told me I should depend upon him; and he was as good as his word quickly after.

While the prince lay at Worcester he made an incursion into Herefordshire, and having made some of the gentlemen prisoners, brought them to Worcester; and though it was an action which had not been usual, they being persons not in arms, yet the like being my father's case who was really not in commission, nor in any military service, having resigned his regiment three years before to me, the prince insisted on exchanging them for such as the Parliament had in custody in like circumstances. The gentlemen seeing no remedy, solicited their own case at the Parliament, and got it passed in their behalf; and by this means my father got his liberty, and by the assistance of the Earl of Denbigh got leave to come to London to make a composition as a delinquent for his estate. This they charged at

£7000, but by the assistance of the same noble person he got off for £4000. Some members of the committee moved very kindly that my father should oblige me to quit the king's service, but that, as a thing which might be out of his power, was not insisted on. The modelling the Parliament army took them up all this winter, and we were in great hopes the divisions which appeared amongst them might have weakened their party; but when they voted Sir Thomas Fairfax to be general, I confess I was convinced the king's affairs were lost and desperate. Sir Thomas, abating the zeal of his party, and the mistaken opinion of his cause, was the fittest man amongst them to undertake the charge. He was a complete general, strict in his discipline, wary in conduct, fearless in action, unwearied in the fatigue of the war, and withal, of a modest, noble, generous disposition. We all apprehended danger from him, and heartily wished him of our own side; and the king was so sensible, though he would not discover it, that when an account was brought him of the choice they had made, he replied, "he was sorry for it; he had rather it had been anybody than he."

The first attempts of this new general and new army were at Oxford, which, by the neighbourhood of a numerous garrison in Abingdon, began to be very much straitened for provisions; and the new forces under Cromwell and Skippon, one lieutenant-general, the other major-general to Fairfax, approaching with a design to block it up, the king left the place, supposing his absence would draw them away, as it soon did.

The king resolving to leave Oxford, marches from thence with all his forces, the garrison excepted, with design to have gone to Bristol; but the plague was in Bristol, which altered the measures, and changed the course of the king's designs, so he marched for Worcester about the beginning of June 1645. The foot, with a train of forty pieces of cannon, marching into Worcester, the horse stayed behind some time in Gloucestershire.

The first action our army did, was to raise the siege of Chester; Sir William Brereton had besieged it, or rather blocked it up, and when his Majesty came to Worcester, he sent Prince Rupert with 4000 horse and dragoons, with orders to join some foot out of Wales, to raise the siege; but Sir William thought fit to withdraw, and not stay for them, and the town was freed without fighting. The governor took care in this interval to furnish himself with all things necessary for another siege; and, as for ammunition and other necessaries, he was in no want. I was sent with a party into Staffordshire, with design to intercept a convoy of stores coming from London, for the use of Sir William Brereton; but they having some notice of the design, stopped, and went out of the road to Burton-upon-Trent, and so I missed them; but that we might not come back quite empty, we attacked Hawkesley House, and took it, where we got good booty, and brought eighty prisoners back to Worcester. From Worcester the king advanced into Shropshire, and took his headquarters at Bridgnorth.

This was a very happy march of the king's, and had his Majesty proceeded, he had certainly cleared the north once more of his enemies, for the country was generally for him. At his advancing so far as Bridgnorth, Sir William Brereton fled up into Lancashire; the Scots brigades who were with him retreated into the north, while yet the king was above forty miles from them, and all things lay open for conquest. The new generals, Fairfax and Cromwell, lay about Oxford, preparing as if they would besiege it, and gave the king's army so much leisure, that his Majesty might have been at Newcastle before they could have been half way to him. But Heaven, when the ruin of a person or party is determined, always so infatuates their counsels as to make them instrumental to it themselves.

The king let slip this great opportunity, as some thought, intending to break into the associated counties of Northampton, Cambridge, Norfolk, where he had some interests forming. What the design was, we knew not, but the king turns eastward, and marches into Leicestershire, and having treated the country but very indifferently, as having deserved no better of us, laid siege to Leicester.

This was but a short siege; for the king, resolving not to lose time, fell on with his great guns, and having beaten down their works, our foot entered, after a vigorous resistance, and took the town by storm. There was some blood shed here, the town being carried by assault; but it was their own faults; for after the town was taken, the soldiers and townsmen obstinately fought us in the market-place; insomuch that the horse was called to enter the town to clear the streets. But this was not all; I was commanded to advance with these horse, being three regiments, and to enter the town; the foot, who were engaged in the streets, crying out, "Horse, horse." Immediately I advanced to the gate, for we were drawn up about musket-shot from the works, to have supported our foot in case of a sally. Having seized the gate, I placed a guard of horse there, with orders to let nobody pass in or out, and dividing my troops, rode up by two ways towards the market-place. The garrison defending themselves in the market-place, and in the churchyard with great obstinacy, killed us a great many men; but as soon as our horse appeared they demanded quarter, which our foot refused them in the first heat, as is frequent in all nations, in like cases, till at last they threw down their arms, and yielded at discretion; and then I can testify to the world, that fair quarter was given them. I am the more particular in this relation having been an eye-witness of the action, because the king was reproached in all the public libels, with which

those times abounded, for having put a great many to death, and hanged the committee of the Parliament, and some Scots, in cold blood, which was a notorious forgery; and as I am sure there was no such thing done, so I must acknowledge I never saw any inclination in his Majesty to cruelty, or to act anything which was not practised by the general laws of war, and by men of honour in all nations.

But the matter of fact, in respect to the garrison, was as I have related; and, if they had thrown down their arms sooner, they had had mercy sooner; but it was not for a conquering army, entering a town by storm, to offer conditions of quarter in the streets.

Another circumstance was, that a great many of the inhabitants, both men and women, were killed, which is most true; and the case was thus: the inhabitants, to show their over-forward zeal to defend the town, fought in the breach; nay, the very women, to the honour of the Leicester ladies, if they like it, officiously did their parts; and after the town was taken, and when if they had had any brains in their zeal, they would have kept their houses, and been quiet, they fired upon our men out of their windows, and from the tops of their houses, and threw tiles upon their heads; and I had several of my men wounded so, and seven or eight killed. This exasperated us to the last degree; and, finding one house better manned than ordinary, and many shot fired at us out of the windows, I caused my men to attack it, resolved to make them an example for the rest; which they did, and breaking open the doors, they killed all they found there, without distinction; and I appeal to the world if they were to blame. If the Parliament committee, or the Scots deputies were here, they ought to have been quiet, since the town was taken; but they began with us, and, I think, brought it upon themselves. This is the whole case so far as came within my knowledge, for which his Majesty was so much abused.

We took here Colonel Gray and Captain Hacker, and about 300 prisoners, and about 300 more were killed. This was the last day of May 1645.

His Majesty having given over Oxford for lost, continued here some days, viewed the town, ordered the fortifications to be augmented, and prepares to make it the seat of war. But the Parliament, roused at this appearance of the king's army, orders their general to raise the siege of Oxford, where the garrison had, in a sally, ruined some of their works, and killed them 150 men, taking several prisoners, and carrying them with them into the city; and orders him to march towards Leicester, to observe the king.

The king had now a small, but gallant army, all brave tried soldiers, and seemed eager to engage the new-modelled army; and his Majesty, hearing that Sir Thomas Fairfax, having raised the siege of Oxford, advanced towards him, fairly saves him the trouble of a long march, and meets him half way.

The army lay at Daventry, and Fairfax at Towcester, about eight miles off. Here the king sends away 600 horse, with 3000 head of cattle, to relieve his people in Oxford; the cattle he might have spared better than the men. The king having thus victualled Oxford, changes his resolution of fighting Fairfax, to whom Cromwell was now joined with 4000 men, or was within a day's march, and marches northward. This was unhappy counsel, because late given. Had we marched northward at first, we had done it; but thus it was. Now we marched with a triumphing enemy at our heels, and at Naseby their advanced parties attacked our rear. The king, upon this, alters his resolution again, and resolves to fight, and at midnight calls us up at Harborough to come to a council of war. Fate and the king's opinion determined the council of war; and 'twas resolved to fight. Accordingly the van, in which was Prince Rupert's brigade of horse, of which my regiment was a part, counter-marched early in the morning.

By five o'clock in the morning, the whole army, in order of battle, began to descry the enemy from the rising grounds, about a mile from Naseby, and moved towards them. They were drawn up on a little ascent in a large common fallow field, in one line extended from one side of the field to the other, the field something more than a mile over, our army in the same order, in one line, with the reserve.

The king led the main battle of foot, Prince Rupert the right wing of the horse, and Sir Marmaduke Langdale the left. Of the enemy Fairfax and Skippon led the body, Cromwell and Rossiter the right, and Ireton the left, the numbers of both armies so equal, as not to differ 500 men, save that the king had most horse by about 1000, and Fairfax most foot by about 500.

The number was in each army about 18,000 men. The armies coming close up, the wings engaged first. The prince with his right wing charged with his wonted fury, and drove all the Parliament's wing of horse, one division excepted, clear out of the field; Ireton, who commanded this wing, give him his due, rallied often, and fought like a lion; but our wing bore down all before them, and pursued them with a terrible execution.

Ireton seeing one division of his horse left, repaired to them, and keeping his ground, fell foul of a brigade of our foot, who coming up to the head of the line, he like a madman charges them with his horse. But they with their pikes tore him to pieces; so that this division was entirely ruined. Ireton himself, thrust through the thigh with a pike, wounded in the face with a halberd, was unhorsed and taken prisoner.

Cromwell, who commanded the Parliament's right wing, charged Sir Marmaduke Langdale with extraordinary fury, but he, an old tried soldier, stood firm, and received the charge with equal gallantry, exchanging all their shot, carabines and pistols and then fell on sword in hand. Rossiter and Whalley had the better on the point of the wing, and routed two divisions of horse, pushed them behind the reserves, where they rallied and charged again, but were at last defeated; the rest of the horse, now charged in the flank, retreated fighting, and were pushed behind the reserves of foot. While this was doing the foot engaged with equal fierceness, and for two hours there was a terrible fire. The king's foot, backed with gallant officers, and full of rage at the rout of their horse, bore down the enemy's brigade led by Skippon. The old man, wounded, bleeding, retreats to their reserves. All the foot, except the general's brigade, were thus driven

129

into the reserves, where their officers rallied them, and bring them on to a fresh charge; and here the horse, having driven our horse above a quarter of a mile from the foot, face about, and fall in on the rear of the foot.

Had our right wing done thus, the day had been secured; but Prince Rupert, according to his custom, following the flying enemy, never concerned himself with the safety of those behind; and yet he returned sooner than he had done in like cases too. At our return we found all in confusion, our foot broken, all but one brigade, which, though charged in the front, flank and rear, could not be broken till Sir Thomas Fairfax himself came up to the charge with fresh men, and then they were rather cut in pieces than beaten, for they stood with their pikes charged every way to the last extremity.

In this condition, at the distance of a quarter of a mile, we saw the king rallying his horse and preparing to renew the fight; and our wing of horse coming up to him, gave him opportunity to draw up a large body of horse, so large that all the enemy's horse facing us stood still and looked on, but did not think fit to charge us till their foot, who had entirely broken our main battle, were put in order again, and brought up to us.

The officers about the king advised his Majesty rather to draw off; for, since our foot were lost, it would be too much odds to expose the horse to the fury of their whole army, and would but be sacrificing his best troops without any hopes of success. The king, though with great regret at the loss of his foot, yet seeing there was no other hope, took this advice, and retreated in good order to Harborough, and from thence to Leicester.

This was the occasion of the enemy having so great a number of prisoners; for the horse being thus gone off, the foot had no means to make their retreat, and were obliged to yield themselves. Commissary-General Ireton being taken by a captain of foot, makes the captain his prisoner, to save his life, and gives him his liberty for his courtesy before.

Cromwell and Rossiter, with all the enemy's horse, followed us as far as Leicester, and killed all that they could lay hold on straggling from the body, but durst not attempt to charge us in a body. The king, expecting the enemy would come to Leicester, removes to Ashby-de-la Zouch, where we had some time to recollect ourselves.

This was the most fatal action of the whole war, not so much for the loss of our cannon, ammunition, and baggage, of which the enemy boasted so much, but as it was impossible for the king ever to retrieve it. The foot, the best that ever he was master of, could never be supplied; his army in the west was exposed to certain ruin, the north overrun with the Scots; in short, the case grew desperate, and the king was once upon the point of bidding us all disband, and shift for ourselves.

We lost in this fight not above 2000 slain, and the Parliament near as many, but the prisoners were a great number; the whole body of foot being, as I have said, dispersed, there were 4500 prisoners, besides 400 officers, 2000 horses, 12 pieces of cannon, 40 barrels of powder, all the king's baggage, coaches, most of his servants, and his secretary, with his cabinet of letters, of which the Parliament made great improvement, and basely enough caused his private letters--between his Majesty and the queen, her Majesty's letters to the king, and a great deal of such stuff--to be printed.

After this fatal blow, being retreated, as I have said, to Ashby-de-la-Zouch in Leicestershire, the king ordered us to divide; his Majesty, with a body of horse, about 3000, went to Lichfield, and through Cheshire into North Wales, and Sir Marmaduke Langdale, with about 2500, went to Newark.

The king remained in Wales for several months; and though the length of the war had almost drained that country of men, yet the king raised a great many men there, recruited his horse regiments, and got together six or seven regiments of foot, which seemed to look like the beginning of a new army. I had frequent discourses with his Majesty in this low ebb of his affairs, and he would often wish he had not exposed his army at Naseby. I took the freedom once to make a proposition to his Majesty, which, if it had taken effect, I verily believe would have given a new turn to his affairs; and that was, at once to slight all his garrisons in the kingdom, and give private orders to all the soldiers in every place, to join in bodies, and meet at two general rendezvous, which I would have appointed to be, one at Bristol, and one at West Chester. I demonstrated how easily all the forces might reach these two places; and both being strong and wealthy places, and both seaports, he would have a free communication by sea with Ireland, and with his friends abroad; and having Wales entirely his own, he might yet have an opportunity to make good terms for himself, or else have another fair field with the enemy.

Upon a fair calculation of his troops in several garrisons and small bodies dispersed about, I convinced the king, by his own accounts, that he might have two complete armies, each of 25,000 foot, 8000 horse, and 2000 dragoons; that the Lord Goring and the Lord Hopton might ship all their forces, and come by sea in two tides, and be with him in a shorter time than the enemy could follow. With two such bodies he might face the enemy, and make a day of it; but now his men were only sacrificed, and eaten up by piecemeal in a party-war, and spent their lives and estates to do him no service. That if the Parliament garrisoned the towns and castles he should quit, they would lessen their army, and not dare to see him in the field: and if they did not, but left them open, then 'twould be no loss to him, but he might possess them as often as he pleased.

This advice I pressed with such arguments, that the king was once going to despatch orders for the doing it; but to be irresolute in counsel is always the companion of a declining fortune; the king was doubtful, and could not resolve till it was too late.

And yet, though the king's forces were very low, his Majesty was resolved to make one adventure more, and it was a strange one; for, with but a handful of men, he made a desperate march, almost 250 miles in the middle of the whole kingdom, compassed about with armies and parties innumerable, traversed the heart of his enemy's country, entered their associated counties, where no army had ever yet come, and in spite of all their victorious troops facing and following him, alarmed even London itself and returned safe to Oxford.

His Majesty continued in Wales from the battle at Naseby till the 5th or 6th of August, and till he had an account from all parts of the progress of his enemies, and the posture of his own affairs.

Here we found, that the enemy being hard pressed in Somersetshire by the Lord Goring, and Lord Hopton's forces, who had taken Bridgewater, and distressed Taunton, which was now at the point of surrender, they had ordered Fairfax and Cromwell, and the whole army, to march westward to relieve the town; which they did, and Goring's troops were worsted, and himself wounded at the fight at Langport.

The Scots, who were always the dead weight upon the king's affairs, having no more work to do in the north, were, at the Parliament's desire, advanced southward, and then ordered away towards South Wales, and were set down to the siege of Hereford. Here this famous Scotch army spent several months in a fruitless siege, ill provided of ammunition, and worse with money; and having sat near three months before the town, and done little but eaten up the country round them, upon the repeated accounts of the progress of the Marquis of Montrose in that kingdom, and pressing instances of their countrymen, they resolved to raise their siege, and go home to relieve their friends.

The king, who was willing to be rid of the Scots, upon good terms, and therefore to hasten them, and lest they should pretend to push on the siege to take the town first, gives it out, that he was resolved with all his forces to go into Scotland, and join Montrose; and so having secured Scotland, to renew the war from thence.

And accordingly his Majesty marches northwards, with a body of 4000 horse; and, had the king really done this, and with that body of horse marched away (for he had the start of all his enemies, by above a fortnight's march), he had then had the fairest opportunity for a general turn of all his affairs, that he ever had in all the latter part of this war. For Montrose, a gallant daring soldier, who from the least shadow of force in the farthest corner of this country, had, rolling like a snowball, spread all over Scotland, was come into the south parts, and had summoned Edinburgh, frighted away their statesmen, beaten their soldiers at Dundee and other places; and letters and messengers in the heels of one another, repeated their cries to their brethren in England, to lay before them the sad condition of the country, and to hasten the army to their relief. The Scots lords of the enemy's party fled to Berwick, and the chancellor of Scotland goes himself to General Leslie, to press him for help.

In this extremity of affairs Scotland lay when we marched out of Wales. The Scots, at the siege of Hereford, hearing the king was gone northward with his horse, conclude he was gone directly for Scotland, and immediately send Leslie with 4000 horse and foot to follow, but did not yet raise the siege. But the king, still irresolute, turns away to the eastward, and comes to Lichfield, where he showed his resentments at Colonel Hastings for his easy surrender of Leicester.

In this march the enemy took heart. We had troops of horse on every side upon us like hounds started at a fresh stag. Leslie, with the Scots, and a strong body followed in our rear, Major-General Poyntz, Sir John Gell, Colonel Rossiter, and others in our way; they pretended to be 10,000 horse, and yet never durst face us. The Scots made one attempt upon a troop which stayed a little behind, and took some prisoners; but when a regiment of our horse faced them they retired. At a village near Lichfield another party of about 1000 horse attacked my regiment. We were on the left of the army, and at a little too far a distance. I happened to be with the king at that time, and my lieutenant-colonel with me, so that the major had charge of the regiment. He made a very handsome defence, but sent messengers for speedy relief. We were on a march, and therefore all ready, and the king orders me a regiment of dragoons and 300 horse, and the body halted to bring us off, not knowing how strong the enemy might be. When I came to the place I found my major hard laid to, but fighting like a lion. The enemy had broke in upon him in two places, and had routed one troop, cutting them off from the body, and had made them all prisoners. Upon this I fell in with the 300 horse, and cleared my major from a party who charged him in the flank; the dragoons immediately lighting, one party of them comes up on my wing, and saluting the enemy with their muskets, put them to a stand, the other party of dragoons wheeling to the left endeavouring to get behind them. The enemy, perceiving they should be overpowered, retreated in as good order as they could, but left us most of our prisoners, and about thirty of their own. We lost about fifteen of our men, and the enemy about forty, chiefly by the fire of our dragoons in their retreat.

In this posture we continued our march; and though the king halted at Lichfield--which was a dangerous article, having so many of the enemy's troops upon his hands, and this time gave them opportunity to get into a body--yet the Scots, with their General Leslie, resolving for the north, the rest of the troops were not able to face us, till, having ravaged the enemy's country through Staffordshire, Warwick, Leicester, and Nottinghamshire, we came to the leaguer before Newark.

The king was once more in the mind to have gone into Scotland, and called a council of war to that purpose; but then it was resolved by all hands that it would be too late to attempt it, for the Scots and Major-General Poyntz were before us, and several strong bodies of horse in our rear; and there was no venturing now, unless any advantage presented to rout one of those parties which attended us.

Upon these and like considerations we resolved for Newark; on our approach the forces which blocked up that town drew off, being too weak to oppose us, for the king was now above 5000 horse and dragoons, besides 300 horse and dragoons he took with him from Newark.

We halted at Newark to assist the garrison, or give them time rather to furnish themselves from the country with what they wanted, which they were very diligent in doing; for in two days' time they filled a large island which lies under the town, between the two branches of the Trent, with sheep, oxen, cows, and horses, an incredible number; and our affairs being now something desperate, we were not very nice in our usage of the country, for really if it was not with a resolution both to punish the enemy and enrich ourselves, no man can give any rational account why this desperate journey was undertaken. 'Tis certain the Newarkers, in the respite they gained by our coming, got above £50,000 from the country round them in corn, cattle, money, and other plunder.

From hence we broke into Lincolnshire, and the king lay at Belvoir Castle, and from Belvoir Castle to Stamford. The swiftness of our march was a terrible surprise to the enemy; for our van being at a village on the great road called Stilton, the country people fled into the Isle of Ely, and every way, as if all was lost. Indeed our dragoons treated the country very coarsely, and all our men in general made themselves rich. Between Stilton and Huntingdon we had a small bustle with some of the associated troops of horse, but they were soon routed, and fled to Huntingdon, where they gave such an account of us to their fellows that they did not think fit to stay for us, but left their foot to defend themselves as well as they could.

While this was doing in the van a party from Burleigh House, near Stamford, the seat of the Earl of Exeter, pursued four troops of our horse, who, straggling towards Peterborough, and committing some disorders there, were surprised before they could get into a posture of fighting; and encumbered, as I suppose, with their plunder, they were entirely routed, lost most of their horses, and were forced to come away on foot; but finding themselves in this condition, they got in a body into the enclosures, and in that posture turning dragoons, they lined the hedges, and fired upon the enemy with their carabines. This way of fighting, though not very pleasant to troopers, put the enemy's horse to some stand, and encouraged our men to venture into a village, where the enemy had secured forty of their horse; and boldly charging the guard, they beat them

133

off, and recovering those horses, the rest made their retreat good to Wansford Bridge; but we lost near 100 horses, and about twelve of our men taken prisoners.

The next day the king took Huntingdon; the foot which were left in the town, as observed by their horse, had posted themselves at the foot of the bridge, and fortified the pass with such things as the haste and shortness of the time would allow; and in this posture they seemed resolute to defend themselves. I confess, had they in time planted a good force here they might have put a full stop to our little army; for the river is large and deep, the country on the left marshy, full of drains and ditches, and unfit for horse, and we must have either turned back, or took the right hand into Bedfordshire; but here not being above 400 foot, and they forsaken of their horse, the resistance they made was to no other purpose than to give us occasion to knock them on the head, and plunder the town.

However, they defended the bridge, as I have said, and opposed our passage. I was this day in the van, and our forlorn having entered Huntingdon without any great resistance till they came to the bridge, finding it barricaded, they sent me word; I caused the troops to halt, and rode up to the forlorn, to view the countenance of the enemy, and found by the posture they had put themselves in, that they resolved to sell us the passage as dear as they could.

I sent to the king for some dragoons, and gave him account of what I observed of the enemy, and that I judged them to be 1000 men; for I could not particularly see their numbers. Accordingly the king ordered 500 dragoons to attack the bridge, commanded by a major; the enemy had 200 musketeers placed on the bridge, their barricade served them for a breastwork on the front, and the low walls on the bridge served to secure their flanks. Two bodies of their foot were placed on the opposite banks of the river, and a reserve stood in the highway on the rear. The number of their men could not have been better ordered, and they wanted not courage answerable to the conduct of the party. They were commanded by one Bennet, a resolute officer who stood in the front of his men on the bridge with a pike in his hand.

Before we began to fall on, the king ordered to view the river, to see if it was nowhere passable, or any boat to be had; but the river being not fordable, and the boats all secured on the other side, the attack was resolved on, and the dragoons fell on with extraordinary bravery. The foot defended themselves obstinately, and beat off our dragoons twice, and though Bennet was killed upon the spot, and after him his lieutenant, yet their officers relieving them with fresh men they would certainly have beat us all off, had not a venturous fellow, one of our dragoons, thrown himself into the river, swam over, and, in the midst of a shower of musket-bullets, cut the rope which tied a great flat-bottom boat, and brought her over. With the help of this boat, I got over 100 troopers first, and then their horses, and then 200 more without their horses; and with this party fell in with one of the small bodies of foot that were posted on that side, and having routed them, and after them the reserve which stood on the road, I made up to the other party. They stood their ground, and having rallied the runaways of both the other parties, charged me with their pikes, and brought me to a retreat; but by this time the king had sent over 300 men more and they coming up to me, the foot retreated. Those on the bridge finding how 'twas, and having no supplies sent them, as before, fainted, and fled; and the dragoons rushing forward, most of them were killed; about 150 of the enemy were killed, of which all the officers at the bridge, the rest run away.

The town suffered for it, for our men left them little of anything they could carry. Here we halted and raised contributions, took money of the country and of the open towns, to exempt them from plunder. Twice we faced the town of Cambridge, and several of our officers advised his Majesty to storm it. But having no foot, and but 1200 dragoons, wiser heads diverted him from it, and leaving Cambridge on the left, we marched to Woburn, in Bedfordshire, and our parties raised money all over the country quite into Hertfordshire, within five miles of St Alban's.

The swiftness of our march, and uncertainty which way we intended, prevented all possible preparation to oppose us, and we met with no party able to make head against us. From Woburn the king went through Buckingham to Oxford; some of our men straggling in the villages for plunder, were often picked up by the enemy. But in all this long march we did not lose 200 men, got an incredible booty, and brought six waggons laden with money, besides 2000 horses and 3000 head of cattle, into Oxford. From Oxford his Majesty moves again into Gloucestershire, having left about 1500 of his horse at Oxford to scour the country, and raise contributions, which they did as far as Reading. Sir Thomas Fairfax was returned from taking Bridgewater, and was sat down before Bristol, in which Prince Rupert commanded with a strong garrison, 2500 foot and 1000 horse. We had not force enough to attempt anything there. But the Scots, who lay still before Hereford, were afraid of us, having before parted with all their horse under Lieutenant-General Leslie, and but ill stored with provisions; and if we came on their backs, were in a fair way to be starved, or made to buy their provisions at the price of their blood.

His Majesty was sensible of this, and had we had but ten regiments of foot, would certainly have fought the Scots. But we had no foot, or so few as was not worth while to march them. However, the king marched to Worcester, and the Scots, apprehending they should be blocked up, immediately raised the siege, pretending it was to go help their brethren in Scotland, and away they marched northwards.

We picked up some of their stragglers, but they were so poor, had been so ill paid, and so harassed at the siege, that they had neither money nor clothes; and the poor soldiers fed upon apples and roots, and ate the very green corn as it grew in the fields, which reduced them to a very sorry condition of health, for they died like people infected with the plague.

'Twas now debated whether we should yet march for Scotland, but two things prevented--(1.) The plague was broke out there, and multitudes died of it, which made the king backward, and the men more backward. (2.) The Marquis of Montrose, having routed a whole brigade of Leslie's best horse, and carried all before him, wrote to his Majesty that he did not now want assistance, but was in hopes in a few days to send a body of foot into England to his Majesty's assistance. This over-confidence of his was his ruin; for, on the contrary, had he earnestly pressed the king to have marched, and fallen in with his horse, the king had done it, and been absolutely master of Scotland in a fortnight's time; but Montrose was too confident, and defied them all, till at last they got their forces together, and Leslie with his horse out of England, and worsted him in two or three encounters, and then never left him till they drove him out of Scotland. While his Majesty stayed at Worcester, several messengers came to him from Cheshire for relief, being exceedingly straitened by the forces of the Parliament; in order to which the king marched, but Shrewsbury being in the enemy's hands, he was obliged to go round by Ludlow, where he was joined by some foot out of Wales. I took this opportunity to ask his Majesty's leave to go by Shrewsbury to my father's, and, taking only two servants, I left the army two days before they marched.

This was the most unsoldier-like action that ever I was guilty of, to go out of the army to pay a visit when a time of action was just at hand; and, though I protest I had not the least intimation, no, not from my own thoughts, that the army would engage, at least before they came to Chester, before which I intended to meet them, yet it looked so ill, so like an excuse or a sham of cowardice, or disaffection to the cause and to my master's interest, or something I know not what, that I could not bear to think of it, nor never had the heart to see the king's face after it.

From Ludlow the king marched to relieve Chester. Poyntz, who commanded the Parliament's forces, follows the king, with design to join with the forces before Chester, under Colonel Jones, before the king could come up. To that end Poyntz passes through Shrewsbury the day that the king marched from Ludlow; yet the king's forces got the start of him, and forced him to engage. Had the king engaged him but three hours sooner, and consequently farther off from Chester, he had ruined him, for Poyntz's men, not able to stand the shock of the king's horse, gave ground, and would in half-an-hour more have been beaten out of the field; but Colonel Jones, with a strong party from the camp, which was within two miles; comes up in the heat of the action, falls on in the king's rear, and turned the scale of the day. The body was, after an obstinate fight, defeated, and a great many gentlemen of quality killed and taken prisoners. The Earl of Lichfield was of the number of the former, and sixty-seven officers of the latter, with 1000 others. The king, with about 500 horse, got into Chester, and from thence into Wales, whither all that could get away made up to him as fast as they could, but in a bad condition. This was the last stroke they struck; the rest of the war was nothing but taking all his garrisons from him one by one, till they finished the war with the captivating his person, and then, for want of other business, fell to fighting with one another.

I was quite disconsolate at the news of this last action, and the more because I was not there. My regiment wholly dispersed, my lieutenant-colonel, a gentleman of a good family, and a near relation to my mother, was prisoner, my major and three captains killed, and most of the rest prisoners.

The king, hopeless of any considerable party in Wales, Bristol being surrendered, sends for Prince Rupert and Prince Maurice, who came to him. With them, and the Lord Digby, Sir Marmaduke Langdale, and a great train of gentlemen, his Majesty marches to Newark again, leaves 1000 horse with Sir William Vaughan to attempt the relief of Chester, in doing whereof he was routed the second time by Jones and his men, and entirely dispersed.

The chief strength the king had in these parts was at Newark, and the Parliament were very earnest with the Scots to march southward and to lay siege to Newark; and while the Parliament pressed them to it, and they sat still and delayed it, several heats began, and some ill blood between them, which afterwards broke out into open war. The English reproached the Scots with pretending to help them, and really hindering their affairs. The Scots returned that they came to fight for them, and are left to be starved, and can neither get money nor clothes. At last they came to this, the Scots will come to the siege if the Parliament will send them money, but not before. However, as people sooner agree in doing ill than in doing well, they came to terms, and the Scots came with their whole army to the siege of Newark.

The king, foreseeing the siege, calls his friends about him, tells them he sees his circumstances are such that they can help him but little, nor he protect them, and advises them to separate. The Lord Digby, with Sir Marmaduke Langdale, with a strong body of horse, attempt to get into Scotland to join with Montrose, who was still in the Highlands, though reduced to a low ebb, but these gentlemen are fallen upon on every side and routed, and at last, being totally broken and dispersed, they fly to the Earl of Derby's protection in the Isle of Man.

Prince Rupert, Prince Maurice, Colonel Gerard, and above 400 gentlemen, all officers of horse, lay their commissions down, and seizing upon Wootton House for a retreat, make proposals to the Parliament to leave the kingdom, upon their parole not to return again in arms against the Parliament, which was accepted, though afterwards the prince declined it. I sent my man post to the prince to be included in this treaty, and for leave for all that would accept of like conditions, but they had given in the list of their names, and could not alter it.

This was a sad time. The poor remains of the king's fortunes went everywhere to wreck. Every garrison of the enemy was full of the Cavalier prisoners, and every garrison the king had was beset with enemies, either blocked up or besieged. Goring and the Lord Hopton were the only remainders of the king's forces which kept in a body, and Fairfax was pushing them with all imaginable vigour with his whole army about Exeter and other parts of Devonshire and Cornwall.

In this condition the king left Newark in the night, and got to Oxford. The king had in Oxford 8000 men, and the towns of Banbury, Farringdon, Donnington Castle, and such places as might have been brought together in twenty-four hours, 15,000 or 20,000 men, with which, if he had then resolved to have quitted the place, and collected the forces in Worcester, Hereford, Lichfield, Ashby-de-la-Zouch, and all the small castles and garrisons he had thereabouts, he might have had near 40,000 men, might have beaten the Scots from Newark, Colonel Jones from Chester, and all, before Fairfax, who was in the west, could be able to come to their relief.

And this his Majesty's friends in North Wales had concerted; and, in order to it, Sir Jacob Ashby gathered what forces he could, in our parts, and attempted to join the king at Oxford, and to have proposed it to him; but Sir Jacob was entirely routed at Stow-on-the-Wold, and taken prisoner, and of 3000 men not above 600 came to Oxford. All the king's garrisons dropped one by one; Hereford, which had stood out against the whole army of the Scots, was surprised by six men and a lieutenant dressed up for country labourers, and a constable pressed to work, who cut the guards in pieces, and let in a party of the enemy. Chester was reduced by famine, all the attempts the king made to relieve it being frustrated.

Sir Thomas Fairfax routed the Lord Hopton at Torrington, and drove him to such extremities, that he was forced up into the farthest corner of Cornwall. The Lord Hopton had a gallant body of horse with him of nine brigades, but no foot; Fairfax, a great army.

Heartless, and tired out with continual ill news, and ill success, I had frequent meetings with some gentlemen who had escaped from the rout of Sir William Vaughan, and we agreed upon a meeting at Worcester, of all the friends we could get, to see if we could raise a body fit to do any service; or, if not, to consider what was to be done. At this meeting we had almost as many opinions as people; our strength appeared too weak to make any attempt, the game was too far gone in our parts to be retrieved; all we could make up did not amount to above 800 horse.

'Twas unanimously agreed not to go into the Parliament as long as our royal master did not give up the cause; but in all places, and by all possible methods, to do him all the service we could. Some proposed one thing, some another; at last we proposed getting vessels to carry us to the Isle of Man to the Earl of Derby, as Sir Marmaduke Langdale, Lord Digby, and others had done. I did not foresee any service it would be to the king's affairs, but I started a proposal that, marching to Pembroke in a body, we should there seize upon all the vessels we could, and embarking ourselves, horses, and what foot we could get, cross the Severn Sea, and land in

Cornwall to the assistance of Prince Charles, who was in the army of the Lord Hopton, and where only there seemed to be any possibility of a chance for the remaining part of our cause.

This proposal was not without its difficulties, as how to get to the seaside, and, when there, what assurance of shipping. The enemy, under Major-General Langhorn, had overrun Wales, and 'twould be next to impossible to effect it.

We could never carry our proposal with the whole assembly; but, however, about 200 of us resolved to attempt it, and [the] meeting being broken up without coming to any conclusion, we had a private meeting among ourselves to effect it.

We despatched private messengers to Swansea and Pembroke, and other places; but they all discouraged us from the attempt that way, and advised us to go higher towards North Wales where the king's interest had more friends, and the Parliament no forces. Upon this we met, and resolved, and having sent several messengers that way, one of my men provided us two small vessels in a little creek near Harlech Castle, in Merionethshire. We marched away with what expedition we could, and embarked in the two vessels accordingly. It was the worst voyage sure that ever man went; for first we had no manner of accommodation for so many people, hay for our horses we got none, or very little, but good store of oats, which served us for our own bread as well as provender for the horses.

In this condition we put off to sea, and had a fair wind all the first night, but early in the morning a sudden storm drove us within two or three leagues of Ireland. In this pickle, sea-sick, our horses rolling about upon one another, and ourselves stifled for want of room, no cabin nor beds, very cold weather, and very indifferent diet, we wished ourselves ashore again a thousand times; and yet we were not willing to go ashore in Ireland if we could help it; for the rebels having possession of every place, that was just having our throats cut at once. Having rolled about at the mercy of the winds all day, the storm ceasing in the evening, we had fair weather again, but wind enough, which being large, in two days and a night we came upon the coast of Cornwall, and, to our no small comfort, landed the next day at St Ives, in the county of Cornwall.

We rested ourselves here, and sent an express to the Lord Hopton, who was then in Devonshire, of our arrival, and desired him to assign us quarters, and send us his farther orders. His lordship expressed a very great satisfaction at our arrival, and left it to our own conduct to join him as we saw convenient.

We were marching to join him, when news came that Fairfax had given him an entire defeat at Torrington. This was but the old story over again. We had been used to ill news a great while, and 'twas the less surprise to us.

Upon this news we halted at Bodmin, till we should hear farther; and it was not long before we saw a confirmation of the news before our eyes, for the Lord Hopton, with the remainder of his horse, which he had brought off at Torrington in a very shattered condition, retreated to Launceston, the first town in Cornwall, and hearing that Fairfax pursued him, came on to Bodmin. Hither he summoned all the troops which he had left, which, when he had got together, were a fine body indeed of 5000 horse, but few foot but what were at Pendennis, Barnstaple, and other garrisons. These were commanded by the Lord Hopton. The Lord Goring had taken shipping for France to get relief a few days before.

138

Here a grand council of war was called, and several things were proposed, but as it always is in distress, people are most irresolute, so 'twas here.

Some were for breaking through by force, our number being superior to the enemy's horse. To fight them with their foot would be desperation and ridiculous; and to retreat would but be to coop up themselves in a narrow place, where at last they must be forced to fight upon disadvantage, or yield at mercy. Others opposed this as a desperate action, and without probability of success, and all were of different opinions. I confess, when I saw how things were, I saw 'twas a lost game, and I was for the opinion of breaking through, and doing it now, while the country was open and large, and not being forced to it when it must be with more disadvantage. But nothing was resolved on, and so we retreated before the enemy. Some small skirmishes there happened near Bodmin, but none that were very considerable.

'Twas the 1st of March when we quitted Bodmin, and quartered at large at Columb, St Dennis, and Truro, and the enemy took his quarters at Bodmin, posting his horse at the passes from Padstow on the north, to Wadebridge, Lostwithiel, and Fowey, spreading so from sea to sea, that now breaking through was impossible. There was no more room for counsel; for unless we had ships to carry us off, we had nothing to do but when we were fallen upon, to defend ourselves, and sell victory as dear as we could to the enemies.

The Prince of Wales seeing the distress we were in, and loth to fall into the enemy's hands, ships himself on board some vessels at Falmouth, with about 400 lords and gentlemen. And as I had no command here to oblige my attendance, I was once going to make one, but my comrades, whom I had been the principal occasion of bringing hither, began to take it ill, that I would leave them, and so I resolved we would take our fate together.

While thus we had nothing before us but a soldier's death, a fair field, and a strong enemy, and people began to look one upon another, the soldiers asked how their officers looked, and the officers asked how their soldiers looked, and every day we expected to be our last, when unexpectedly the enemy's general sent a trumpet to Truro to my Lord Hopton, with a very handsome gentlemanlike offer:--

That since the general could not be ignorant of his present condition, and that the place he was in could not afford him subsistence or defence; and especially considering that the state of our affairs were such, that if we should escape from thence we could not remove to our advantage, he had thought good to let us know, that if we would deliver up our horses and arms, he would, for avoiding the effusion of Christian blood, or the putting any unsoldierly extremities upon us, allow such honourable and safe conditions, as were rather better than our present circumstances could demand, and such as should discharge him to all the world, as a gentleman, as a soldier, and as a Christian.

After this followed the conditions he would give us, which were as follows, viz.:--That all the soldiery, as well English as foreigners, should have liberty to go beyond the seas, or to their own dwellings, as they pleased; and to such as shall choose to live at home, protection for their liberty, and from all violence and plundering of soldiers, and to give them bag and baggage, and all their goods, except horses and arms. That for officers in commissions, and gentlemen of quality, he would allow them horses for themselves and one servant, or more, suitable to their quality, and such arms as are suitable to gentlemen of such quality travelling in times of peace; and such officers as would go beyond sea, should take with them their full arms and number of horses as are allowed in the army to such officers.

That all the troopers shall receive on the delivery of their horses, 20s. a man to carry them home; and the general's pass and recommendation to any gentleman who desires to go to the Parliament to settle the composition for their estates.

Lastly, a very honourable mention of the general, and offer of their mediation to the Parliament, to treat him as a man of honour, and one who has been tender of the country, and behaved himself with all the moderation and candour that could be expected from an enemy.

Upon the unexpected receipt of this message, a council of war was called, and the letter read; no man offered to speak a word; the general moved it, but every one was loth to begin.

At last an old colonel starts up, and asked the general what he thought might occasion the writing this letter? The general told him, he could not tell; but he could tell, he was sure, of one thing, that he knew what was not the occasion of it, viz., that is, not any want of force in their army to oblige us to other terms. Then a doubt was started, whether the king and Parliament were not in any treaty, which this agreement might be prejudicial to.

This occasioned a letter to my Lord Fairfax, wherein our general returning the civilities and neither accepting nor refusing his proposal, put it upon his honour, whether there was not some agreement or concession between his Majesty and the Parliament, in order to a general peace, which this treaty might be prejudicial to, or thereby be prejudicial to us. The Lord Fairfax ingenuously declared, he had heard the king had made some concessions, and he heartily wished he would make such as would settle the kingdom in peace, that Englishmen might not wound and destroy one another; but that he declared he knew of no treaty commenced, nor anything passed which could give us the least shadow of hope for any advantage in not accepting his conditions; at last telling us, that though he did not insult over our circumstances, yet if we thought fit, upon any such supposition, to refuse his offers, he was not to seek in his measures.

And it appeared so, for he immediately advanced his forlorns, and dispossessed us of two advanced quarters, and thereby straitened us yet more.

We had now nothing to say, but treat, and our general was so sensible of our condition that he returned the trumpet with a safe-conduct for commissioners at twelve o'clock that night upon which a cessation of arms was agreed on, we quitting Truro to the Lord Fairfax, and he left St Allen to us to keep our headquarters.

The conditions were soon agreed on; we disbanded nine full brigades of horse, and all the conditions were observed with the most honour and care by the enemy that ever I saw in my life.

Nor can I omit to make very honourable mention of this noble gentleman, though I did not like his cause; but I never saw a man of a more pleasant, calm, courteous, downright, honest behaviour in my life; and for his courage and personal bravery in the field, that we had felt enough of. No man in the world had more fire and fury in him while in action, or more temper and softness out of it. In short, and I cannot do him greater honour, he exceedingly came near the character of my foreign hero, Gustavus Adolphus, and in my account is, of all the soldiers in Europe, the fittest to be reckoned in the second place of honour to him.

I had particular occasion to see much of his temper in all this action, being one of the hostages given by our general for the performance of the conditions, in which circumstance the general did me several times the honour to send to me to dine with him; and was exceedingly pleased to discourse with me about the passages of the wars in Germany, which I had served in, he having been at the same time in the Low Countries in the service of Prince Maurice; but I observed if at any time my civilities extended to commendations of his own actions, and especially to comparing him to Gustavus Adolphus, he would blush like a woman, and be uneasy, declining the discourse, and in this he was still more like him.

Let no man scruple my honourable mention of this noble enemy, since no man can suspect me of favouring the cause he embarked in, which I served as heartily against as any man in the army; but I cannot conceal extraordinary merit for its being placed in an enemy.

This was the end of our making war, for now we were all under parole never to bear arms against the Parliament; and though some of us did not keep our word, yet I think a soldier's parole ought to be the most sacred in such case, that a soldier may be the easier trusted at all times upon his word. For my part, I went home fully contented, since I could do my royal master no better service, that I had come off no worse.

The enemy going now on in a full current of success, and the king reduced to the last extremity, and Fairfax, by long marches, being come back within five miles of Oxford, his Majesty, loth to be cooped up in a town which could on no account hold long out, quits the town in a disguise, leaving Sir Thomas Clemham governor, and being only attended with Mr Ashburnham and one more, rides away to Newark, and there fatally committed himself to the honour and fidelity of the Scots under General Leven.

There had been some little bickering between the Parliament and the Scots commissioners concerning the propositions which the Scots were for a treaty with the king upon, and the Parliament refused it. The Parliament, upon all proposals of peace, had formerly invited the king to come and throw himself upon the honour, fidelity, and affection of his Parliament.

And now the king from Oxford offering to come up to London on the protection of the Parliament for the safety of his person, they refused him, and the Scots differed from them in it, and were for a personal treaty. This, in our opinion, was the reason which prompted the king to throw himself upon the fidelity of the Scots, who really by their infidelity had been the ruin of all his affairs, and now, by their perfidious breach of honour and faith with him, will be virtually and mediately the ruin of his person.

The Scots were, as all the nation besides them was, surprised at the king's coming among them; the Parliament began very high with them, and send an order to General Leven to send the king to Warwick Castle; but he was not so hasty to part with so rich a prize. As soon as the king came to the general, he signs an order to Colonel Bellasis, the governor of Newark, to surrender it, and immediately the Scots decamp homewards, carrying the king in the camp with them, and marching on, a house was ordered to be provided for the king at Newcastle.

And now the Parliament saw their error, in refusing his Majesty a personal treaty, which, if they had accepted (their army was not yet taught the way of huffing their masters), the kingdom might have been settled in peace.

Upon this the Parliament send to General Leven to have his Majesty not be sent, which was their first language, but be suffered to come to London to treat with his Parliament; before it was, "Let the king be sent to Warwick Castle"; now 'tis, "To let his Majesty come to London to treat with his people."

But neither one or the other would do with the Scots; but we who knew the Scots best knew that there was one thing would do with them, if the other would not, and that was money, and therefore our hearts ached for the king.

The Scots, as I said, had retreated to Newcastle with the king, and there they quartered their whole army at large upon the country; the Parliament voted they had no farther occasion for the Scots, and desired them to go home about their business. I do not say it was in these words, but in whatsoever good words their messages might be expressed, this and nothing less was the English of it. The Scots reply, by setting forth their losses, damages, and dues, the substance of which was, "Pay us our money and we will be gone, or else we won't stir." The Parliament call for an account of their demands, which the Scots give in, amounting to a million; but, according to their custom, and especially finding that the army under Fairfax inclined gradually that way, fall down to £500,000, and at last to

£400,000; but all the while this is transacting a separate treaty is carried on at London with the commissioners of Scotland, and afterwards at Edinburgh, by which it is given them to understand that, whereas upon payment of the money, the Scots army is to march out of England, and to give up all the towns and garrisons which they hold in this kingdom, so they are to take it for granted that 'tis the meaning of the treaty that they shall leave the king in the hands of the English Parliament.

To make this go down the better, the Scotch Parliament, upon his Majesty's desire to go with their army into Scotland, send him for answer, that it cannot be for the safety of his Majesty or of the State to come into Scotland, not having taken the Covenant, and this was carried in their Parliament but by two voices.

The Scots having refused his coming into Scotland, as was concerted between the two Houses, and their army being to march out of England, the delivering up the king became consequence of the thing--unavoidable, and of necessity.

His Majesty, thus deserted of those into whose hands he had thrown himself, took his leave of the Scots general at Newcastle, telling him only, in few words, this sad truth, that he was bought and sold. The Parliament commissioners received him at Newcastle from the Scots, and brought him to Holmby House, in Northamptonshire; from whence, upon the quarrels and feuds of parties, he was fetched by a party of horse, commanded by one Cornet Joyce, from the army, upon their mutinous rendezvous at Triplow Heath; and, after this, suffering many violences and varieties of circumstances among the army, was carried to Hampton Court, from whence his Majesty very readily made his escape; but not having notice enough to provide effectual means for his more effectual deliverance, was obliged to deliver himself to Colonel Hammond in the Isle of Wight. Here, after some very indifferent usage, the Parliament pursued a farther treaty with him, and all points were agreed but two: the entire abolishing Episcopacy, which the king declared to be against his conscience and his coronation oath; and the sale of the Church lands, which he declared, being most of them gifts to God and the Church, by persons deceased, his Majesty thought could not be alienated without the highest sacrilege, and if taken from the uses to which they were appointed by the wills of the donors, ought to be restored back to the heirs and families of the persons who bequeathed them.

And these two articles so stuck with his Majesty, that he ventured his fortune, and royal family, and his own life for them. However, at last, the king condescended so far in these, that the Parliament voted his Majesty's concessions to be sufficient to settle and establish the peace of the nation.

This vote discovered the bottom of all the counsels which then prevailed; for the army, who knew if peace were once settled, they should be undone, took the alarm at this, and clubbing together in committees and councils, at last brought themselves to a degree of hardness above all that ever this nation saw; for calling into question the proceedings of their masters who employed them, they immediately fall to work upon the Parliament, remove Colonel Hammond, who had the charge of the king, and used him honourably, place a new guard upon him, dismiss the commissioners, and put a stop to the treaty; and, following their blow, march to London, place regiments of foot at the Parliament-house door, and, as the members came up, seize upon all those whom they had down in a list as promoters of the settlement and treaty, and would not suffer them to sit; but the rest who, being of their own stamp, are permitted to go on, carry on the designs of the army, revive their votes of non-addresses to the king, and then, upon the army's petition to bring all delinquents to justice, the mask was thrown off, the word all is declared to be meant the king, as well as every man else they pleased. 'Tis too sad a story, and too much a matter of grief to me, and to all good men, to renew the blackness of those days, when law and justice was under the feet of power; the army ruled the Parliament, the private officers their generals, the common soldiers their officers, and confusion was in every part of the government. In this hurry they sacrificed their king, and shed the blood of the English nobility without mercy. The history of the times will supply the particulars which I omit, being willing to confine myself to my own accounts and observations. I was now no more an actor, but a melancholy observator of the misfortunes of the times. I had given my parole not to take up arms against the Parliament, and I saw nothing to invite me to engage on their side. I saw a world of confusion in all their counsels, and I always expected that in a chain of distractions, as it generally falls out, the last link would be destruction; and though I pretended to no prophecy, yet the progress of affairs have brought it to pass, and I have seen Providence, who suffered, for the correction of this nation, the sword to govern and devour us, has at last brought destruction by the sword upon the head of most of the party who first drew it.

* * * * *

If together with the brief account of what concern I had in the active part of the war, I leave behind me some of my own remarks and observations, it may be pertinent enough to my design, and not unuseful to posterity.

1. I observed by the sequel of things that it may be some excuse to the first Parliament, who began this war, to say that they manifested their designs were not aimed at the monarchy, nor their quarrel at the person of the king; because, when they had in their power, though against his will, they would have restored both his person and dignity as a king, only loading it with such clogs of the people's power as they at first pretended to, viz., the militia, and power of naming the great officers at court, and the like; which powers, it was never denied, had been stretched too far in the beginning of this king's reign, and several things done illegally, which his Majesty had been sensible of, and was willing to rectify; but they having obtained the power by victory, resolved so to secure themselves, as that, whenever they laid down their arms, the king should not be able to do the like again. And thus far they were not to be so much blamed, and we did not on our own part blame them, when they had obtained the power, for parting with it on good

terms. But when I have thus far advocated for the enemies, I must be very free to state the crimes of this bloody war by the events of it. 'Tis manifest there were among them from the beginning a party who aimed at the very root of the government, and at the very thing which they brought to pass, viz., the deposing and murdering of their sovereign; and, as the devil is always master where mischief is the work, this party prevailed, turned the other out of doors, and overturned all that little honesty that might be in the first beginning of this unhappy strife.

The consequence of this was, the Presbyterians saw their error when it was too late, and then would gladly have joined the royal party to have suppressed this new leaven which had infected the lump; and this is very remarkable, that most of the first champions of this war who bore the brunt of it, when the king was powerful and prosperous, and when there was nothing to be got by it but blows, first or last, were so ill used by this independent, powerful party, who tripped up the heels of all their honesty, that they were either forced by ill treatment to take up arms on our side, or suppressed and reduced by them. In this the justice of Providence seemed very conspicuous, that these having pushed all things by violence against the king, and by arms and force brought him to their will, were at once both robbed of the end, their Church government, and punished for drawing their swords against their masters, by their own servants drawing the sword against them; and God, in His due time, punished the others too. And what was yet farther strange, the punishment of this crime of making war against their king, singled out those very men, both in the army and in the Parliament, who were the greatest champions of the Presbyterian cause in the council and in the field. Some minutes, too, of circumstances I cannot forbear observing, though they are not very material, as to the fatality and revolutions of days and times. A Roman Catholic gentleman of Lancashire, a very religious man in his way, who had kept a calculate of times, and had observed mightily the fatality of times, places, and actions being at my father's house, was discoursing once upon the just judgment of God in dating His providences, so as to signify to us His displeasure at particular circumstances; and, among an infinite number of collections he had made, these were some which I took particular notice of and from whence I began to observe the like:-- 1. That King Edward VI. died the very same day of the same month in which he caused the altar to be taken down, and the image of the Blessed Virgin in the Cathedral of St Paul's.

2. That Cranmer was burnt at Oxford the same day and month that he gave King Henry VIII. advice to divorce his Queen Catherine.

3. That Queen Elizabeth died the same day and month that she resolved, in her Privy Council, to behead the Queen of Scots.

4. That King James died the same day that he published his book against Bellarmine.

5. That King Charles's long Parliament, which ruined him, began the very same day and month which that Parliament began, that at the request of his predecessor robbed the Roman Church of all her revenues, and suppressed abbeys and monasteries.

How just his calculations were, or how true the matter of fact, I cannot tell, but it put me upon the same in several actions and successes of this war.

And I found a great many circumstances, as to time or action, which befell both his Majesty and his parties first;

Then others which befell the Parliament and Presbyterian faction, which raised the war

144

Then the Independent tyranny which succeeded and supplanted the first party;

Then the Scots who acted on both sides;

Lastly, the restoration and re-establishment of the loyalty and religion of our ancestors.

1. For King Charles I.; 'tis observable, that the charge against the Earl of Strafford, a thing which his Majesty blamed himself for all the days of his life, and at the moment of his last suffering, was first read in the Lords' House on the 30th of January, the same day of the month six years that the king himself was brought to the block.

2. That the king was carried away prisoner from Newark, by the Scots, May 10, the same day six years that, against his conscience and promise, he passed the bill of attainder against the loyal, noble Earl of Strafford.

3. The same day seven years that the king entered the House of Commons for the five members, which all his friends blamed him for, the same day the Rump voted bringing his Majesty to trial, after they had set by the Lords for not agreeing to it, which was the 3rd of January 1648.

4. The 12th of May 1646, being the surrender of Newark, the Parliament held a day of thanksgiving and rejoicing, for the reduction of the king and his party, and finishing the war, which was the same day five years that the Earl of Strafford was beheaded.

5. The battle at Naseby, which ruined the king's affairs, and where his secretary and his office was taken, was the 14th of June, the same day and month the first commission was given out by his Majesty to raise forces.

6. The queen voted a traitor by the Parliament the 3rd of May, the same day and month she carried the jewels into France.

7. The same day the king defeated Essex in the west, his son, King Charles II., was defeated at Worcester.

8. Archbishop Laud's house at Lambeth assaulted by the mob, the same day of the same month that he advised the king to make war upon the Scots.

9. Impeached the 15th of December 1640, the same day twelvemonth that he ordered the Common Prayer-book of Scotland to be printed, in order to be imposed upon the Scots, from which all our troubles began. But many more, and more strange, are the critical junctures of affairs in the case of the enemy, or at least more observed by me:--

1. Sir John Hotham, who repulsed his Majesty and refused him admittance into Hull before the war, was seized at Hull by the same Parliament for whom he had done it, the same 10th day of August two years that he drew the first blood in that war.

2. Hampden of Buckinghamshire killed the same day one year that the mob petition from Bucks was presented to the king about him, as one of the five members.

3. Young Captain Hotham executed the 1st of January, the same day that he assisted Sir Thomas Fairfax in the first skirmish with the king's forces at Bramham Moor.

145

4. The same day and month, being the 6th of August 1641, that the Parliament voted to raise an army against the king, the same day and month, anno 1648, the Parliament were assaulted and turned out of doors by that very army, and none left to sit but who the soldiers pleased which were therefore called the Rump.

5. The Earl of Holland deserted the king, who had made him general of the horse, and went over to the Parliament, and the 9th of March 1641, carried the Commons' reproaching declaration to the king; and afterwards taking up arms for the king against the Parliament, was beheaded by them the 9th of March 1648, just seven years after.

6. The Earl of Holland was sent by the king to come to his assistance and refused, the 11th of July 1641, and that very day seven years after was taken by the Parliament at St Neots.

7. Colonel Massey defended Gloucester against the king, and beat him off the 5th of September 1643; was taken after by Cromwell's men fighting for the king, on the 5th of September 1651, two or three days after the fight at Worcester. 8. Richard Cromwell resigning because he could not help it, the Parliament voted a free Commonwealth, without a single person or House of Lords. This was the 25th of May 1658; the 25th of May 1660, the king landed at Dover, and restored the government of a single person and House of Lords.

9. Lambert was proclaimed a traitor by the Parliament April the 20th, being the same day he proposed to Oliver Cromwell to take upon him the title of king.

10. Monk being taken prisoner at Nantwich by Sir Thomas Fairfax, revolted to the Parliament the same day nineteen years he declared for the king, and thereby restored the royal authority.

11. The Parliament voted to approve of Sir John Hotham's repulsing the king at Hull the 28th of April 1642; the 28th of April 1660, the Parliament first debated in the House the restoring the king to the crown.

12. The agitators of the army formed themselves into a cabal, and held their first meeting to seize on the king's person, and take him into their custody from Holmby, the 28th of April 1647; the same day, 1660, the Parliament voted the agitators to be taken into custody, and committed as many of them as could be found.

13. The Parliament voted the queen a traitor for assisting her husband, the king, May the 3rd, 1643; her son, King Charles II., was presented with the votes of Parliament to restore him, and the present of £50,000, the 3rd of May 1660.

14. The same day the Parliament passed the Act for recognition of Oliver Cromwell, October 13th, 1654, Lambert broke up the Parliament and set up the army, 1659, October the 13th.

Some other observations I have made, which, as not so pertinent, I forbear to publish among which I have noted the fatality of some days to parties, as-- The 2nd of September: The fight at Dunbar; the fight at Worcester; the oath against a single person passed; Oliver's first Parliament called. For the enemy.

The 2nd of September: Essex defeated in Cornwall; Oliver died; city works demolished. For the king.

The 29th of May: Prince Charles born; Leicester taken by storm; King Charles II. restored. Ditto.

Fatality of circumstances in this unhappy war, as--

1. The English Parliament call in the Scots, to invade their king, and are invaded themselves by the same Scots, in defence of the king whose case, and the design of the Parliament, the Scots had mistaken.

2. The Scots, who unjustly assisted the Parliament to conquer their lawful sovereign, contrary to their oath of allegiance, and without any pretence on the king's part, are afterwards absolutely conquered and subdued by the same Parliament they assisted.

3. The Parliament, who raised an army to depose their king, deposed by the very army they had raised.

4. The army broke three Parliaments, and are at last broke by a free Parliament; and all they had done by the military power, undone at once by the civil.

5. Abundance of the chief men, who by their fiery spirits involved the nation in a civil war, and took up arms against their prince, first or last met with ruin or disgrace from their own party.

(1.) Sir John Hotham and his son, who struck the first stroke, both beheaded or hanged by the Parliament. (2.) Major-General Massey three times taken prisoner by them, and once wounded at Worcester.

(3.) Major-General Langhorn, (4.) Colonel Poyer, and (5.) Colonel Powell, changed sides, and at last taken, could obtain no other favour than to draw lots for their lives; Colonel Poyer drew the dead lot, and was shot to death.

(6.) Earl of Holland: who, when the House voted who should be reprieved, Lord Goring, who had been their worst enemy, or the Earl of Holland, who excepting one offence, had been their constant servant, voted Goring to be spared, and the Earl to die.

(7.) The Earl of Essex, their first general; (8.) Sir William Waller;

(9.) Lieutenant-General Ludlow; (10.) The Earl of Manchester;

--all disgusted and voted out of the army, though they had stood the first shock of the war, to make way for the new model of the army, and introduce a party.

* * * * *

In all these confusions I have observed two great errors, one of the king, and one of his friends.

Of the king, that when he was in their custody, and at their mercy, he did not comply with their propositions of peace, before their army, for want of employment, fell into heats and mutinies; that he did not at first grant the Scots their own conditions, which, if he had done, he had gone into Scotland; and then, if the English would have fought the Scots for him, he had a reserve of his loyal friends, who would have had room to have fallen in with the Scots to his assistance, who were after dispersed and destroyed in small parties attempting to serve him.

While his Majesty remained at Newcastle, the queen wrote to him, persuading him to make peace upon any terms; and in politics her Majesty's advice was certainly the best. For, however low he was brought by a peace, it must have been better than the condition he was then in.

The error I mention of the king's friends was this, that after they saw all was lost, they could not be content to sit still, and reserve themselves for better fortunes, and wait the happy time when the divisions of the enemy would bring them to certain ruin; but must hasten their own miseries by frequent fruitless risings, in the face of a victorious enemy, in small parties; and I always found these effects from it:--

1. The enemy, who were always together by the ears, when they were let alone, were united and reconciled when we gave them any interruption; as particularly, in the case of the first assault the army made upon them, when Colonel Pride, with his regiment, garbled the House, as they called it. At that time a fair opportunity offered; but it was omitted till it was too late. That insult upon the House had been attempted the year before, but was hindered by the little insurrection of the royal party, and the sooner they had fallen out, the better.

2. These risings being desperate, with vast disadvantages, and always suppressed, ruined all our friends; the remnants of the Cavaliers were lessened, the stoutest and most daring were cut off, and the king's interest exceedingly weakened, there not being less than 30,000 of his best friends cut off in the several attempts made at Maidstone, Colchester, Lancashire, Pembroke, Pontefract, Kingston, Preston, Warrington, Worcester, and other places. Had these men all reserved their fortunes to a conjunction with the Scots, at either of the invasions they made into this kingdom, and acted with the conduct and courage they were known masters of, perhaps neither of those Scots armies had been defeated.

But the impatience of our friends ruined all; for my part, I had as good a mind to put my hand to the ruin of the enemy as any of them, but I never saw any tolerable appearance of a force able to match the enemy, and I had no mind to be beaten and then hanged. Had we let them alone, they would have fallen into so many parties and factions, and so effectually have torn one another to pieces, that whichsoever party had come to us, we should, with them, have been too hard for all the rest.

This was plain by the course of things afterwards; when the Independent army had ruffled the Presbyterian Parliament, the soldiery of that party made no scruple to join us, and would have restored the king with all their hearts, and many of them did join us at last.

And the consequence, though late, ended so; for they fell out so many times, army and Parliament, Parliament and army, and alternately pulled one another down so often till at last the Presbyterians who began the war, ended it, and, to be rid of their enemies, rather than for any love to the monarchy, restored King Charles the Second, and brought him in on the very day that they themselves had formerly resolved the ruin of his father's government, being the 29th of May, the same day twenty years that the private cabal in London concluded their secret league with the Scots, to embroil his father King Charles the First.

Made in the USA
Coppell, TX
21 January 2021

48538044R00083